COACHING TRANSITION PLAY

Vol.2 - Full Sessions from the Tactics of Pochettino, Sarri, Jardim & Sampaoli

WRITTEN BY
MICHAIL TSOKAKTSIDIS

PUBLISHED BY

COACHING TRANSITION PLAY

Vol.2 - Full Sessions from the Tactics of Pochettino, Sarri, Jardim & Sampaoli

First Published October 2018 by SoccerTutor.com

info@soccertutor.com | www.SoccerTutor.com

UK: 0208 1234 007 | **US:** (305) 767 4443 | **ROTW:** +44 208 1234 007

ISBN: 978-1-910491-22-5

Copyright: SoccerTutor.com Limited © 2018. All Rights Reserved.

All rights reserved. No part of this publication may be reproduced, stored in a retrieval system, or transmitted in any form or by any means, electronic, mechanical, photocopy, recording or otherwise, without prior written permission of the copyright owner. Nor can it be circulated in any form of binding or cover other than that in which it is published and without similar condition including this condition being imposed on a subsequent purchaser.

Author
Michail Tsokaktsidis © 2018

Edited by
Alex Fitzgerald - SoccerTutor.com

Cover Design by
Alex Macrides, Think Out Of The Box Ltd.
Email: design@thinkootb.com Tel: +44 (0) 208 144 3550

Diagrams
Diagram designs by SoccerTutor.com. All the diagrams in this book have been created using SoccerTutor.com Tactics Manager Software available from **www.SoccerTutor.com**

Note: While every effort has been made to ensure the technical accuracy of the content of this book, neither the author nor publishers can accept any responsibility for any injury or loss sustained as a result of the use of this material.

CONTENTS

Meet The Author 8
Coaching Format 9
Key 9

CHAPTER 1: THE TRANSITION PHASES 10
The Transition Phases 11
The Low, Middle and High Zones 12
How Important are the Transition Phases? 13
Mauricio Pochettino's Tactics in the Transition Phases (Tottenham Hotspur) 14
Maurizio Sarri's Tactics in the Transition Phases (S.S.C. Napoli) 16
Leonardo Jardim's Tactics in the Transition Phases (AS Monaco) 18
Jorge Sampaoli's Tactics in the Transition Phases (Sevilla FC) 19

CHAPTER 2: HOW TO COACH AND PLAY IN THE TRANSITION PHASES 20
Creating a Game Model 21
Philosophy, Objectives of the Team and Adopting the Game Model 23
Transition Training: What is Needed? 24
Creating a "Thinking Player" 25
Creating a Practice 26

THE TRANSITION FROM DEFENCE TO ATTACK 27

CHAPTER 3: TECHNICAL & TACTICAL REQUIREMENTS IN THE TRANSITION FROM DEFENCE TO ATTACK 28
Coaching the Transition from Defence to Attack 29
Transition from Defence to Attack Flow Chart 30
Technical and Tactical Requirements 32

CHAPTER 4: TRANSITION FROM DEFENCE TO ATTACK IN THE LOW ZONE 33

TACTICAL SITUATION 1 (MAURICIO POCHETTINO TACTICS) 36
ANALYSIS: Exploiting Free Space in the Opposition Half with Fast Combination Play ... 37

SESSION FOR THIS TACTICAL SITUATION
1. Pressing to Win the Ball and then Keep Possession in a 4 (+1) v 4 Transition Game ... 38
2. Pressing to Win the Ball and then Keep Possession in a Two Zone Transition Game ... 39
3. Exploiting Free Space in the Opposition Half with Fast Combination Play in a Dynamic Game ... 40
4. Exploiting Free Space in the Opposition Half with Fast Combination Play in a Tactical Game ... 41

TACTICAL SITUATION 2 (MAURIZIO SARRI TACTICS) 42
ANALYSIS: Exploiting Free Space in the Opposition Half with a Fast Break Attack ... 43

SESSION FOR THIS TACTICAL SITUATION
1. Exploiting Free Space in the Opposition Half with a Fast Break Attack in a Dynamic 3 Team Transition Game .. 44
2. Exploiting Free Space in the Opposition Half with a Fast Break Attack in a Dynamic Small Sided Game 45

3. Exploiting Free Space in the Opposition Half with a Fast Break Attack in a 2 Zone Game (4-3-3 vs 4-3-3)........46

TACTICAL SITUATION 3 (JORGE SAMPAOLI TACTICS)..47
ANALYSIS: Counter Attack with a Forward Pass, Lay-Off and Supporting Runs 48

SESSION FOR THIS TACTICAL SITUATION
1. Counter Attack with a Forward Pass, Lay-Off and Supporting Runs in a Functional Practice 49
2. Counter Attack with a Forward Pass, Lay-Off and Supporting Runs in a 2 Zone Game.........................50
3. Counter Attack with a Forward Pass, Lay-Off and Supporting Runs in a Tactical Game 51

CHAPTER 5: TRANSITION FROM DEFENCE TO ATTACK IN THE MIDDLE ZONE 52

TACTICAL SITUATION 1 (LEONARDO JARDIM TACTICS)...55
ANALYSIS: Fast and Direct Counter Attacks with Through Ball in Behind..56

SESSION FOR THIS TACTICAL SITUATION
1. Fast Counter Attacks with Through Ball in Behind in a Dynamic 3 Zone Possession Game.....................57
2. Fast Counter Attacks with Through Ball in Behind in a 3 Zone Transition Game 58
3. Fast Counter Attacks with Through Ball in Behind in a Dynamic Small Sided Game 59
4. Press in Middle Zone + Fast Counter Attacks with Through Ball in Behind (Tactical Game) 60

TACTICAL SITUATION 2 (JORGE SAMPAOLI TACTICS)..62
ANALYSIS: Direct Counter Attack with Driving Support Runs..63

SESSION FOR THIS TACTICAL SITUATION
1. Direct Counter Attacks with Driving Support Runs in a 5 v 5 (+2) Dynamic 2 Zone Transition Game 64
2. Direct Counter Attacks with Driving Support Runs in a 5 v 5 (+1) Dynamic 2 Zone Transition Game 65
3. Direct Counter Attacks with Driving Support Runs in a Position Specific 2 Zone Game........................66
4. Direct Counter Attacks with Driving Support Runs in a Dynamic "5-5-5 Rule Game" (3-4-3 vs 4-2-3-1) 67

TACTICAL SITUATION 3 (MAURIZIO SARRI TACTICS)...68
ANALYSIS: Fast Break Attack when the Opposition is Disorganised 69

SESSION FOR THIS TACTICAL SITUATION
1. Fast Transition Play in a 4 (+4) v 4 Possession Game 70
2. Fast Break Attack when the Opposition is Disorganised in a 4 (+4) v 4 Dynamic Zonal Game..................71
3. Fast Supporting Runs to Finish in an 8 v 8 (+3) Dynamic Zonal Game 73
4. Fast Break Attack when the Opposition is Disorganised in a Dynamic Tactical Game.........................75

TACTICAL SITUATION 4 (MAURICIO POCHETTINO TACTICS) 76
ANALYSIS: High Intensity Pressing and Fast Break Attack from the Middle Zone 77

SESSION FOR THIS TACTICAL SITUATION
1. One-Touch Combination Play in a Continuous Short Passing Circuit (1) 79
2. One-Touch Combination Play in a Continuous Short Passing Circuit (2) 80
3. Collective Pressing and Transition to Attack with Fast Break 81
4. High Intensity Pressing in the Middle Zone and Fast Break Attack in a Tactical Practice 82
5. High Intensity Pressing in the Middle Zone and Fast Break Attack in a 3 Zone Game.........................83

TACTICAL SITUATION 5 (JORGE SAMPAOLI TACTICS)..84
ANALYSIS: Fast Break Attacking Overload from the Middle Zone 85

SESSION FOR THIS TACTICAL SITUATION
1. Fast Break Attack 1 v 0 (+1) to 4 v 3 (+1) Overload Game..86

2. Fast Break Attack Overload Game with Crossing and Finishing..................................88
3. Fast Break Attacking Overloads in a Position Specific Zonal Game 89
4. Fast Break Attacking Overloads in a Position Specific 9 v 9 Tactical Game 90

TACTICAL SITUATION 6 (LEONARDO JARDIM TACTICS)..91
ANALYSIS: Fast Break Attacks with Many Support Players 92

SESSION FOR THIS TACTICAL SITUATION
1. Continuous One-Touch Combination Play in a Passing Practice...............................95
2. Possession and Fast Support Play in a Dynamic 2 Zone Transition Game......................96
3. Fast Break Attacks with Support Players in a Position Specific Small Sided Game............97
4. Fast Break Attacks with Many Support Players in an 11 v 11 Tactical Game (4-4-2 vs 4-2-3-1 or 4-4-2).........98

CHAPTER 6: TRANSITION FROM DEFENCE TO ATTACK IN THE HIGH ZONE 99

TACTICAL SITUATION 1 (MAURICIO POCHETTINO TACTICS) 102
ANALYSIS: High Press to Win the Ball + Fast Attack.. 103

SESSION FOR THIS TACTICAL SITUATION
1. High Press to Win the Ball + Keep Possession in a Dynamic 2 Zone Transition Game 105
2. High Press to Win the Ball + Fast Attack in a Dynamic 2 Zone Small Sided Game........... 106
3. High Press to Win the Ball + Fast Attack in a Dynamic Game with Target Players 107
4. High Press to Win the Ball + Fast Attack in a Tactical 2 Zone Game (3-1-4-2 vs 3-4-2-1) 108

TACTICAL SITUATION 2 (MAURIZIO SARRI TACTICS).. 109
ANALYSIS: High Press and Fast Attack with Third Man Run 110

SESSION FOR THIS TACTICAL SITUATION
1. Quick Passing Combination, Third Man Run, Final Ball and Finish 111
2. Possession Play and Pressing to Win the Ball in a Dynamic 2 Zone Transition Game........ 112
3. High Press and Fast Attack with Third Man Run in a Position Specific Game 113
4. High Press and Fast Attack with Third Man Run in a 9 v 9 Small Sided Game............... 114
5. High Press and Fast Attack with Third Man Run in a Tactical Transition Game (4-3-3 vs 4-2-3-1)............. 115

THE TRANSITION FROM ATTACK TO DEFENCE 116

CHAPTER 7: TECHNICAL & TACTICAL REQUIREMENTS IN THE TRANSITION FROM ATTACK TO DEFENCE 117
Coaching the Transition from Attack to Defence.. 118
Transition from Attack to Defence Flow Chart 119
Technical Requirements... 120
Tactical Requirements.. 121

CHAPTER 8: TRANSITION FROM ATTACK TO DEFENCE IN THE LOW ZONE 122

TACTICAL SITUATION 1 (LEONARDO JARDIM TACTICS)....................................... 125
ANALYSIS: Condensing the Space After Losing Possession in the Low Zone 126

SESSION FOR THIS TACTICAL SITUATION
1. Condensing the Space After Losing Possession in a 5 v 3 Transition Game................. 127
2. Condensing the Space After Losing Possession in a 5 v 3 Transition Game with Goals 128
3. Condensing the Space After Losing Possession in a Dynamic Possession Practice 129

4. Condensing the Space After Losing Possession in the Low Zone in a Dynamic Game 131
5. Condensing the Space After Losing Possession in the Low Zone with a Numerical Disadvantage 132

TACTICAL SITUATION 2 (MAURICIO POCHETTINO TACTICS) 133
ANALYSIS: Defensive Adjustments to Defend a Through Ball in Behind in the Transition to Defence 134

SESSION FOR THIS TACTICAL SITUATION
1. Quick Reactions and Tracking Back in a Dynamic Transition Game 135
2. Defensive Adjustments to Defend a Through Ball in Behind in the Transition to Defence (4 v 4 Practice)..... 137
2. Defensive Adjustments to Defend a Through Ball in Behind in the Transition to Defence (6 v 6 Practice)..... 138
4. Defensive Adjustments to Defend a Through Ball in Behind in a Positional Game......................... 139
5. Defensive Adjustments to Defend a Through Ball in Behind in an 11 v 11 Game 141

TACTICAL SITUATION 3 (JORGE SAMPAOLI TACTICS) 142
ANALYSIS: Reactions when Defenders Lose Possession Trying to Pass into Midfield 143

SESSION FOR THIS TACTICAL SITUATION
1. Reactions when Defenders Lose Possession Trying to Pass into Midfield in a Dynamic Transition Game 144
2. Reactions when Defenders Lose Possession Trying to Pass into Midfield in a Positional Transition Game 145
3. Reactions when Defenders Lose Possession Trying to Pass into Midfield in an End to End Possession Game . 146
4. Fast Transition to Defence in the Low Zone in a Dynamic End to End Possession Game 148

TACTICAL SITUATION 4 (JORGE SAMPAOLI TACTICS) 149
ANALYSIS: Fast Reactions to Defend the Centre of the Pitch After Losing Possession 150

SESSION FOR THIS TACTICAL SITUATION
1. Open the Space in Possession and Close the Space in the Transition to Defence (Dynamic 8 v 8 Practice).... 151
2. Fast Reactions to Defend the Centre of the Pitch After Losing Possession in a Positional 8 v 9 Game......... 152
3. Fast Reactions to Defend the Centre of the Pitch After Losing Possession in a Specific Game Scenario....... 153
4. Fast Reactions to Defend the Centre of the Pitch with Changing Game Situations in an 11 v 11 Game....... 154

CHAPTER 9: TRANSITION FROM ATTACK TO DEFENCE IN THE MIDDLE ZONE 155

TACTICAL SITUATION 1 (MAURIZIO SARRI TACTICS) 158
ANALYSIS: Tracking Back and Forcing Opponents Wide to Protect the Goal................................. 159

SESSION FOR THIS TACTICAL SITUATION
1. Tracking Back and Forcing Opponents Wide to Protect the Goal in a 5 v 4 Practice........................ 160
2. Tracking Back and Forcing Opponents Wide to Protect the Goal in a Functional Practice (1)................ 161
3. Tracking Back and Forcing Opponents Wide to Protect the Goal in a Functional Practice (2)................ 162
4. Tracking Back and Forcing Opponents Wide to Protect the Goal in a Dynamic Zonal Game 163
5. Tracking Back and Forcing Opponents Wide to Protect the Goal in an 11 v 11 Game...................... 164

TACTICAL SITUATION 2 (JORGE SAMPAOLI TACTICS) 165
ANALYSIS: Fast Transition with Midfielders Tracking Back to Get Behind the Ball 166

SESSION FOR THIS TACTICAL SITUATION
1. Fast Transition with Midfielders Tracking Back to Get Behind the Ball in a 2 Zone Possession Game 168
2. Fast Transition with Midfielders Tracking Back to Get Behind the Ball in a Dynamic Zonal Game (1) 169
3. Fast Transition with Midfielders Tracking Back to Get Behind the Ball in a Dynamic Zonal Game (2) 170
4. Fast Transition with Midfielders Tracking Back to Get Behind the Ball in an 11 v 11 Tactical Game 171

TACTICAL SITUATION 3 (LEONARDO JARDIM TACTICS) 172
ANALYSIS: Quickly Returning into Defensive Shape After Losing Possession 173

SESSION FOR THIS TACTICAL SITUATION

1. Unopposed Combination Play and Quickly Returning into Defensive Shape (Warm Up) 174
2. Unopposed Combination Play and Quickly Reorganising in Relation to the New Ball Position. 176
3. Quickly Returning into Defensive Shape After an Attack in a Dynamic 11 v 6 Practice 177
4. Quickly Returning into Defensive Shape After an Attack in a Dynamic 11 v 11 Game 178

CHAPTER 10: TRANSITION FROM ATTACK TO DEFENCE IN THE HIGH ZONE 179

TACTICAL SITUATION 1 (MAURIZIO SARRI TACTICS) 182
ANALYSIS: High Press from Multiple Angles to Create a Numerical Advantage Around the Ball 183

SESSION FOR THIS TACTICAL SITUATION

1. Unopposed Combination Play + High Press from Multiple Angles to Create a Numerical Advantage Around the Ball 184
2. High Press from Multiple Angles to Create a Numerical Advantage Around the Ball in a Dynamic Game..... 186
3. High Press from Multiple Angles to Create a Numerical Advantage Around the Ball in a Positional SSG...... 187
4. High Press from Multiple Angles to Create a Numerical Advantage Around the Ball in a Tactical Game 188

TACTICAL SITUATION 2 (JORGE SAMPAOLI TACTICS) 189
ANALYSIS: Recovering the Ball as Quickly as Possible with a High Press. 190

SESSION FOR THIS TACTICAL SITUATION

1. Recovering the Ball as Quickly as Possible with Collective Pressing in a Dynamic 6 v 5 Possession Game 191
2. Recovering the Ball as Quickly as Possible with a High Press in a Dynamic 2 Zone Game................... 192
3. Recovering the Ball as Quickly as Possible with a High Press in an 11 v 11 Game with Passing Gates......... 193
4. Switching the Point of Defence to Recover the Ball as Quickly as Possible in a Dynamic Game 194

MEET THE AUTHOR

MICHAIL TSOKAKTSIDIS

- **UEFA 'A' Coaching Licence**
- **Bachelor Degree in Physical & Sports Education** (Specialising in Soccer Conditioning).
- **10 years as a professional player in Greece** (Doxa Dramas, Iltex Likoi (WOLVES), Olympiakos Volou, Agrotikos Asteras, Ethnikos K. and Pandramaikos).

m.tsokaktsidis@gmail.com

- Author of **José Mourinho Attacking Sessions** (2013)
- 114 Practices from Goal Analysis of Real Madrid's 4-2-3-1
- Learn how to coach your team to play like "the best counter attacking team in the world" with 30 ready-made sessions

- Author of **Spain Attacking Sessions** (2014)
- 140 Practices from Goal Analysis of the Spanish National Team
- Learn how to coach your team to play like "one of the best national teams in history" with 31 ready-made sessions

- Author of **Coaching Transition Play Vol.1** (2017)
- Learn to "Coach Transition Play" with 98 Practices based on 32 Transition Game Situations from the Tactics of: Diego Simeone, Pep Guardiola, Jürgen Klopp, José Mourinho and Claudio Ranieri

For this book (volume 2), I have studied the following coaches and teams: **Mauricio Pochettino** (Tottenham), **Maurizio Sarri** (Napoli), **Leonardo Jardim** (Monaco) and **Jorge Sampaoli** (Sevilla). We split the content into the transition from defence to attack and the transition from attack to defence. All possible situations encountered in a football match in these phases of the game are split into sub-categories of the 3 basic zones - low, middle and high. At the beginning of each session, we present analysis of a top coach and team in the transition phase. We then present specific practices to train for that exact tactical situation. These practices make up full progressive training sessions with detailed and clear instructions.

To the greatest mentor and teacher of my life, my mother, because everything she did for me, taught me, and all her actions, she did it with love...Thank you for all Mum

COACHING FORMAT

1. **TACTICAL SITUATION AND ANALYSIS**
2. **FULL TRAINING SESSION FROM THE TACTICAL SITUATION**

- Functional Practices / Transition Games
- Game Situations
- Rules, Coaching Points, Variations & Progressions (if applicable)

KEY

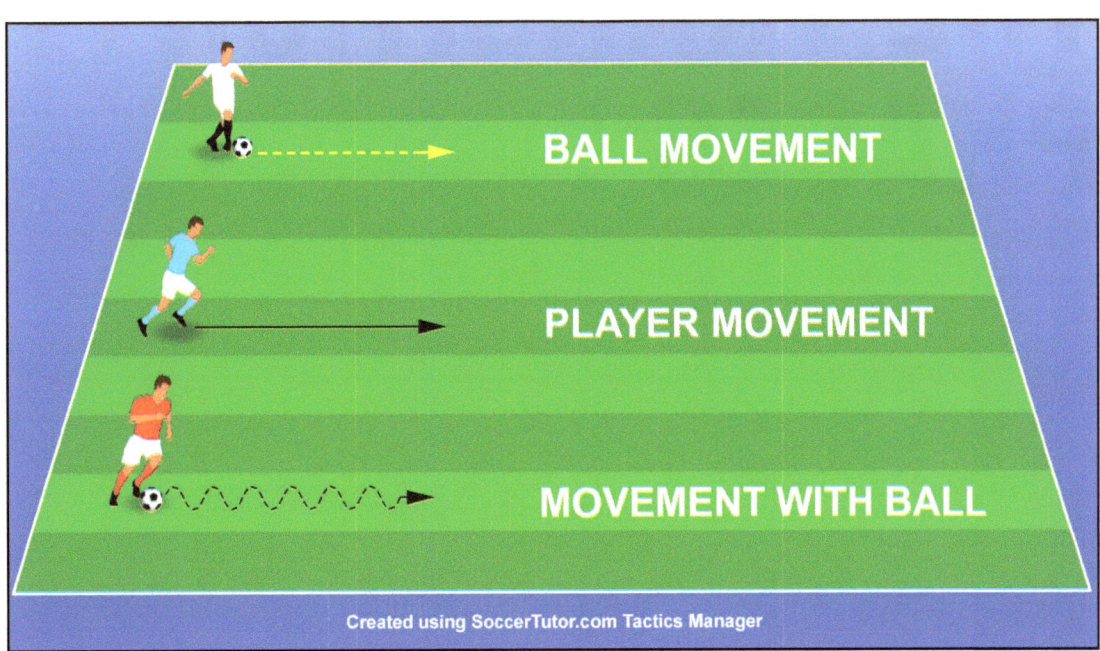

CHAPTER 1

THE TRANSITION PHASES

THE TRANSITION PHASES

In every football match, whether it be at amateur level, professional level or even the UEFA Champions League final, we can see the same specific and repeated game situations within the transition phases of the game.

THE 2 TRANSITION PHASES:

- **Transition from Defence to Attack:** The moment a team wins the ball from their opponents, we enter the transition from defence to attack (positive transition).
- **Transition from Attack to Defence:** The moment a team loses the ball to their opponents, we enter the transition from attack to defence (negative transition).

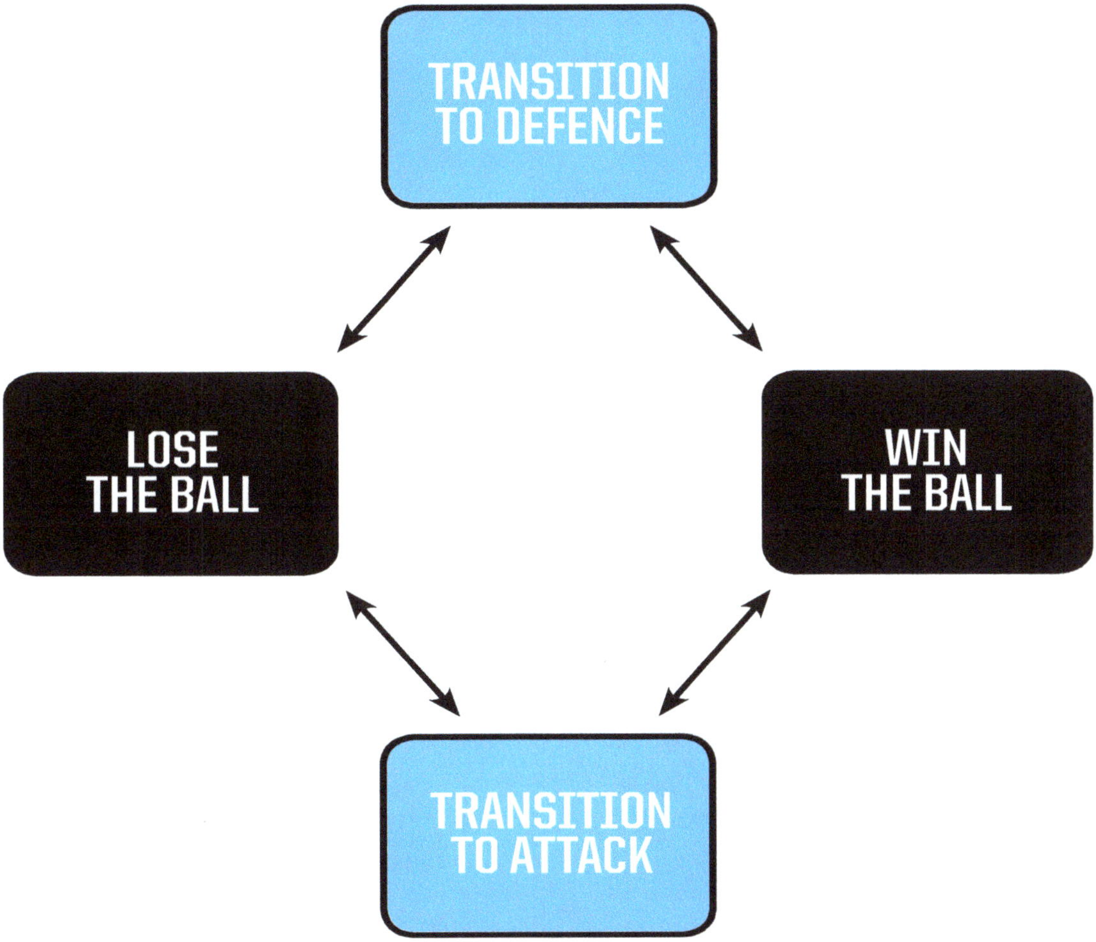

THE TRANSITION PHASES

THE LOW, MIDDLE AND HIGH ZONES

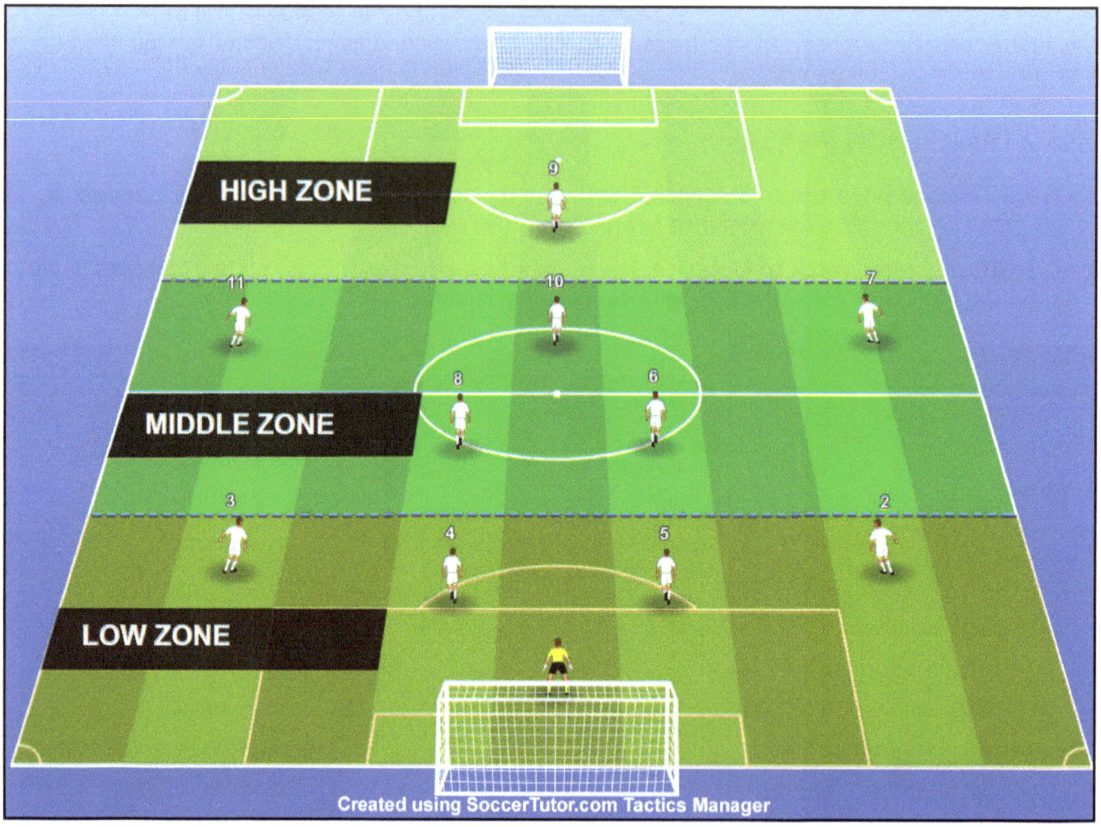

For this book, we have divided the chapters by which zone the transition starts in. There are 3 zones/thirds - high, middle and low. The zone always refers to the team we are focussing on.

In the *'Transition from Defence to Attack'* section, the zone refers to where that team wins the ball. In the *'Transition from Attack to Defence'* section, the zone refers to where that team loses the ball:

TRANSITION FROM DEFENCE TO ATTACK

- **High Zone** - The team win the ball high up the pitch and close to goal, then attack.
- **Middle Zone** - The team win the ball in the middle of the pitch and then attack.
- **Low Zone** - The team win the ball deep in their own half and far from the opponent's goal, then attack.

TRANSITION FROM ATTACK TO DEFENCE

- **High Zone** - The team lose the ball high up the pitch and must defend.
- **Middle Zone** - The team lose the ball in the middle of the pitch and must defend.
- **Low Zone** - The team lose the ball deep in their own half and must defend with their opponents close to their goal.

THE TRANSITION PHASES

HOW IMPORTANT ARE THE TRANSITION PHASES?

Football is a game of constant turnovers of possession. We always have one team defending, trying to win back possession of the ball. The other team is therefore in the attacking phase, trying to create goal scoring opportunities. These transitions happen continuously throughout a game and can happen extremely quickly.

Whether a team will be successful or not is largely down to whether they are capable of exploiting the unbalanced defence of the opposition when they win the ball and whether they can close down space and limit the options of the opposition when they lose the ball. In the modern game, the faster you are able to react as a team in the transition phases, the more successful you will be!

TRANSITION FROM DEFENCE TO ATTACK

After winning the ball, a team should look to exploit the tactical situation as quickly as possible. It is important to move the ball forward before the opposition are able to close down the ball carrier and mark the potential receivers of the next pass.

The transition from defence to attack requires quick reactions, anticipation, technical accuracy, visual awareness of the space to play into, intelligent movement and good decision making. This means that the players need to demonstrate physical speed and speed of thought.

The aim is to train your teams in the transition from defence to attack at high intensity so they learn to play at high speeds. The faster they are able to make this transition, the more successful the team will be.

TRANSITION FROM ATTACK TO DEFENCE

After losing the ball, it is important to apply immediate pressure to the new ball carrier before he can get his head up to be able to dribble or pass forward. This should be done with the player that lost the ball and at least one more player closing the area around the ball zone. The rest of the players make sure to mark the potential receivers and block the passing lanes.

The players need to react immediately after losing possession and anticipate the positioning/movements of their opponents. This has to be worked on in training sessions to make sure that the defensive movements are coordinated as a team, with good cohesion and communication. As like the positive transition, the negative transition (from attack to defence) needs to be done at a high intensity and speed - making sure that the opposition are unable to exploit the team's lack of balance and launch a successful fast break attack.

TOP COACHES IN THE TRANSITION PHASES

There are many teams and many coaches who have put particular emphasis on the transition phase of the game and have been able to achieve great success in football. We studied some of the most important coaches for the first volume: "Coaching Transition Play - Full Sessions from the Tactics of Simeone, Guardiola, Klopp, Mourinho & Ranieri."

For this second volume, I decided to again focus on coaches who have had the greatest influence in the transition phases in the last few years. For this book, I have studied the following coaches and teams from the 2016/17 season:

- **Mauricio Pochettino** (Tottenham Hotspur)
- **Maurizio Sarri** (Napoli)
- **Leonardo Jardim** (Monaco)
- **Jorge Sampaoli** (Sevilla)

* On the following pages, each coach's ideas and tactics are presented.

THE TRANSITION PHASES

MAURICIO POCHETTINO'S TACTICS IN THE TRANSITION PHASES (TOTTENHAM HOTSPUR)

Mauricio Pochettino

"The players have told me since that, even today, they still hear Jesus [Poch's assistant] yelling out 'press, press, press' in their dreams."

"I like football to be played well from the back, to have movement both in and out of possession, to pressure high up the pitch, and to be attacking."[1]

1 Balague, G 2018, Brave New World: Inside Pochettino's Spurs, Orion Publishing Group, Limited

TRANSITION FROM DEFENCE TO ATTACK

In the transition from defence to attack from the low zone, there would normally be a quick pass to a free teammate in a central position in Tottenham's half. From that point, the player with the ball would dribble forward and 2-3 other players would make fast runs forward into the space in the opposition's half to support him. After the ball carrier dribbled up to an opponent, he would use the correct decision making for when/how to pass to a teammate:

1. A final pass to a teammate in the space in behind for a shot at goal.
2. Pass into space for a teammate in a wide position, who with 1 or 2 touches, can provide an assist for a third upcoming player to finish.

In the transition from defence to attack from the middle and high zones using the 4-2-3-1, Tottenham looked for a quick forward pass to the forward (Kane) and he would be supported quickly by the attacking midfielder who would receive the ball back off of him. Immediately, the 2 wingers would sprint forward to receive in space, often joined by a central midfielder making a run from deep. In addition, after passing the ball back, Kane would make a curved run to either side to provide the ball carrier with another passing option. If he did receive, Kane would often dribble forward, drawing in defenders and then make the final pass to the player in the best position.

When they used the 4-1-4-1, a quick pass was still played to the forward again in 3 different ways:

A. Into the space between the full backs and centre backs: 2 midfielders from this side run up to support the forward (Kane) and 2 midfielders from the other side run quickly to receive the final pass or hit a short cross into the space to finish the attack.

B. Into forward's feet on one side: 1 central midfielder from that side runs forward to support him from behind and the wide midfielder on that side + 2 other midfielders from the opposite side run into the space to try and receive the ball in behind the defensive line.

C. Into forward's feet centrally: The central midfielders run into the space between the full backs and centre backs. This is usually with combination play + third man run between:

- Forward, 1 central midfielder and 1 wide midfielder
- Forward and 2 central midfielders
- Forward, 1 central midfielder and the defensive midfielder

During the last part of the 2016-2017 season, Tottenham started to use 3 at the back in a 3-4-3, 3-4-2-1 or 3-4-1-2 formation, finally using a 5-3-2 (or 3-5-2) with V in the centre during the 2017-2018 season. The tactics remained very similar.

THE TRANSITION PHASES

TRANSITION FROM ATTACK TO DEFENCE

When possession was lost in the high or middle zone and the opposition easily passed the ball into Tottenham's half, then the reaction of the defenders was to not take too many risks and not rush towards the ball.

Pochettino wanted to stop the opposition's attacking players from getting the opportunity of playing in 1 v 1 situations. They would delay the attack and retain balance with a controlled defensive shape, making sure to always be behind the ball. This would give time to the other players to track back and provide defensive support, creating a numerical superiority near and around the ball, forcing the opponents to operate under pressure without free spaces to view in front of them (for a possible shot or final pass).

Pochettino's tactics in the transition from attack to defence in the low zone are very similar to that of Maurizio Sarri's Napoli (see page 17).

Pochettino's Tottenham players press immediately to limit the options for the ball carrier - the nearest player presses him and all the other players move very quickly to close off the dangerous channels to goal and provide cover.

The other players who are not immediately involved track back as quickly as possible to provide defensive support, reduce the distances and restore cohesion in the defensive and midfield lines.

MAURIZIO SARRI'S TACTICS IN THE TRANSITION PHASES (S.S.C. NAPOLI)

Dries Mertens (Napoli)

"The thing I love the most about his style of football is the way he organises the phases when we are off the ball and structures the pressure we put on opponents when they've got the ball at their feet. It feels like he has already played the game out in his head and on the field you have an extra man."

Maurizio Sarri's Napoli team are characterised by a high energy style of play with good rhythm in all phases of the game. More specifically, in the transitions phases, Sarri's Napoli were a very active team with the focus on fast reactions (speed) and actions both when they win the ball, and when they lose it.

TRANSITION FROM DEFENCE TO ATTACK IN THE HIGH ZONE

Sarri's Napoli mainly defended in the high zone, pressing their opponents from the start of their build up play from the back:

When Napoli won the ball in the high zone, the player that won it would immediately look to pass to the forward Mertens. He would move into space in the penalty area, trying to gain an advantage against the opposing centre backs and finish the attack with an individual effort.

Alternatively, the player that won the ball would play the ball into Mertens' feet when he had his back to goal. In this situation, Napoli would use quick combination play, with fast supporting runs from the midfielders who would receive off of Mertens. Mertens is very adept at playing first time passes in between the centre back and full back into the penalty area, most often for the runs of the 2 wingers Insigne and Callejón. One of these players would receive and shoot or deliver a short cross for the oncoming runners - most often for the other winger and the forward Mertens.

In the third situation, the ball is played to one of the two wingers (Insigne or Callejón) immediately. They would use their dribbling skills to make the opponents come to them, moving defenders out of position and creating space. The wingers would either dribble into the box or out wide, but either way, they would time their final pass in behind to the forward Mertens, the attacking midfielders or the winger on the opposite side.

TRANSITION FROM DEFENCE TO ATTACK IN THE MIDDLE ZONE

When Sarri's Napoli won the ball in the middle zone, they had the same objectives, but the initial decision making changed, as they were further away from their opponent's goal.

Now the player that won the ball would look to dribble forward into any available space and then proceed with the solutions explained for the high zone.

If there was no free space to dribble into, Napoli applied very quick and effective one touch combination play with continuous short and direct passes to feet, with good coordination and synchronisation. Many players would make well-timed runs in behind the defensive line, with other players running forward quickly to provide support and different options to finish the counter attack.

THE TRANSITION PHASES

TRANSITION FROM DEFENCE TO ATTACK IN THE LOW ZONE

When Sarri's Napoli won the ball in the low zone, their first choice was to pass the ball out wide to the wingers (Insigne and Callejón). These two players would then run with the ball, draw opponents out of position and create space. This gave their teammates time to make forward supporting runs.

Napoli usually had 2 scenarios:

1. Napoli would concentrate 2-4 players on one side to create a numerical superiority - they would then use 1-2 combinations and third man runs to exploit the advantage. These tactics would lead to a player receiving a final pass in behind the defensive line - this player would most often receive in a wide position and deliver a cross for oncoming runners to finish (normally attacker from other side).

2. In the second scenario, after the ball goes out wide to the wingers (Insigne or Callejón), and when the opposition had left free space in the centre of the pitch, they would pass the ball to a central midfielder. That midfielder could then dribble the ball forward to advance Napoli up the pitch. Depending on the actions of the opponents, the midfielder could then pass into space for the forward (Mertens) or the winger on the other side.

TRANSITION FROM ATTACK TO DEFENCE IN THE HIGH ZONE

In the transition from attack to defence in the high zone, Sarri's Napoli most often applied a quick high press. The ball carrier would be immediately closed down by the nearest player - this had the aim of stopping that player getting their head up and quickly playing the ball into Napoli's half, where there was a lot of space in behind the defensive line to exploit.

Sarri also wanted to recover the ball as quickly as possible or at least make the opponent act under pressure of time and space - this would force mistakes and lead to the indirect recovery of the ball.

The other main objective was to force the opponents out wide and then create a numerical superiority around the ball zone, which would reduce the space available and their options.

TRANSITION FROM ATTACK TO DEFENCE IN THE MIDDLE ZONE

In the transition from attack to defence in the middle zone, the nearest player again presses the ball carrier. All the other players (except for the forward) must quickly run across or back towards the ball area, closing off the dangerous channels to goal.

If Napoli were unable to achieve this and the opposition passed the ball behind the midfield line, this would leave only the back 4 in position to defend the counter attack. In this situation, the back 4 worked excellently with synchronised movements and the correct body shape to delay their opponents and push them away from goal. Once teammates running back had recovered into defensive positions, one of the defenders in the back 4 would move to press the ball carrier and the other 3 would provide cover.

TRANSITION FROM ATTACK TO DEFENCE IN THE LOW ZONE

Sarri's players act very quickly and instantly to the loss of the ball with the basic aim of limiting the options for the ball carrier - the nearest defender presses him to prevent the player dribbling, shooting or passing to a teammate in a better position e.g. A player making a well-timed run into the penalty area.

All other players move very quickly to close off the dangerous channels to goal and provide cover. Normally in this situation, it is the back 4 and defensive midfielder who take part in the first instance.

Of course, all the other players who are not immediately involved track back as quickly as possible to provide defensive support, reduce the distances and to restore cohesion in the defensive and midfield lines.

THE TRANSITION PHASES

LEONARDO JARDIM'S TACTICS IN THE TRANSITION PHASES (AS MONACO)

In the defensive phase, Monaco tried to have very short distances between the midfield and defensive lines, using a compact defensive block. This made it very hard for opponents to break through using combination play - this meant that they were often forced into making individual efforts, using long passes and delivering crosses from deep positions. These actions often led to Monaco being able to win the ball and then launch a counter attack (transition from defence to attack).

TRANSITION FROM DEFENCE TO ATTACK

After winning the ball, the first Monaco pass was quick and forward, leading to a fast break attack with equal numbers of players (2 v 2, 3 v 3 and 4 v 4) or with a numerical advantage/overload situation (3 v 2, 4 v 3, 2 [+1] v 2 and 3 [+1] v 3).

When Monaco won the ball near the sides of the pitch, the objective was to move the ball quickly to the winger (Lemar or Bernardo Silva). If this happened from the low zone, the winger would run forward quickly with the ball. He would be able to exploit the movements of the 2 quick forwards into space.

If this happened from the middle zone, the wingers could receive the ball in space and in more advanced positions. The wingers would exploit their speed and dribble into the box, or pass in behind for oncoming runners in the centre (or the other side of the pitch), to finish the attack. There were 2 scenarios when Jardim's Monaco won the ball in the centre of the pitch:

1. From the low zone, the new ball carrier passes forward quickly to a free teammate in the centre of the pitch and moves forward to support. Monaco would then pass to the winger in the best position (free in space). Many players would run forward to provide support and the attack would be finished in the same ways described previously.

2. From the low zone, the new ball carrier would dribble forward to draw in opponents and create space. He would then pass to one of the 2 forwards who moved in behind the defensive line, or pass into space out wide for one of the wingers who sprinted forward rapidly to receive. If the winger received out wide, he would cross into the box for the 2 forwards and the other winger.

TRANSITION FROM ATTACK TO DEFENCE

Jardim's Monaco looked to press the new ball carrier immediately to delay and close off options. When successful, the other players would also apply pressure around the ball area to win the ball back or push the play towards one side. But the most important characteristic of Monaco's transition to defence is when the opponent had space to move forward - the Monaco full backs and central midfielders would quickly run back to provide safety and balance in the 4-4-2 formation. They have high levels of concentration and cohesion in central areas and close the channels to their goal, creating a 6 player defensive block in front of the box. If for example, the left back was high up the pitch and unable to get back, there were 2 situations:

1. If the attack was on Monaco's left side, the LCB moves across to take the LB position, the RCB takes the LCB position and a CM (RCM in this case) runs back to take the RCB position. Monaco therefore have a 4 + 1 defensive line.

2. If the attack was on Monaco's right side, the RB, RCB and RCM normally stayed in their positions. There would then be communication between the LCB and LCM to take up the other 2 positions in the back 4. Monaco again had a 4 + 1 defensive line.

THE TRANSITION PHASES

JORGE SAMPAOLI'S TACTICS IN THE TRANSITION PHASES (SEVILLA FC)

Jorge Sampaoli

"My teams are characterised by pressing in the opposition half, circulating the ball well and attacking from the wings."

Sampaoli's Sevilla played a game based on energy, rhythm and physicality. Sevilla played at a high tempo with and without the ball. Sampaoli's game model is highly focussed on the transition from defence to attack.

TRANSITION FROM DEFENCE TO ATTACK

In this phase of the game, Sampaoli's players tried to apply a very fast transition from defence to attack and exploit all the free spaces that were available.

If the ball was won in the low or middle zone, the players were focussed on making a quick first pass to the player in the best position and in the most space. Normally, this player tried to exploit this free space with quick and creative dribbling. All the other players (usually 3-5) would make very fast forward runs to support him and ask for the ball in the most dangerous areas in behind the defensive line. These unmarking and support movements are made with great determination and energy at a high tempo. Sampaoli's Sevilla normally finished such transitions in the following ways:

1. With one final pass from the ball carrier to a teammate in behind, who finishes the attack.

2. With a pass from the ball carrier* to a teammate in a better position, closer to the opposition's penalty area (normally in behind the defensive line). This player then makes the final pass, which may be a short cross from the side of the box for an oncoming teammate running from deep, to finish on the move.

* Ball carrier: *The player who receives the first pass from the player that won the ball.*

If the ball was won in the high zone, then the ball carrier would look to play a quick forward pass to a teammate in a better position, higher up the pitch. Sevilla would then use quick combination play with fast and accurate passes, as well as continuous support movements/runs. Once Sevilla were able to move the ball into a more advanced position, the other aims and ways to attack were then the same as when they won the ball in the low or middle zone.

TRANSITION FROM ATTACK TO DEFENCE

Sampaoli's Sevilla moved very quickly from attack to defence and pressed the new ball carrier with the aim of recovering the ball as soon as possible. For this reason, they pressed the opponent immediately and stopped him from being able to dribble or pass the ball forward.

Sampaoli's players reduce the size of the pitch and the time for any possible action, while also creating a numerical superiority and strong side near and around the ball with aggressive marking, and often double marking, of the ball carrier and players near the ball. This marking made it very difficult for their opponents, limiting their choices and often leading to them making the wrong decisions and losing the ball.

CHAPTER 2

HOW TO COACH AND PLAY IN THE TRANSITION PHASES

CREATING A GAME MODEL

- How can you train for the transition phases?
- How can you organise your training of transition play better?
- What is the best way to coach transition play?

To answer these questions, we must first look at what the appropriate training is. My personal view is that good training has to be game realistic (taken from the game and for the game).

This creates substantial training and gives us the results that we want - it is the most effective method to organise your team and work on specific match scenarios. This helps our players and the team to apply exactly what we want from them on the pitch.

- How can we make sure our training is game realistic?
- What is our guide?

For each training session we need to focus on meeting our targets we want to apply on the pitch. The objective creates the practices, but the talent of the players and the coach's ability is what defines and differentiates the training.

The game itself is the guide, but not any game, it must be our own game - how we want to play from the moment we lose the ball and how we want to play from the moment that we win the ball. Before creating specific practices, we must first create our own 'Game Model' which will be our guide for the tactics and training of our team (see diagram below).

THE KEY FEATURES OF THE GAME MODEL

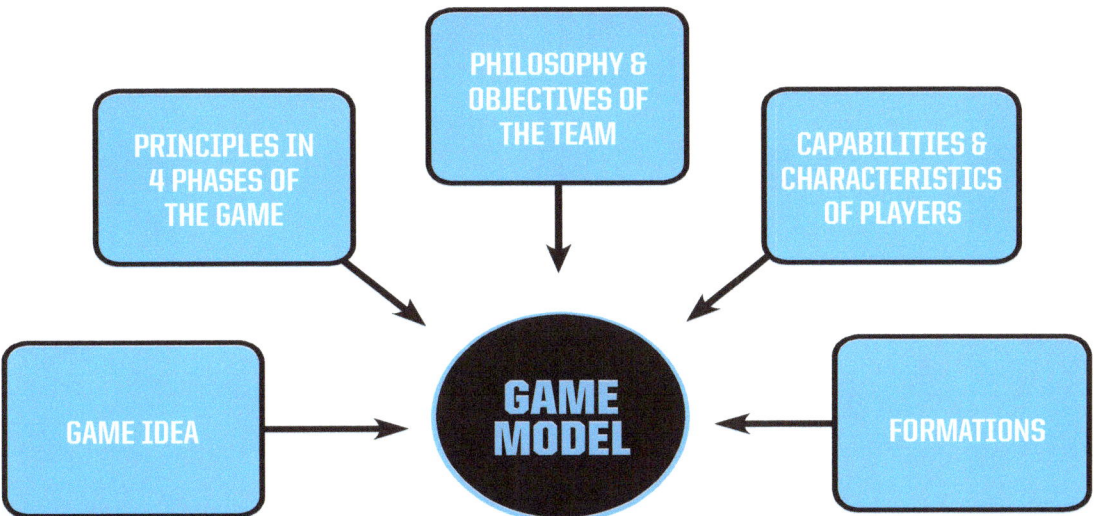

The key features are described fully on the next page.

Game Idea

How do we want to play football? This includes the style of play in every phase of the game.

Principles in 4 Phases of the Game

Those who want to succeed in all 4 phases of the game start with the fundamentals and basic principles, working through sub-principles step by step. Football is played in specific areas and specific zones, so the training should not be general and unspecific - it must be specific and concrete.

Philosophy & Objectives of the Team

The purpose, vision, mission, short-term goals, medium-term goals and long-term goals of the team.

Capabilities & Characteristics of the Players

What players do we have in our team? What tactical, technical and physical skills do they have? What are their strengths and weaknesses? Analysis of all of these elements can help us to create a path to follow in our work and in relation to the transition phases.

Formations

With this in our minds, we must find the appropriate formations that can best utilise our players to achieve the team goals and be directly linked to the basic principles of our game model. We need to specifically focus on transition play and become more effective and efficient.

PHILOSOPHY, OBJECTIVES OF THE TEAM AND ADOPTING THE GAME MODEL

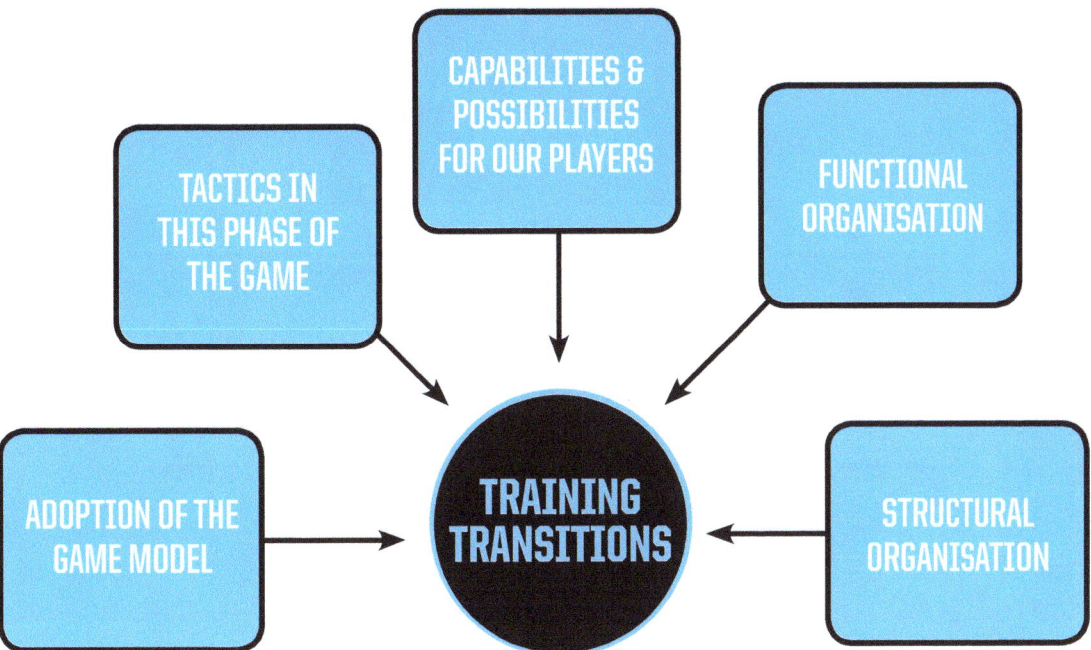

Adoption of the Game Model

Adoption and implementation of the game model which should be decided upon after analysing the factors presented on the previous page 'Creating a Game Model'.

Tactics in this Phase of the Game

Our specific idea about the transition phases - how do we want to play in these phases of the game? We need to combine all the elements that we want to characterise us as individuals and as a team when winning or losing the ball.

Capabilities & Possibilities for Our Players

We have to take the analysis of the 'Capabilities & Characteristics' seriously and then proceed with the design of where and how we want to behave when we lose the ball and when we win it.

Functional Organisation

Here we include all the specific details. We must work out in which zone (low, middle or high) we will we start our defence, how we will react when we win the ball and how we will recover the ball in the negative transition. This includes how to act when we lose the ball as individuals, as a small group and as a full team, depending on the zone we are playing in.

Structural Organisation

All the previous information should be used to form our defensive and attacking formations against the formation of our opponents. The emphasis is on exploiting our strengths in relation to the weaknesses of the opposition.

TRANSITION TRAINING: WHAT IS NEEDED?

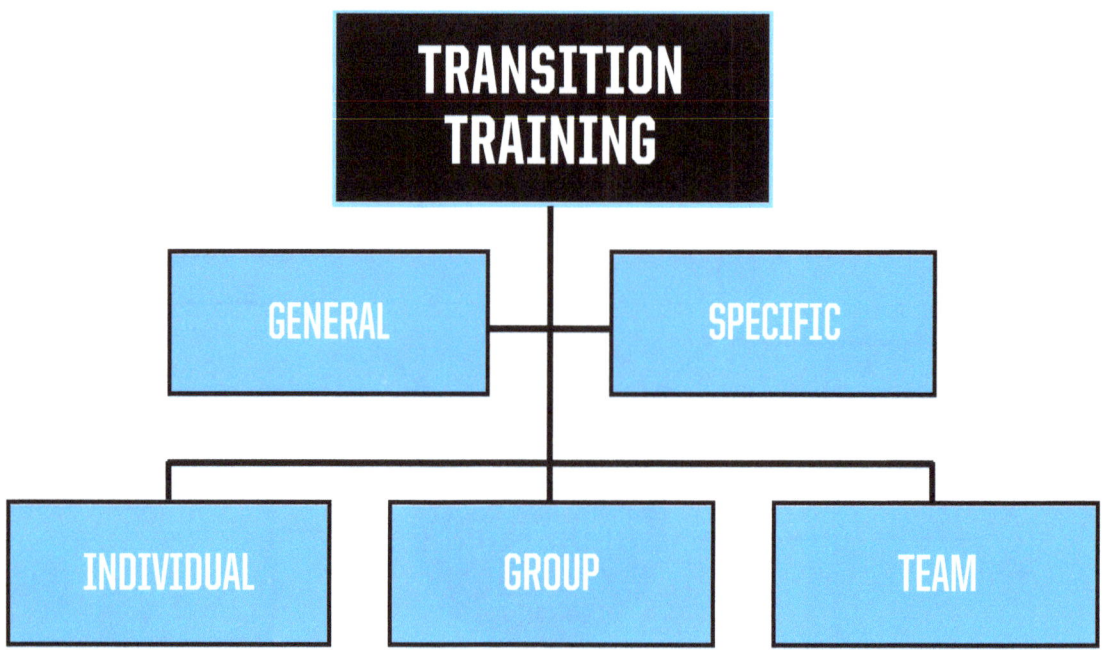

General Training

In general training practices (individual, group and as a team) we focus on improving the starting points for these tactical situations. We also work on quick reactions and decision making, combined with the efficiency and effectiveness of our work against the opposition.

Specific Training

In specific training practices we apply all these ideas into game scenarios vs active opponents using formations, positioning within zones of the pitch and directional play. This is more realistic and tailored to competitive games and the real situations that the players will encounter.

What is Needed?

The transitions themselves are situations that require intensity, rhythm, energy and speed (in all its forms) and above all, quick decision making. That is why they are the most exciting phases during a football match.

These changing game situations contain combination play, individuality, aggression and determination. So it is very natural for the training of such situations to involve intensity, energy, change of pace and direction, and speed/power training. This training should be done on the days when we can work with high intensity.

Our basic and most important goal should be to produce players, groups and teams which understand, decide and act very quickly and effectively. And of course, this must be done faster than the opponent!

HOW TO COACH AND PLAY IN THE TRANSITION PHASES

CREATING A "THINKING PLAYER"

To train transition play well, specialised and specific coaching is needed with intense workouts. This is the only way to produce a team with exceptional rhythm, good decision making and effectiveness on the pitch, showing more speed and enthusiasm than the opposition.

In the practices and sessions provided in this book we have a continuous and progressive flow to our training, with high rhythm and intensity. This results in a very quick improvement of the players' tactical and technical level.

It is in training where you can imprint ideas and gain the interest of the players, which then improves the required speed and efficiency of their decision making - creating the 'Thinking Player'.

- SPEED OF AWARENESS
- SPEED OF PERCEPTION
- SPEED OF DECISION
- TACTICAL PROBLEM
- SPEED OF ACTION
- TECHNICAL PROBLEM

CREATING A THINKING PLAYER

CREATING A PRACTICE

Rules & Directions: All rules and directions under which players have to work in during the practice, with the aim to drive them towards the desired objective and development.

Pitch Dimensions: The necessary dimensions of the created space in which we will perform the practice to have the greatest possible benefit.

Duration: The total and optimum working time of the practice.

Number of Players: The total number of players required for the execution of the practice.

Objective of Practice: What is the main objective? What do we want to work on and improve in this practice?

Methods: The coaching and training methods to follow so the execution of the practice give us the desired results.

Coaching Points: What are the key coaching points to which we should focus our players for the correct execution of the practice? At what points should we emphasise these and offer feedback to our players?

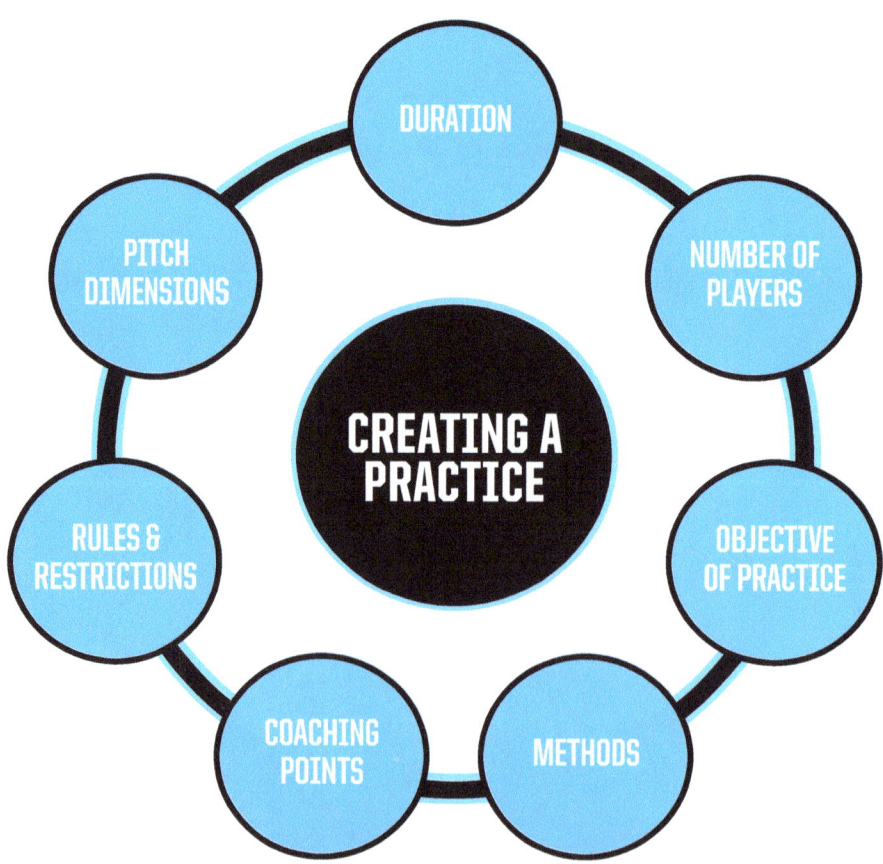

THE TRANSITION FROM DEFENCE TO ATTACK

CHAPTER 3

TECHNICAL & TACTICAL REQUIREMENTS IN THE TRANSITION FROM DEFENCE TO ATTACK

COACHING THE TRANSITION FROM DEFENCE TO ATTACK

In this phase of the game we should first and foremost think about where we start our defence, which zone of the pitch we apply our pressure, and finally in which zone we have the best chance to pass quickly from defence to attack.

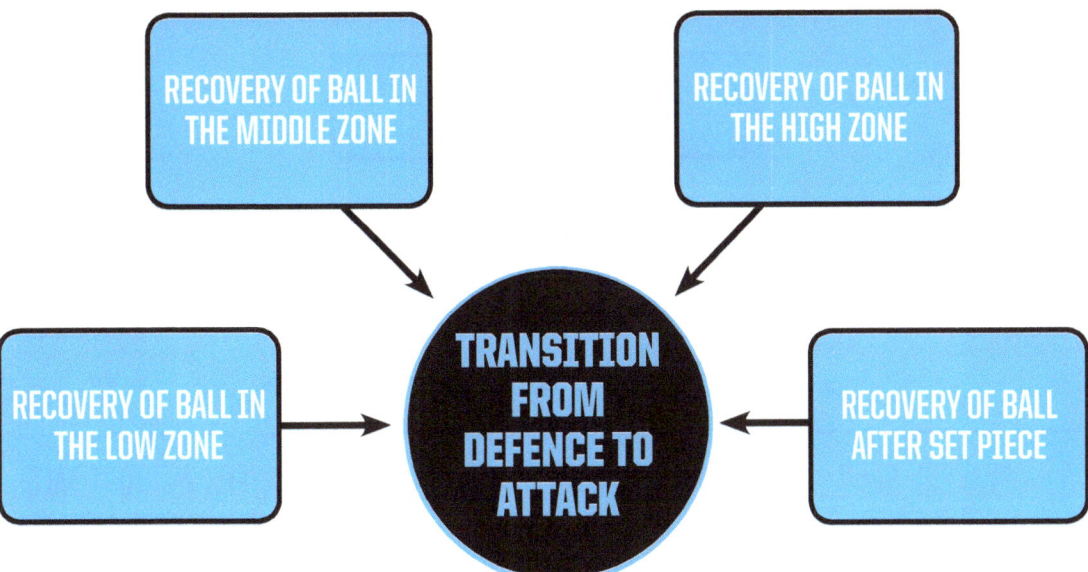

Based on this, every coach should be targeting his team's training on the recovery of the ball in specific zones.

We then work on how he wants to attack from that point, based on what kind of players we have in our team and what kind of players the opposition have. We must utilise the individual strengths of our players and our strengths as a group, against the weaknesses of our opponents.

TECHNICAL & TACTICAL REQUIREMENTS IN THE TRANSITION FROM DEFENCE TO ATTACK

TRANSITION FROM DEFENCE TO ATTACK FLOW CHART

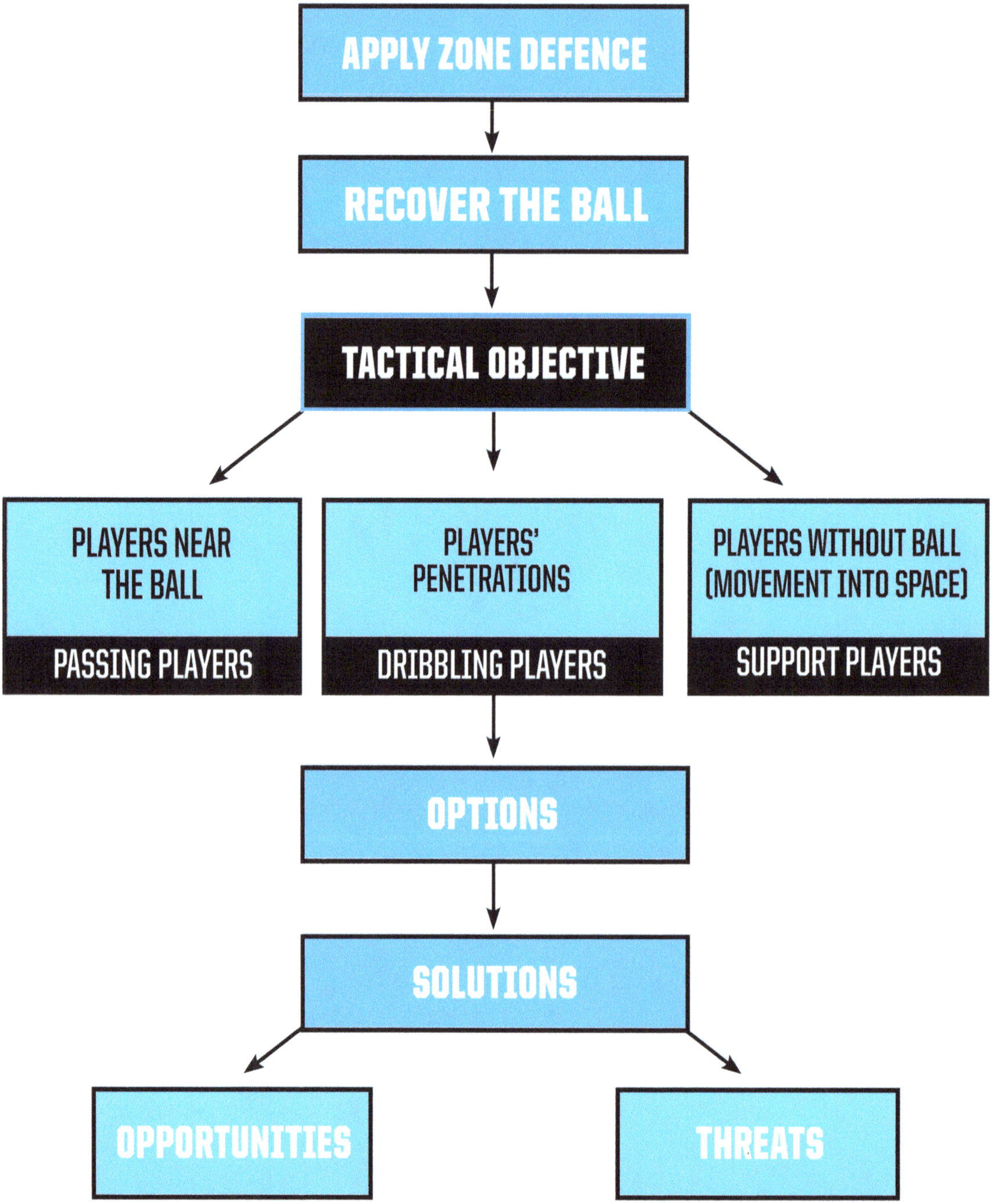

```
APPLY ZONE DEFENCE
        ↓
RECOVER THE BALL
        ↓
TACTICAL OBJECTIVE
   ↓      ↓       ↓
```

- **PLAYERS NEAR THE BALL** — PASSING PLAYERS
- **PLAYERS' PENETRATIONS** — DRIBBLING PLAYERS
- **PLAYERS WITHOUT BALL (MOVEMENT INTO SPACE)** — SUPPORT PLAYERS

```
        ↓
     OPTIONS
        ↓
    SOLUTIONS
     ↓      ↓
OPPORTUNITIES   THREATS
```

TECHNICAL & TACTICAL REQUIREMENTS IN THE TRANSITION FROM DEFENCE TO ATTACK

Apply Zone Defence

The zone we decide to apply our defensive press in a specific match depends on our tactical/technical characteristics and formation against our opponent.

Recover the Ball

We must decide which zone and area of the pitch our team should try to win/recover the ball.

Tactical Objective

What are the tactical objectives that we have in this situation as individuals, as a group and as a whole team?

Decision Making

- The player in possession who should pass - where, how, when?
- The player in possession who should drive forward with the ball (dribbling) - where, how, when?
- The player without the ball - what movement should he make? Should he run forward, move to support, create space for himself or for teammates? - Where, how, when?

Options

What are the basic objectives and options in all of these situations and how can we exploit them?

Solutions

What solutions do we have and how can we use them to exploit this situation? (We can provide the players with 1-3 solutions for each situation in training).

Opportunities

What are the opportunities in these tactical situations and how can we exploit them to get the best results?

Threats

What are the threats we must pay attention to which the opposition may be able to exploit?

TECHNICAL AND TACTICAL REQUIREMENTS

TECHNICAL REQUIREMENTS

- When the opposition try to make passes in behind or cross the ball into the box, we don't want our players to clear the ball aimlessly or off the pitch. We want them to clear the ball towards a teammate or into space for a teammate to run onto, so we can quickly attack (transition).

- Correct body shape when pressing and technique when tackling or intercepting the ball.

- Accurate passes - to feet or into space.

- Weight, timing and speed of passes.

- Excellent directional first touch and control of the ball.

- Fast dribbling with close control of the ball.

- Accurate crossing (short, long) or final pass into the box.

- Accurate finishing (shooting or heading) in all forms, under pressure of time and space.

TACTICAL REQUIREMENTS

- Effective defence (individually, as a group and as a team).

- Creating and exploiting space (from the player who won the ball or another player).

- Creating and exploiting a numerical advantage or overload situation.

- Dribble the ball at the opposition to unbalance them.

- The ability to work effectively with a numerical disadvantage or with equal numbers.

- Exploiting the weak side and the weakness of the opposition's defensive line.

- Exploiting the space and time before the opposition are able to reorganise.

CHAPTER 4

TRANSITION FROM DEFENCE TO ATTACK IN THE LOW ZONE

TRANSITION FROM DEFENCE TO ATTACK IN THE LOW ZONE

We have divided the chapters by which zone the transition starts in. There are 3 zones:

1. **Low Zone**
2. **Middle Zone**
3. **High Zone**

This diagram shows an example of a team that has won the ball in the low zone. In this situation, we have players behind the ball when defending. To win the ball, they need to limit their opponent's time/space, block potential passing options and demonstrate good anticipation.

The red team are attacking and have entered the final third, trying to find solutions to get in behind the defence and score. The white centre back No.5 intercepts the left winger's (11) pass towards the striker (9) near the edge of the penalty area.

The centre back (5) immediately passes forward to No.10 which immediately leaves 5 red players behind the ball and takes them out of the game. No.10 plays a first time pass into the path of No.8, who runs forward with the ball. The winger (11) and the striker (9) make runs into the space out wide and in the centre respectively.

The red centre back (5) is forced to close down white No.8 who then has 2 very good passing options in behind the defensive line, both of which would end up with a player through on goal, and with a great chance to score.

TRANSITION FROM DEFENCE TO ATTACK IN THE LOW ZONE

What is the Tactical Situation?

- The opposition have many players high up and in our half of the pitch.

- Our team would often be defending with many players behind the ball.

- Our defenders have a numerical superiority or equality of numbers against their opponents.

- There is a long distance to the opposition's goal.

- We usually only have 1-2 attacking solutions at the top of the attacking line.

- The 1-2 players at the top of the attacking line can be supported by 1-3 players (maximum) running up from the back.

- Our attackers have an equality of numbers or a numerical disadvantage against their opponents. There could also be an overload situation e.g. 2 (+1) v 2.

- There is a lot of free space to exploit in the opposition half.

What Objectives Should We Have?

- To defend well in our own half and limit the space and time our opponents have to make decisions, with the basic aim of winning the ball.

- To quickly pass the ball forward after winning it and neutralise the immediate pressure from the opposition.

- To play through the lines so that many opposition players are left behind the ball.

- To move the ball into space quickly and effectively to the right players in attacking positions.

- When the transition from defence to attack takes place in the low zone, there is often a lot of space in the opponent's half to exploit - this means the team can get quickly in behind the defensive line to create scoring opportunities.

- Support our forwards with players making fast runs from deep positions.

- Play the ball into the spaces so that we can implement a fast break attack. Take advantage of the space and our speed of movement against the opposing defenders.

- Counter attacks from the low zone (from the time we win the ball to the finish) take 8-12 seconds on average.

What Practices/Sessions Can We Create for this Tactical Situation?

- We must practice our defensive organisation and cohesive movements in our own half against an organised attack. We aim to block the channels to our goal and win the ball.

- Once the ball is won, we need to work on passing the ball quickly forward into the spaces where we can be most effective.

- We work on fast and effective transitions from defence to attack - practicing various tactical situations with equality of numbers or with a numerical advantage (overload situations).

TACTICAL SITUATION 1

POCHETTINO TACTICS

Exploiting Free Space in the Opposition Half with Fast Combination Play

Content taken from Analysis of Tottenham Hotspur during the 2016/2017 Season

The analysis is based on recurring patterns of play observed within the Tottenham team. Once the same phase of play occurred a number of times (at least 10), the tactics would be seen as a pattern. The analysis on the next page is an example of the team's tactics being used effectively, taken from a specific game.

Each action, pass, individual movement with or without the ball, and the positioning of each player on the pitch including their body shape, are presented.

The analysis is then used to create a full progressive session to coach this specific tactical situation.

Tactical Analysis of POCHETTINO - Transition from Defence to Attack (Low Zone)

Analysis Taken from 'Tottenham vs Swansea - 3rd Dec 2016 (Premier League)'

Exploiting Free Space in the Opposition Half with Fast Combination Play (4-2-3-1 vs 4-3-3)

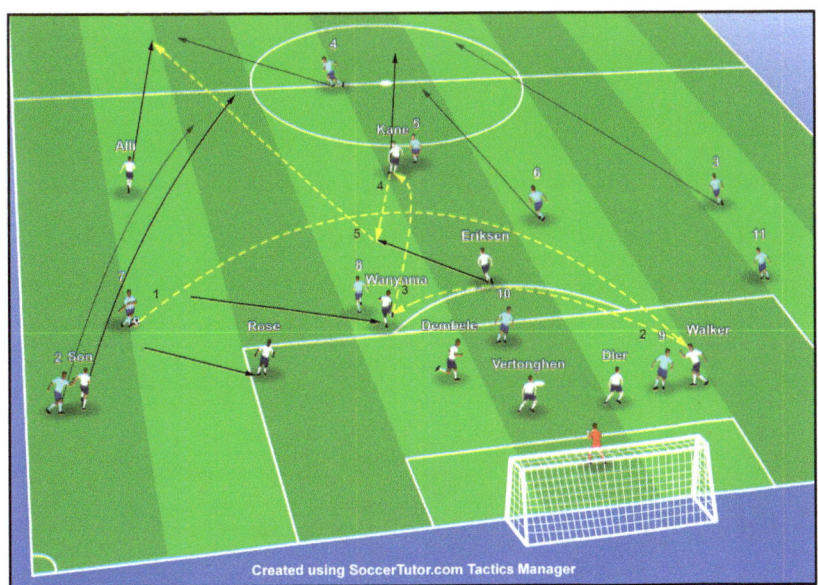

The Swansea winger (7) crosses into the box. The Tottenham right back Walker heads the ball out and Wanyama (defensive midfielder) receives as shown.

He plays forward to the striker Kane, who lays it off for the attacking midfielder Eriksen to run onto.

Eriksen then plays forward for Dele Alli out wide, as he runs into the space in the opposition's half.

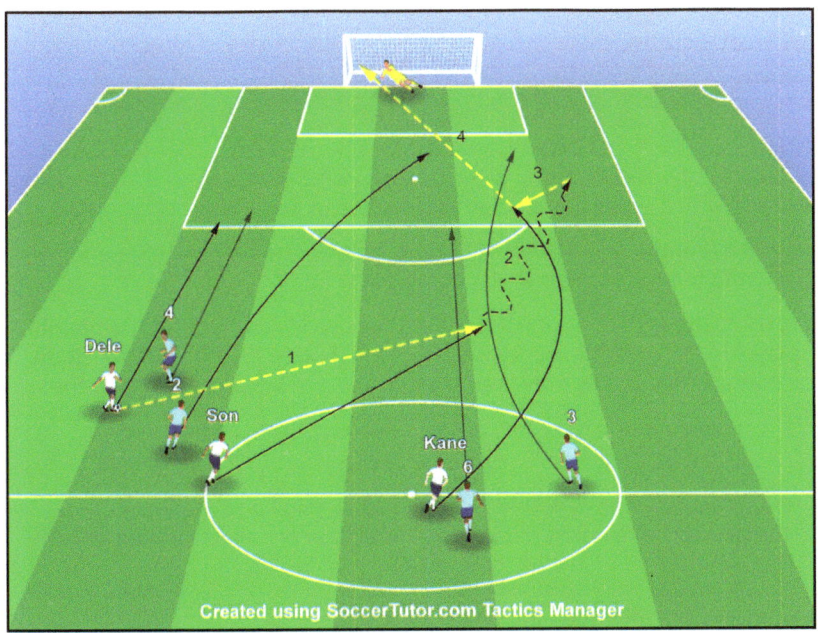

Dele Alli is tracked by the centre back (4) but he has 2 teammates running forward to support in a 3 v 4 situation.

Dele plays inside for Son (tracked by No.3), who receives on the move and dribbles into the box. Kane sprints forward to support.

Son tries to cut inside but takes a heavy touch. Kane is there to stroke the ball home into the far corner with 1 touch.

Session to Practice POCHETTINO Tactics - Transition from Defence to Attack (Low Zone)

SESSION FOR THIS TACTICAL SITUATION (4 PRACTICES)
1. Pressing to Win the Ball and then Keep Possession in a 4 (+1) v 4 Transition Game

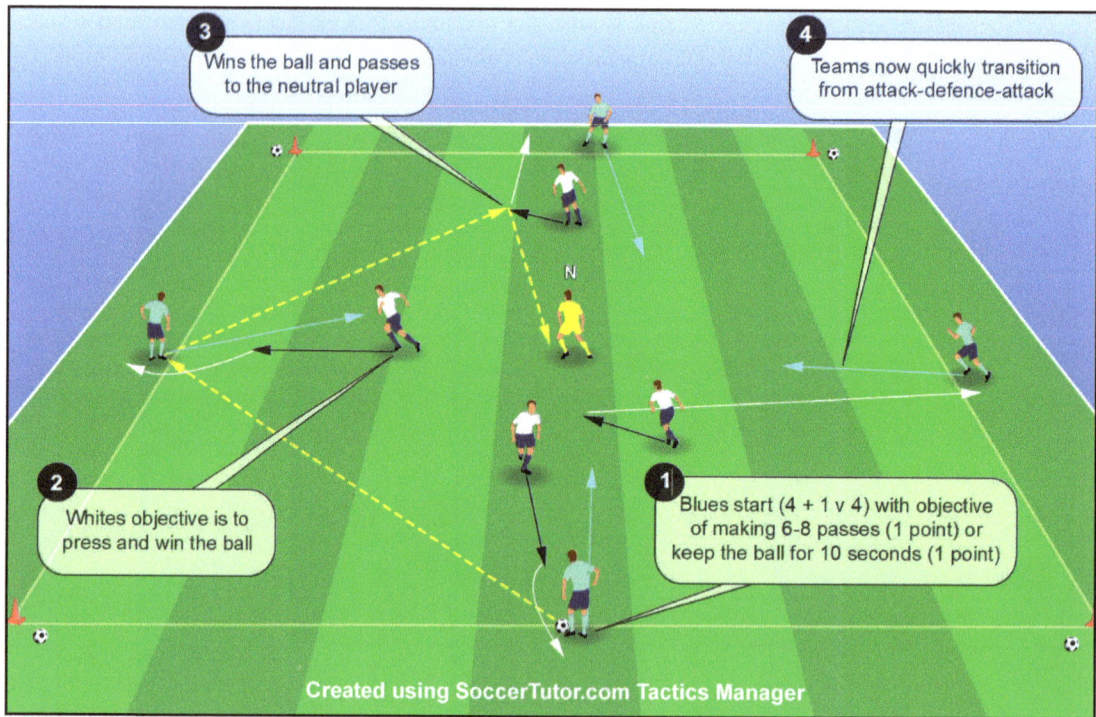

Description

In a 25 yard square, we have 2 teams of 4 and 1 neutral player (inside) who always plays with the team in possession. The team that starts with the ball has all their players at the sides (blues in diagram).

The objective for the blue team is to complete 6-8 passes (1 point) or keep the ball for 10 seconds (1 point). The objective for the white team is to press and win the ball.

If they win the ball, the whites try to move to the outside positions as quickly as possible, maintaining possession with the neutral player in the meantime (1 point). They must open the pitch in transition from defence to attack. Once they are all outside, they then try to complete 6-8 passes or keep the ball for 10 seconds (1 point).

Rules
1. Players are limited to 2-3 touches and the neutral player has 1-2 touches.
2. In the transition to attack, the players have unlimited touches until they are all positioned outside.

Coaching Points
1. The defending team need to press as a unit to limit space/time and win the ball.
2. After a team wins the ball (transition), focus on: Quality of pass (ideally 1 touch), correct decision making, appropriate angles and distances for support play + good communication.

PROGRESSION

2. Pressing to Win the Ball and then Keep Possession in a Two Zone Transition Game

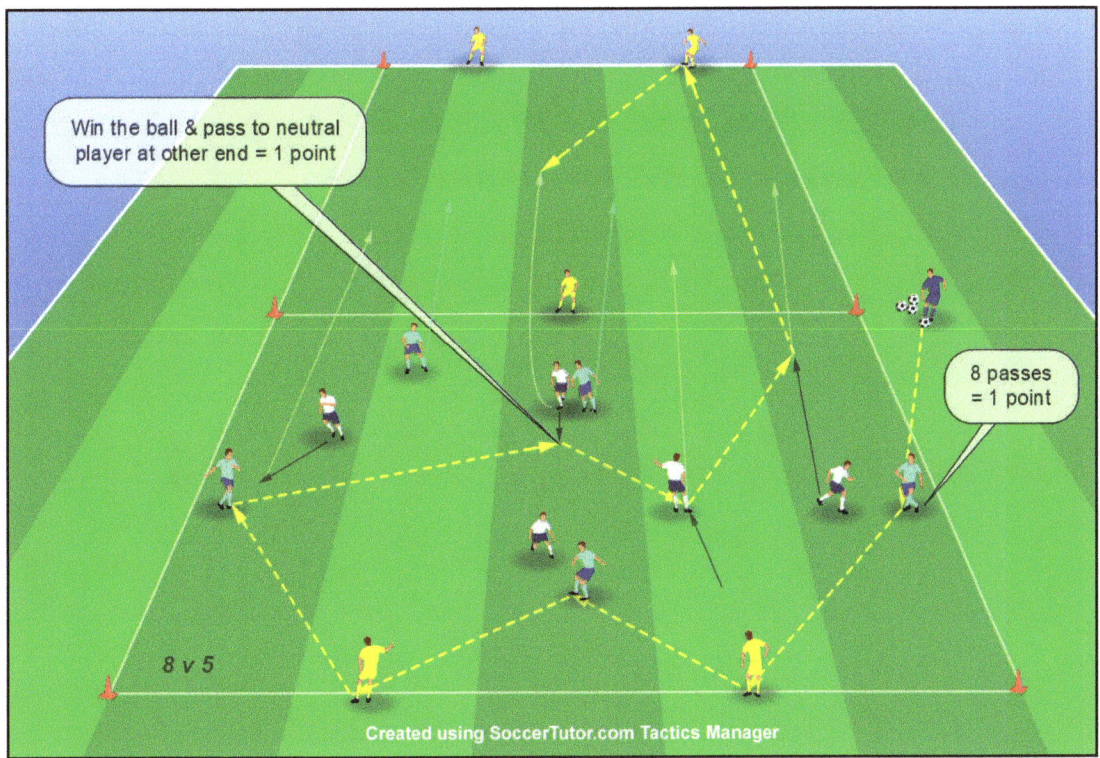

Description

In a 25 x 45 yard area, we divide the pitch into 2 equal zones and work with 15 players. There are 2 teams of 5 and 5 extra neutral players (yellows - 2 at each end line and 1 on the middle line).

The practice starts in one zone with the blues in possession and an 8 v 5 numerical advantage. Their objective is to complete 8 passes (1 point).

The objective for the white defending team is to press, win the ball and pass to a neutral player at the end of the other zone (1 point). All the white and blue players then move across - the whites make a transition from defence to attack. The team roles are reversed with the whites now trying to complete 8 consecutive passes.

Rule: Players have unlimited (or 2-3) touches and the neutrals have 1-2 touches.

Coaching Points
1. After winning the ball (transition), change direction of the game with a quick pass to other zone.
2. Follow this with quick movements to support, using the correct distances and angles to receive.

Session to Practice **POCHETTINO** Tactics - Transition from Defence to Attack (Low Zone)

PROGRESSION

3. Exploiting Free Space in the Opposition Half with Fast Combination Play in a Dynamic Game

Description

Using a full pitch, we mark out an end zone (third of pitch) with a full sized goal and goalkeeper. We have 3 mini goals at the other end and the rest of the players start within 2/3 of the pitch as shown. Within this area, we mark out 2 wide channels for the yellow neutral players.

The white team use a 4-2-3-1 formation and the blues use a 4-3-3 formation. The neutral players play with the team in possession and take up the roles of the full backs in both systems. The practice always starts from the blue goalkeeper with the aim to build up and score in one of the mini goals.

The white team defend the mini goals and try to win the ball. When they win the ball, their second aim is to launch a quick counter attack. They should use fast combination play and then exploit the space in behind with a correctly weighted pass and well-timed run.

Rules

1. As soon as the ball is played into the end zone, all players can move freely to attack/defend.
2. From the moment they win the ball, the whites must score within 10-12 seconds.
3. All players have unlimited touches and the neutrals have 2 touches.

Session to Practice **POCHETTINO** Tactics - Transition from Defence to Attack (Low Zone)

PROGRESSION

4. Exploiting Free Space in the Opposition Half with Fast Combination Play in a Tactical Game (4-2-3-1 vs 4-3-3)

Description

In this progression of the previous practice, we remove the wide channels, the neutral players and the 3 mini goals. We therefore add full backs (2 & 3) for both teams and a large goal and goalkeeper for the white team. The white team are using a 4-2-3-1 formation and the blues use a 4-3-3 formation. The aims and rules are the same as the previous practice.

Coaching Points

1. Press in and around the ball area to limit time/space and exploit the numerical advantage in the low zone (apply as much pressure as possible).
2. In the transition to attack, players need to demonstrate good decision making, movement/runs with rhythm at a high tempo, intelligence, good awareness and good communication.
3. In the transition from defence to attack, we should look to play quickly to the forward (9) or No.10. From this point, we then need quick support runs from a central midfielder (6 or 8) and the 2 wingers (7 & 11), as well as accurate combination play.
4. If an attacking player is able to receive in space within the end zone, the other attacking players must run forward to support them in the penalty area for quick and effective finishing.

TACTICAL SITUATION 2

MAURIZIO SARRI TACTICS

Exploiting Free Space in the Opposition Half with a Fast Break Attack

Content taken from Analysis of Napoli during the 2016/2017 Season

The analysis is based on recurring patterns of play observed within the Napoli team. Once the same phase of play occurred a number of times (at least 10) the tactics would be seen as a pattern. The analysis on the next page is an example of the team's tactics being used effectively, taken from a specific game.

Each action, pass, individual movement with or without the ball, and the positioning of each player on the pitch including their body shape, are presented.

The analysis is then used to create a full progressive session to coach this specific tactical situation.

Tactical Analysis of MAURIZIO SARRI - Transition from Defence to Attack (Low Zone)

Analysis Taken from 'AC Milan vs Napoli - 21st Jan 2017 (Serie A)'

Exploiting Free Space in the Opposition Half with a Fast Break Attack (4-3-3 vs 4-3-3)

In this example, Napoli's defensive midfielder Jorginho intercepts a pass from the Milan left winger (11) and lays the ball off to central midfielder Allan.

Allan dribbles into the space ahead and looks up. He can see that the opposition's defensive line is extremely high and there is lots of space in behind.

Allan plays a pass for the forward Mertens to run onto in space.

Mertens is tracked well by the Milan centre back (5) but there is lots of space to exploit.

As the opposition's defence is very disorganised, Mertens plays a first time pass in behind and across for the left winger Insigne to run onto.

Insigne is able to take a good first touch away from the defenders and score with a left footed strike.

Session to Practice MAURIZIO SARRI Tactics - Transition from Defence to Attack (Low Zone)

SESSION FOR THIS TACTICAL SITUATION (3 PRACTICES)
1. Exploiting Free Space in the Opposition Half with a Fast Break Attack in a Dynamic 3 Team Transition Game

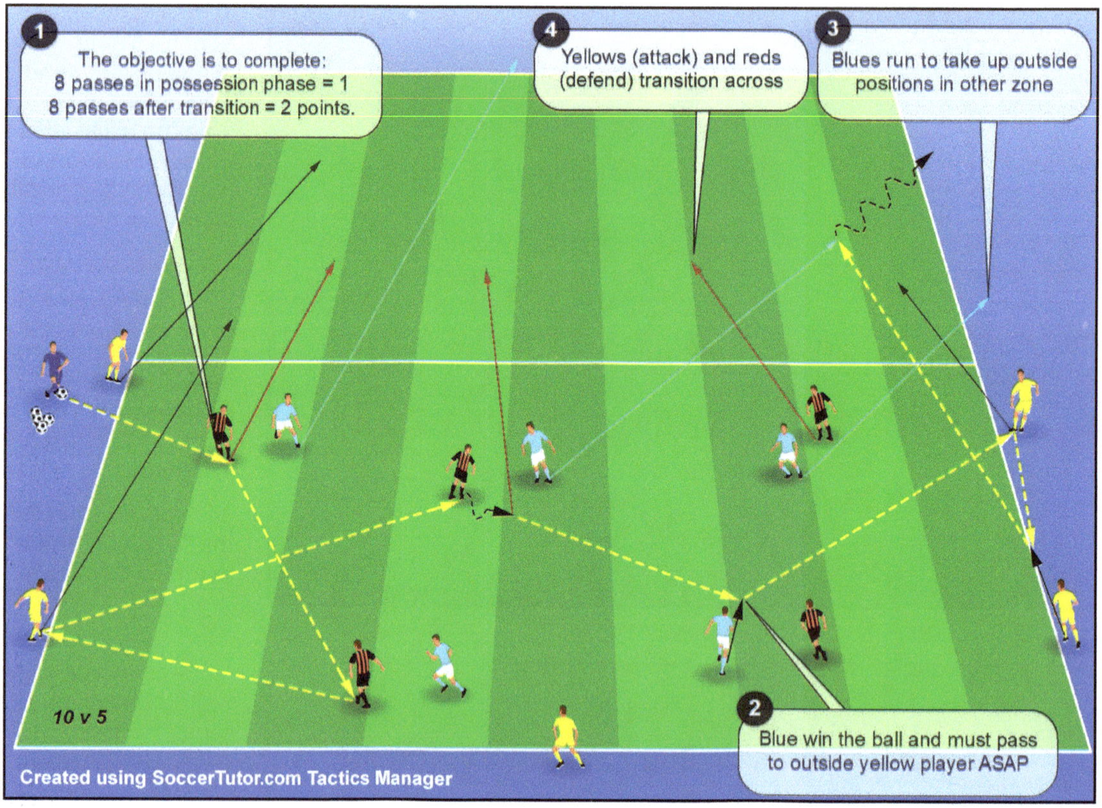

1 The objective is to complete:
8 passes in possession phase = 1
8 passes after transition = 2 points.

4 Yellows (attack) and reds (defend) transition across

3 Blues run to take up outside positions in other zone

2 Blue win the ball and must pass to outside yellow player ASAP

10 v 5

Description

In a 40 x 50 yard area, we divide the pitch into 2 equal zones. We have 3 teams of 5 players. Two teams (blues and reds) start inside the first zone and the yellow team start outside as neutral players.

The red team try to keep possession of the ball with the yellows (10 v 5) and the blues try to win the ball. If the blues win the ball, the following happens:

- The blues pass to an outside yellow player as soon as possible.
- All the blue players run to take up the outside positions in the other zone.
- All the other players move across. We now have the blues (outside) and the yellows (inside) in the other zone trying to keep possession in a 10 v 5 situation, with the reds trying to win it back.

Rules

1. All players have unlimited touches or all players are limited to 2-3 touches.
2. Inside players have 2-3 touches and the outside players have 1 touch.
3. Complete 8 passes in possession phase = 1 point / Complete 8 passes after transition = 2 points.

Session to Practice MAURIZIO SARRI Tactics - Transition from Defence to Attack (Low Zone)

PROGRESSION

2. Exploiting Free Space in the Opposition Half with a Fast Break Attack in a Dynamic Small Sided Game

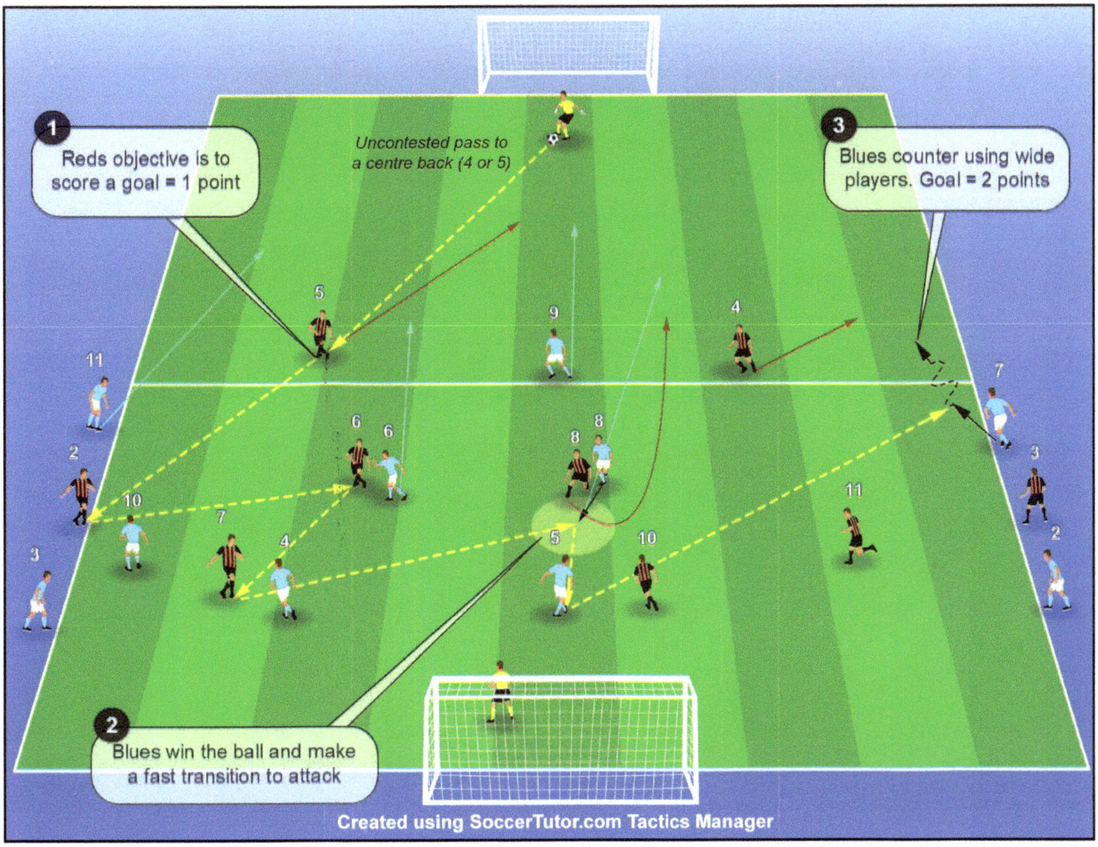

Description

In this progression of the previous practice, we now only have 2 teams. The red team have 9 outfield players + GK. They have 5 players inside the blue's half (3 central midfielders & 2 wingers). They also have 2 full backs outside and 2 centre backs in their half, as shown.

The blue team have a full 11 players. They have 5 players in their own half (2 centre backs & 3 central midfielders), 4 players outside (2 full backs & 2 wingers) and 1 forward in the other half.

The practice starts with an uncontested pass from the red team's GK to a centre back (4 or 5). The red team try to score a goal (1 point). The blues try to win the ball and make a fast transition to attack. They exploit the open space in the other half and utilise their players at the sides to score (2 points).

Rules

1. All players are free to move into the other half as soon as the ball is played in there.
2. The blues have a limited time to finish their attack e.g. 8-12 seconds.
3. When the transition is finished, change the team roles and start from the opposite end.

Session to Practice MAURIZIO SARRI Tactics - Transition from Defence to Attack (Low Zone)

PROGRESSION

3. Exploiting Free Space in the Opposition Half with a Fast Break Attack in a 2 Zone Game (4-3-3 vs 4-3-3)

Blue must score within 15 seconds of winning the ball = 2 points

Description

As we progress to playing on a full pitch, both teams are using the 4-3-3 formation. The practice starts with an uncontested pass from the red team's GK to a centre back (4 or 5).

The reds try to score (1 point). The blues try to win the ball and make a fast transition to attack. They exploit the open space in the opposition's half and in behind the defensive line.

As soon as the blues win the ball, they have 15 seconds to score (2 points). After 10-15 minutes, change the team roles.

Coaching Points

1. Blues need to have a good defensive shape, use ball oriented defence, keep compact lines and apply collective pressing to win the ball.
2. In the transition to attack, there needs to be good awareness, decision making, forward passes and combination play, fast running (quick support movements from the back) and aggression.
3. Look to play passes outside the 2 centre backs, timed with a good run in behind.

TACTICAL SITUATION 3

JORGE SAMPAOLI TACTICS

Counter Attack with a Forward Pass, Lay-Off and Supporting Runs

Content taken from Analysis of Sevilla during the 2016/2017 season

The analysis is based on recurring patterns of play observed within the Sevilla team. Once the same phase of play occurred a number of times (at least 10) the tactics would be seen as a pattern. The analysis on the next page is an example of the team's tactics being used effectively, taken from a specific game.

Each action, pass, individual movement with or without the ball, and the positioning of each player on the pitch including their body shape, are presented.

The analysis is then used to create a full progressive session to coach this specific tactical situation.

Tactical Analysis of JORGE SAMPAOLI - Transition from Defence to Attack (Low Zone)

Analysis Taken from 'Sevilla vs FC Barcelona - 6th Nov 2016 (La Liga)'

Counter Attack with a Forward Pass, Lay-Off and Supporting Runs (4-1-4-1 vs 4-3-3)

In this example, Sevilla are very deep and Neymar (11) has the ball in the box. He tries to pass to Suarez (9), but plays the ball behind him.

The Sevilla left back Escudero is able to track back and clear the ball towards the right winger Sarabia.

Sarabia plays the ball forward to Vazquez who is in a centre forward's position. He lays the ball off for Sarabia to run onto (one-two).

Sarabia receives the pass back unmarked and there is lots of space in behind the Barcelona defensive line.

The left winger Vitolo makes a run outside the Barca right back (2) and receives a perfectly weighted pass from Sarabia.

Vitolo dribbles into the box, close to the goalkeeper and then prods the ball past him to score.

Session to Practice **JORGE SAMPAOLI** Tactics - Transition from Defence to Attack (Low Zone)

SESSION FOR THIS TACTICAL SITUATION (3 PRACTICES)
1. Counter Attack with a Forward Pass, Lay-Off and Supporting Runs in a Functional Practice

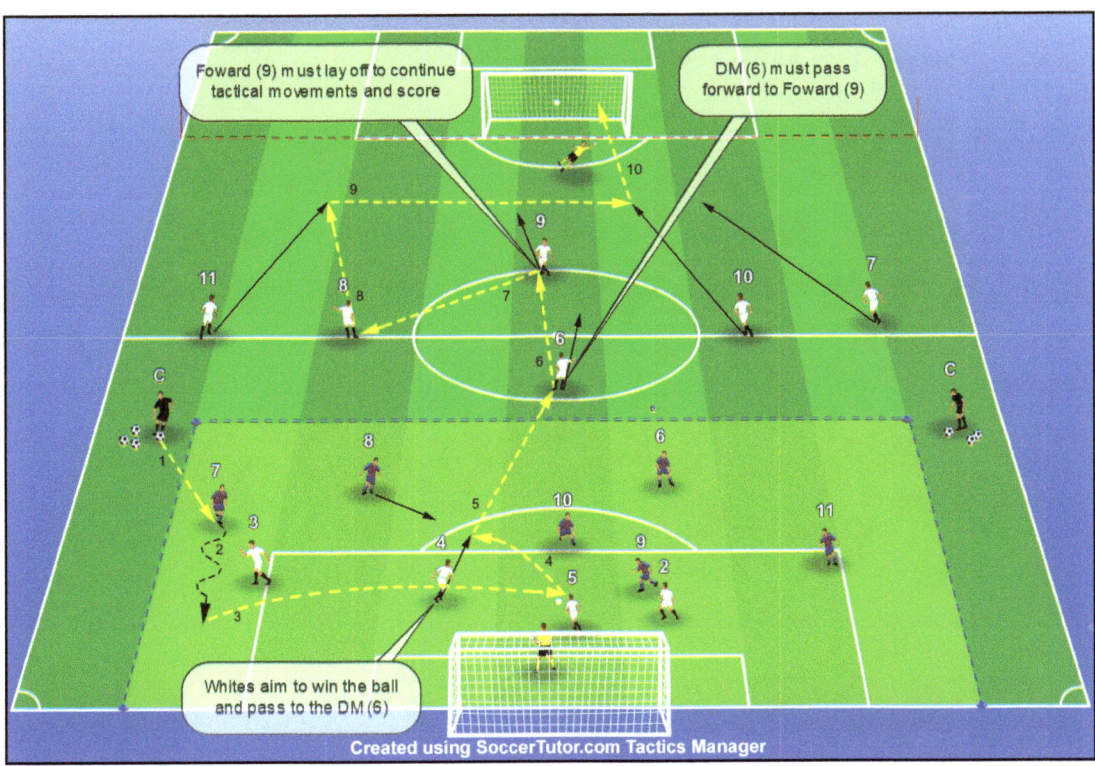

Objective: Tactical attacking movements, solutions and combinations: Forward pass, lay-off, support.

Description
For this practice, the white team have 11 players and the other team have 7 players. We mark out a low zone as shown - within this zone we have the white back 4 against 6 attackers (from 4-3-3).

The practice starts with the coach's pass inside and the blue/reds try to score a goal. The aim for the whites is to win the ball and then pass to the defensive midfielder (6) who is waiting just outside.

From this point, No.6 must pass to the forward (9) who lays it off to an oncoming runner (6, 8 or 10). From here, the 6 white attacking players must use tactical movements and combinations that we want for our players and team, and try to score a goal.

Different Rules
1. All players have unlimited touches / Limit the players to 2 or 3 touches.
2. Blue/reds have unlimited time to finish attack / Blue/reds have 12 seconds to finish their attack.
3. After winning the ball (transition), the whites have 10-12 seconds to finish their counter attack.

Session to Practice JORGE SAMPAOLI Tactics - Transition from Defence to Attack (Low Zone)

PROGRESSION

2. Counter Attack with a Forward Pass, Lay-Off and Supporting Runs in a 2 Zone Game

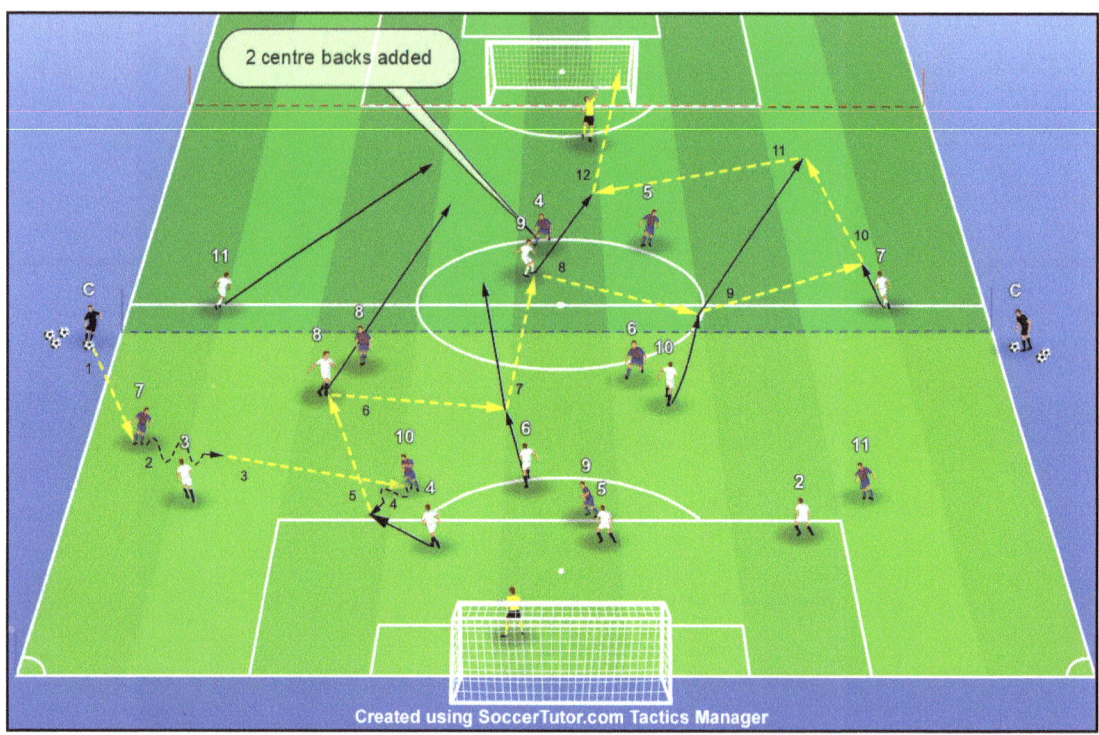

Description

In this progression of the previous practice, we increase the low zone area as shown and the initial situation is now 6 v 7 (+GK) for the blue/red's attack.

After winning the ball in this zone, the whites now play directly to the forward (9) who lays the ball off for an oncoming runner (6, 8 or 10). They then try to score, as in the last practice.

We add 2 blue/red centre backs (4 & 5) which makes it more difficult for the whites to combine and finish the counter attacks, as there is now defensive pressure. However, as the whites still have a 6 v 2 numerical advantage, they should still score the majority of the time.

Coaching Points

1. The white team use ball oriented defence in the low zone and press as a unit to limit the time and space available for their opponents.
2. They need to demonstrate good communication when pressing and exploit the numerical superiority they have.
3. In the transition to attack, a hard and precise forward pass is needed into the forward.
4. In the attacking half, the players need to be aggressive and play at a very high speed/tempo, using the required tactical movements/combinations + quick and effective finishing.

Session to Practice **JORGE SAMPAOLI** Tactics - Transition from Defence to Attack (Low Zone)

PROGRESSION

3. Counter Attack with a Forward Pass, Lay-Off and Supporting Runs in a Tactical Game (4-1-4-1 vs 4-3-3)

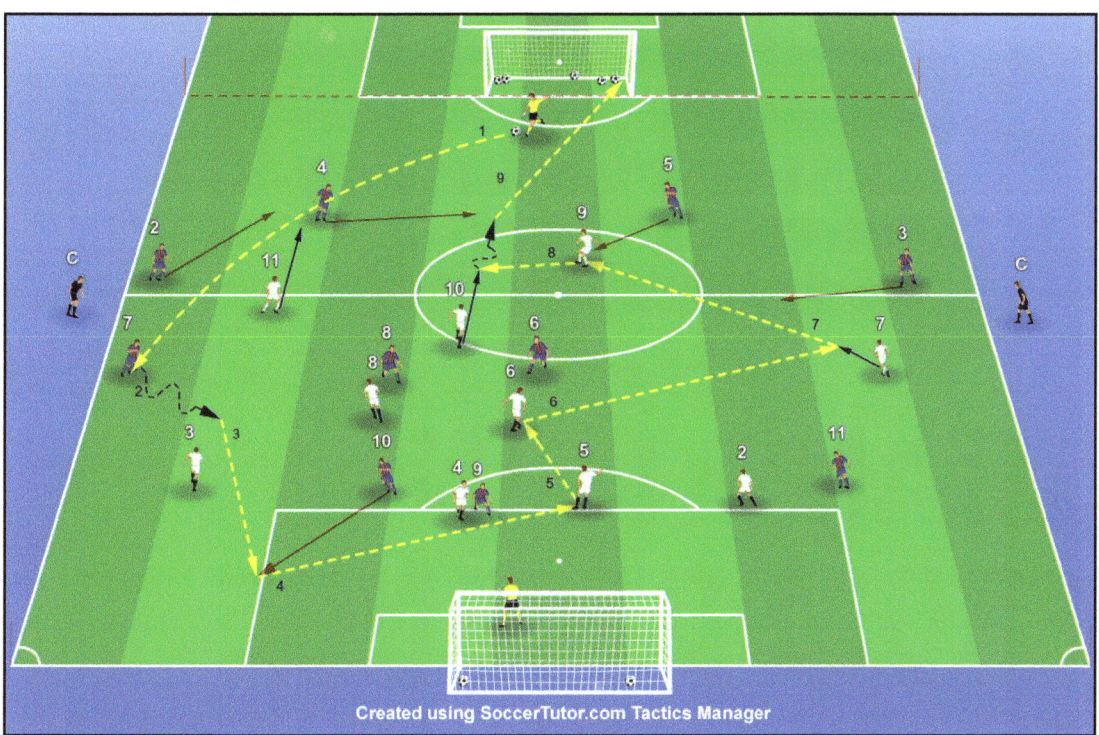

Description

In this progression, we remove the zone and now play in the full area, as shown.

We also add 2 full backs (2 & 3) for the blue/red team so the game is a fully competitive 11 v 11 tactical situation.

The practice now starts from the blue/red team's goalkeeper.

The aims, objectives and coaching points remain the same.

CHAPTER 5

TRANSITION FROM DEFENCE TO ATTACK IN THE MIDDLE ZONE

TRANSITION FROM DEFENCE TO ATTACK IN THE MIDDLE ZONE

For this book, we have divided the chapters by which zone the transition starts in. There are 3 zones:

1. **Low Zone**
2. **Middle Zone**
3. **High Zone**

This diagram shows a team winning the ball in the middle zone. In this situation, the white team have players behind the ball when defending. To win the ball, they need to limit their opponent's time/space, block potential passing options and demonstrate good anticipation.

The red team are trying to build up play from the back. The right back (2) had received a pass from the centre back and is closed down by the white team's left winger (11). The attempted pass inside to red No.8 is intercepted by the white No.10.

The No.10 runs forward with the ball and the red team are left unbalanced. The striker (9) makes a run out wide and receives the pass. The red centre back (4) has to follow him, which creates space in the centre for the No.10 to run into. No.9 dribbles towards the box and passes the ball across to No.10 to finish. The right winger (7) also makes a run into the box to support the attack.

The aim after winning the ball in the middle zone should always be to pass/move the ball forward quickly to exploit the disorganised defence of the opposition, before they have time to recover.

TRANSITION FROM DEFENCE TO ATTACK IN THE MIDDLE ZONE

What is the Tactical Situation?

- Our team defends higher up the pitch and further from our goal, compared to when we defend in the low zone.

- There are many players from both teams in the centre of the pitch.

- We are now closer to the opponent's goal when we win the ball.

- We have the option of many attacking solutions when we win the ball.

- We can attack with up to 5 or 6 players.

- 2-3 players can more easily run beyond the forwards to offer options.

- Quick attacks from the middle zone have a higher chance of success than the low zone. The opposition are often disorganised when they lose the ball in this area.

- There is often free space behind the opponent's defensive line to exploit.

- There are possibilities to create a numerical advantage (overload situation).

- The attacks (transition from defence to attack) take 8 seconds on average.

What Objectives Should We Have?

- To defend well in our own half, limiting the time and space our opponents have while pressing to win the ball.

- To quickly pass the ball forward and exploit the disorganised defence of our opponents.

- Quick combination play - one-touch passing and passes into space.

- To run forward with the ball at speed, drawing opponents in and beating them or creating space for teammates to run into before passing to them.

- To quickly run up from behind, to support our striker, ask for the ball to be played into the space and finish the attacks.

- Quick, quality and synchronised movements inside the penalty area to finish the attacks effectively.

What Practices/Sessions Can We Create for this Tactical Situation?

- Work on defensive situations in the middle zone versus opponents trying to attack in behind the defensive line, with the primary aim to win the ball.

- The players need to learn how to move and pass the ball quickly forward to players in advanced positions, so that we can attack quickly while the opposition are still unbalanced.

- The main focus of the practices needs to be on fast and effective transitions from defence to attack with equal numbers or with a numerical advantage (overload situations).

TACTICAL SITUATION 1

LEONARDO JARDIM TACTICS

Fast and Direct Counter Attacks with Through Ball in Behind

Content taken from Analysis of Monaco during the 2016/2017 season

The analysis is based on recurring patterns of play observed within the Monaco team. Once the same phase of play occurred a number of times (at least 10) the tactics would be seen as a pattern. The analysis on the next page is an example of the team's tactics being used effectively, taken from a specific game.

Each action, pass, individual movement with or without the ball, and the positioning of each player on the pitch including their body shape, are presented.

The analysis is then used to create a full progressive session to coach this specific tactical situation.

Tactical Analysis of LEONARDO JARDIM - Transition from Defence to Attack (Middle Zone)

Analysis Taken from 'AS Monaco vs Fenerbahçe - 3rd Aug 2016 (Champions League)'
Fast and Direct Counter Attacks with Through Ball in Behind

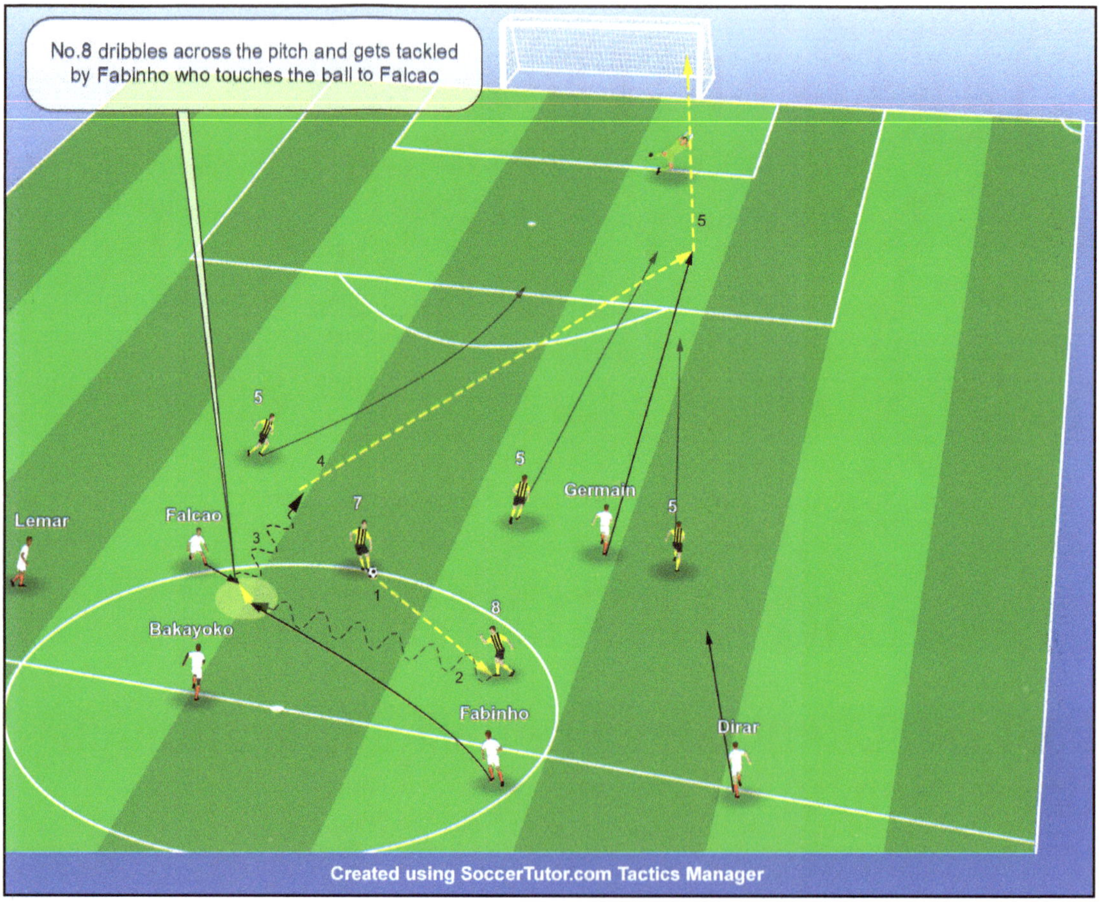

No.8 dribbles across the pitch and gets tackled by Fabinho who touches the ball to Falcao

In this situation, the Fenerbahçe central midfielder (8) receives and dribbles inside. No.8 is closed down by 2 Monaco central midfielders (Fabinho and Bakayoko) and the forward Falcao - he is left with nowhere to go.

The Fenerbahçe No.8 is tackled by the Monaco central midfielder Fabinho, who touches the ball to the forward (Falcao).

Falcao dribbles forward into the space and the Fenerbahçe centre backs (and defensive midfielder No.6) are in unbalanced positions and running back towards their own goal.

The other Monaco forward Germain sprints forward into the space behind the defensive line. Falcao's pass is perfectly timed and weighted for Germain to run onto finish first time past the goalkeeper.

Session to Practice **LEONARDO JARDIM** Tactics - Transition from Defence to Attack (Middle Zone)

SESSION FOR THIS TACTICAL SITUATION (4 PRACTICES)
1. Fast Counter Attacks with Through Ball in Behind in a Dynamic 3 Zone Possession Game

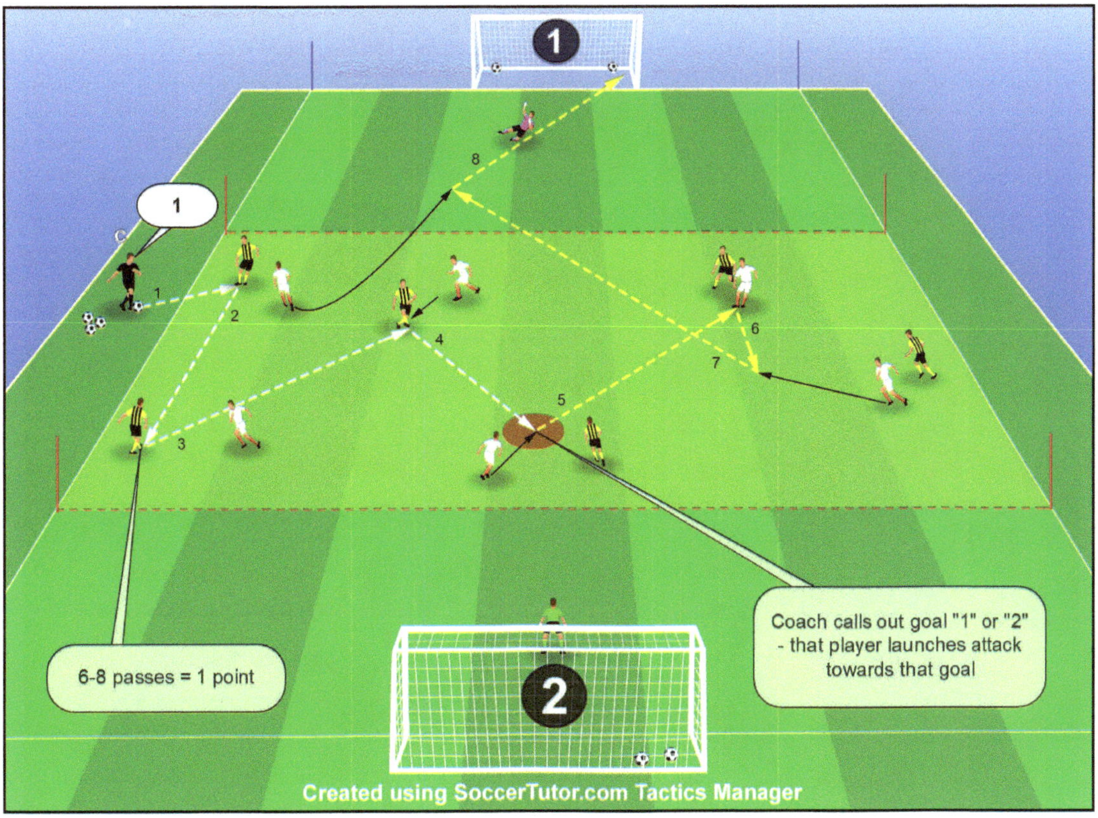

6-8 passes = 1 point

Coach calls out goal "1" or "2" - that player launches attack towards that goal

Description

In a 40 x 60 yard area, we mark out a 40 x 30 yard middle zone. We have 6 v 6 in the middle zone and we also have 2 goalkeepers in large goals. When the coach passes the ball in, the players play a 6 v 6 possession game within the middle zone. If a team completes 6-8 passes, they score 1 point.

The coach allows possession to change hands a few times and then calls out either "1" or "2" in reference to the goals which are numbered. At this point, the player in possession launches a fast break attack for his team (whites in diagram) towards the goal that was called out.

Rules

1. The attack must include a through ball from the middle zone into the end zone.
2. If a team scores within 8 seconds of the coach's signal, the goal counts double.
3. If the attack is too slow, the coach can call out the other goal so the team has to change the direction of their attack.

Coaching Points: These are the same as the next practice (see page 58).

Session to Practice **LEONARDO JARDIM** Tactics - Transition from Defence to Attack (Middle Zone)

VARIATION

2. Fast Counter Attacks with Through Ball in Behind in a 3 Zone Transition Game

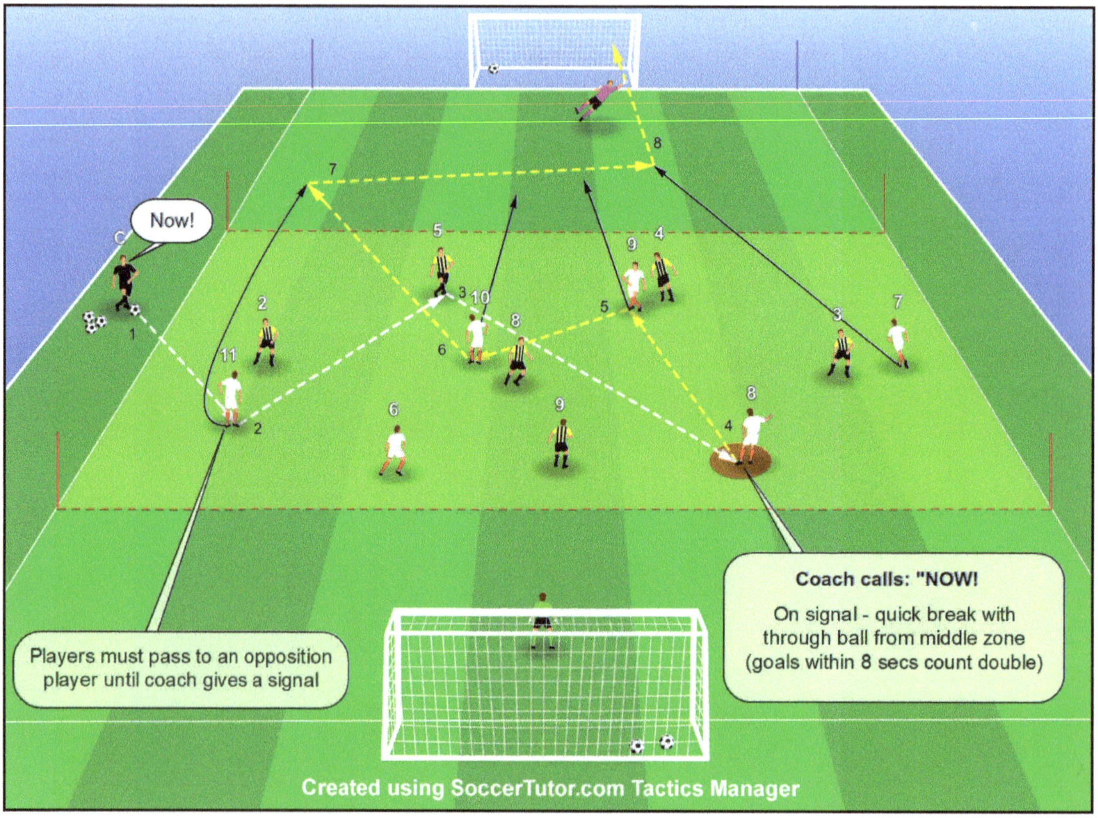

Description

In this variation of the previous practice, the players for both teams now form a tactical shape. The yellows use a 2-3-1 formation and the whites use a 4-2.

The practice starts with the coach's pass into the middle zone. The players must pass to an opposition player continuously until the coach gives a signal, trying to always keep in their tactical shape. On this signal, the player in possession launches a fast break attack for his team (whites in diagram).

Rules: 1. The attack must include a through ball from the middle zone into the end zone.
2. If a team scores within 8 seconds of the coach's signal, the goal counts double.

Coaching Points

1. Players need to react quickly, demonstrate good decision making, movement and intelligent runs.
2. Players must work at a high tempo, with accurate passes, synchronised movements, precise combination play, good communication and one-touch finishing.
3. Decision making is key - when to pass to feet or into space, the weight of pass and timing of runs.

Session to Practice **LEONARDO JARDIM** Tactics - Transition from Defence to Attack (Middle Zone)

PROGRESSION

3. Fast Counter Attacks with Through Ball in Behind in a Dynamic Small Sided Game

Coach waits for team to win the ball and signals for fast break attack

Objective: Winning the ball in the middle zone and fast break attacks with through ball in behind.

Description

In this progression of the previous practice, we now play a directional game with the teams defending one goal and trying to score in the other.

When the coach passes the ball in, the players play a 6 v 6 possession game within the middle zone. The coach waits for the right moment when a player has just won the ball from the opposition and then gives his signal. At this point, the player in possession launches a fast break attack for his team (whites in diagram).

Rules

1. The attack must include a through ball from the middle zone into the end zone.
2. If a team scores within 8 seconds of the coach's signal, the goal counts double.

Coaching Points: These are the same as the previous practice.

Session to Practice **LEONARDO JARDIM** Tactics - Transition from Defence to Attack (Middle Zone)

PROGRESSION

4. Press in Middle Zone + Fast Counter Attacks with Through Ball in Behind (Tactical Game)

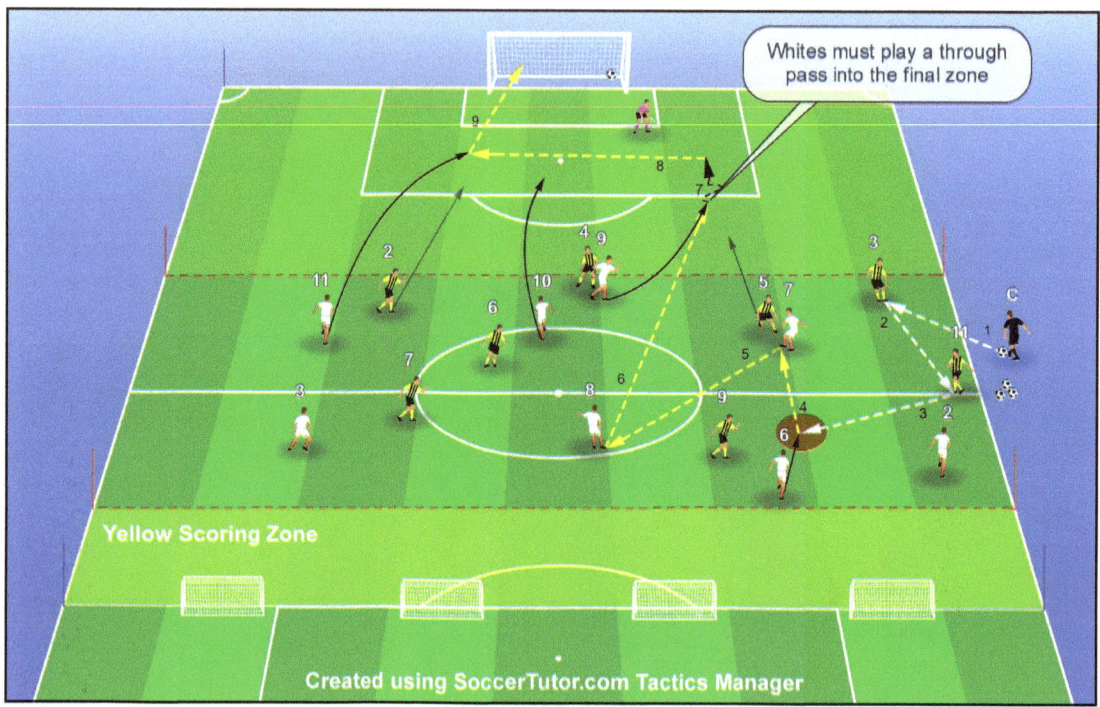

Objective: Winning the ball in the middle zone and fast break attacks with a through ball in behind.

Description

Using the area shown, we divide the pitch into 3 zones. All of the outfield players start in the middle zone. We play 8 v 8 - the yellows are in a 4-1-3 formation. The white team are in a 2-4-2 formation with 2 full backs (2 & 3), 2 central midfielders (6 & 8), 2 wingers (7 & 11) and 2 forwards (9 & 10).

The practice starts from the coach, as shown. The yellow team attack and try to play the ball into the "Yellow Scoring Zone" (or dribble inside) and then score in one of the 4 mini goals.

The white team apply ball oriented defence, try to win the ball and then launch a fast break attack with a through ball in behind the defensive line, as in the previous practices in this session.

Rules

1. The yellow team cannot defend in the low zone before the ball is played in there.
2. From the moment they win the ball, the whites have 10 seconds to finish their counter attack.
3. The white's counter attack must include a through ball from the middle zone into the end zone.

Session to Practice **LEONARDO JARDIM** Tactics - Transition from Defence to Attack (Middle Zone)

Variation

Simply remove the 4 mini goals and replace them with a large goal and goalkeeper.

Coaching Points

1. The white team use ball oriented defence and press as a unit to limit the time and space available for their opponents, trying to win the ball as quickly as possible.

2. Defensive cover is needed to prevent possible passes, as well as quick changes of defensive positioning.

3. Monitor the correct distances between the players when pressing.

4. In the transition from defence to attack, the passes and dribbling should be performed at a high tempo with one-touch combinations and finishing.

5. The rhythm and timing of the movement and passing needs to be coordinated to break through the lines of defence effectively.

6. Players need good awareness, movement, communication, quick support and decision making.

TACTICAL SITUATION 2

JORGE SAMPAOLI TACTICS

Direct Counter Attacks with Driving Support Runs

Content taken from Analysis of Sevilla during the 2016/2017 season

The analysis is based on recurring patterns of play observed within the Sevilla team. Once the same phase of play occurred a number of times (at least 10) the tactics would be seen as a pattern. The analysis on the next page is an example of the team's tactics being used effectively, taken from a specific game.

Each action, pass, individual movement with or without the ball, and the positioning of each player on the pitch including their body shape, are presented.

The analysis is then used to create a full progressive session to coach this specific tactical situation.

Tactical Analysis of JORGE SAMPAOLI - Transition from Defence to Attack (Middle Zone)

Analysis Taken from 'Sevilla vs Leganes - 11th Mar 2017 (La Liga)'

Direct Counter Attacks with Driving Support Runs (3-4-3 vs 4-2-3-1)

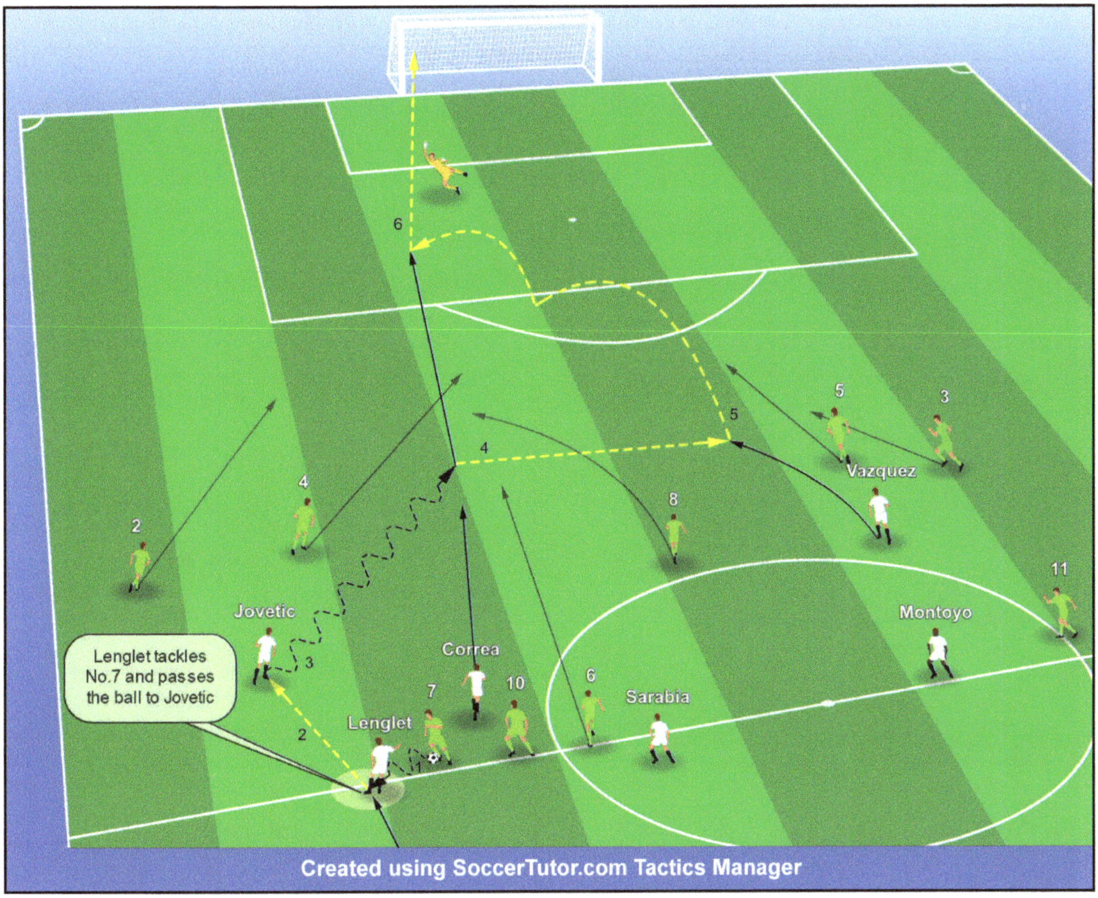

In this situation, the Leganes right winger (7) is dispossessed by the Sevilla left centre back Lenglet, who has stepped up to apply pressure.

Lenglet plays a short pass to the forward Jovetic, who is able to drive forward into the space as the Leganes defenders drop back.

Jovetic then demonstrates great awareness and intelligence to play a one-two combination with oncoming right forward Vazquez.

The pass is perfectly timed to the run and Jovetic scores. The Leganes defence was left static, as they tried to play offside.

Session to Practice **JORGE SAMPAOLI** Tactics - Transition from Defence to Attack (Middle Zone)

SESSION FOR THIS TACTICAL SITUATION (4 PRACTICES)
1. Direct Counter Attacks with Driving Support Runs in a 5 v 5 (+2) Dynamic 2 Zone Transition Game

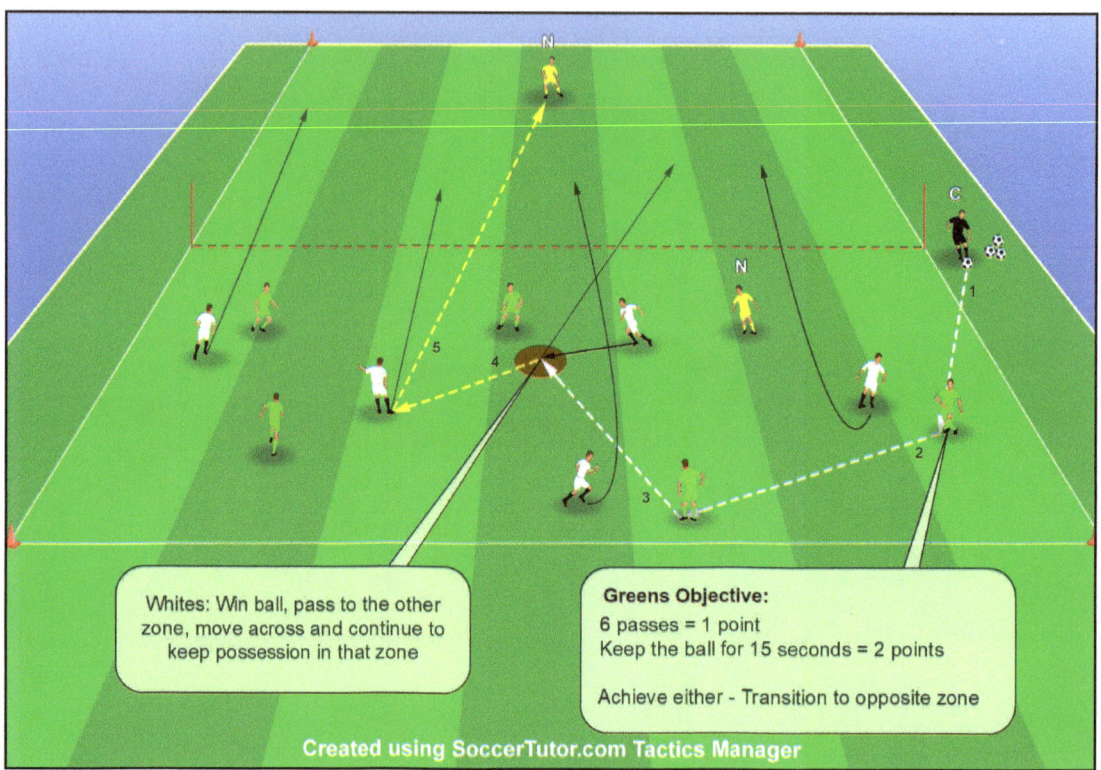

Whites: Win ball, pass to the other zone, move across and continue to keep possession in that zone

Greens Objective:
6 passes = 1 point
Keep the ball for 15 seconds = 2 points

Achieve either - Transition to opposite zone

Objective: Quick play in transition from defence to attack with driving support runs.

Description

In a 25 x 35 yard area, we have 2 equal zones. All 5 players from both teams start in one zone and there are also 2 neutral players (1 in each zone).

The team that starts in possession (greens in diagram) try to complete 6 passes (1 point) and keep the ball for 15 seconds (2 points). If they achieve either of these objectives, they can then pass to the other zone, move across (fast driving support running) and continue to keep possession in that zone.

The objective for the white defending team is to press, win the ball and then quickly pass to the neutral player in the other zone. At this point, all the players move across (fast driving support running) and the practice continues in the other zone with the team roles reversed.

Rules

1. If a team wins the ball, passes to other zone + all players move across within 6-8 seconds = 1 point.
2. If a team loses the ball and wins it back within same zone before it is passed across = 2 points.

Session to Practice JORGE SAMPAOLI Tactics - Transition from Defence to Attack (Middle Zone)

VARIATION

2. Direct Counter Attacks with Driving Support Runs in a 5 v 5 (+1) Dynamic 2 Zone Transition Game

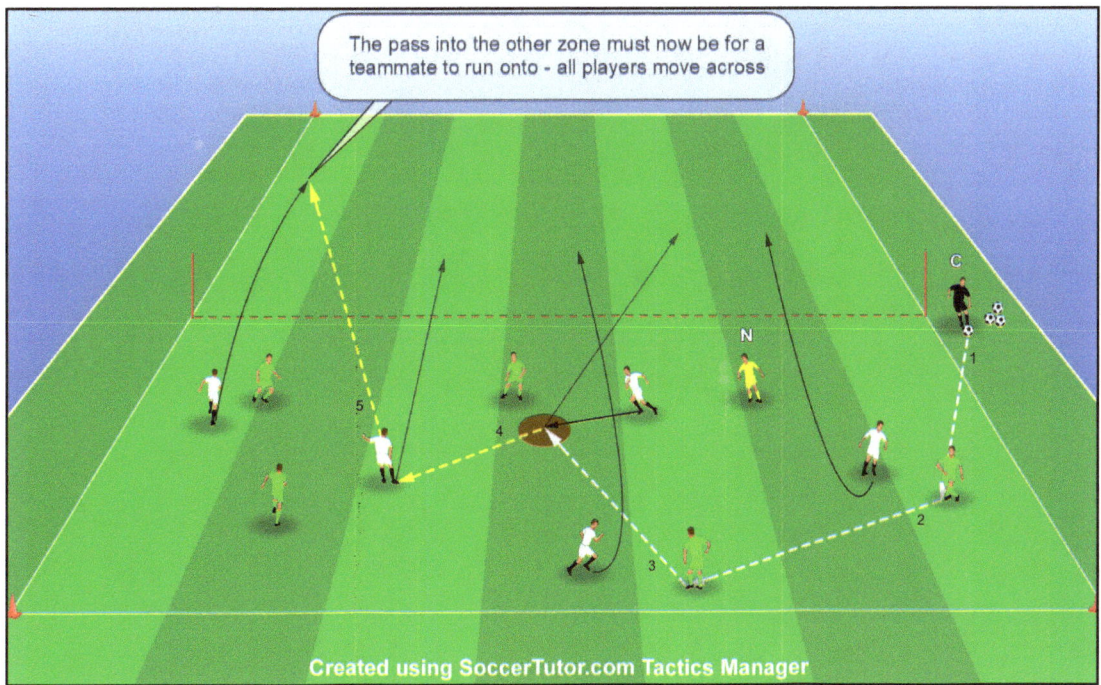

Description

For this variation, we simply remove the second neutral player. The teams now have to pass the ball across to the other zone, weighted well for a teammate to run onto.

All players then move across including the neutral player.

Variation

We play without neutral players and the teams play with equal numbers (5 v 5). The teams still have to pass the ball across to the other zone after winning it, well weighted for a teammate to run onto.

All players then move across to the other zone with the team roles reversed.

Coaching Points

1. The defending team must try to reduce the space for their opponents and apply as much collective pressing as possible, to eliminate the numerical disadvantage and win the ball.
2. In the transition from defence to attack, there needs to be good awareness, quick decision making, high tempo actions, fast support play and movement.
3. Once a pass has been played to the other zone, the players must run quickly to provide support, offering to receive the ball at the correct angles and distances to maintain possession for their team.

Session to Practice **JORGE SAMPAOLI** Tactics - Transition from Defence to Attack (Middle Zone)

PROGRESSION

3. Direct Counter Attacks with Driving Support Runs in a Position Specific 2 Zone Game

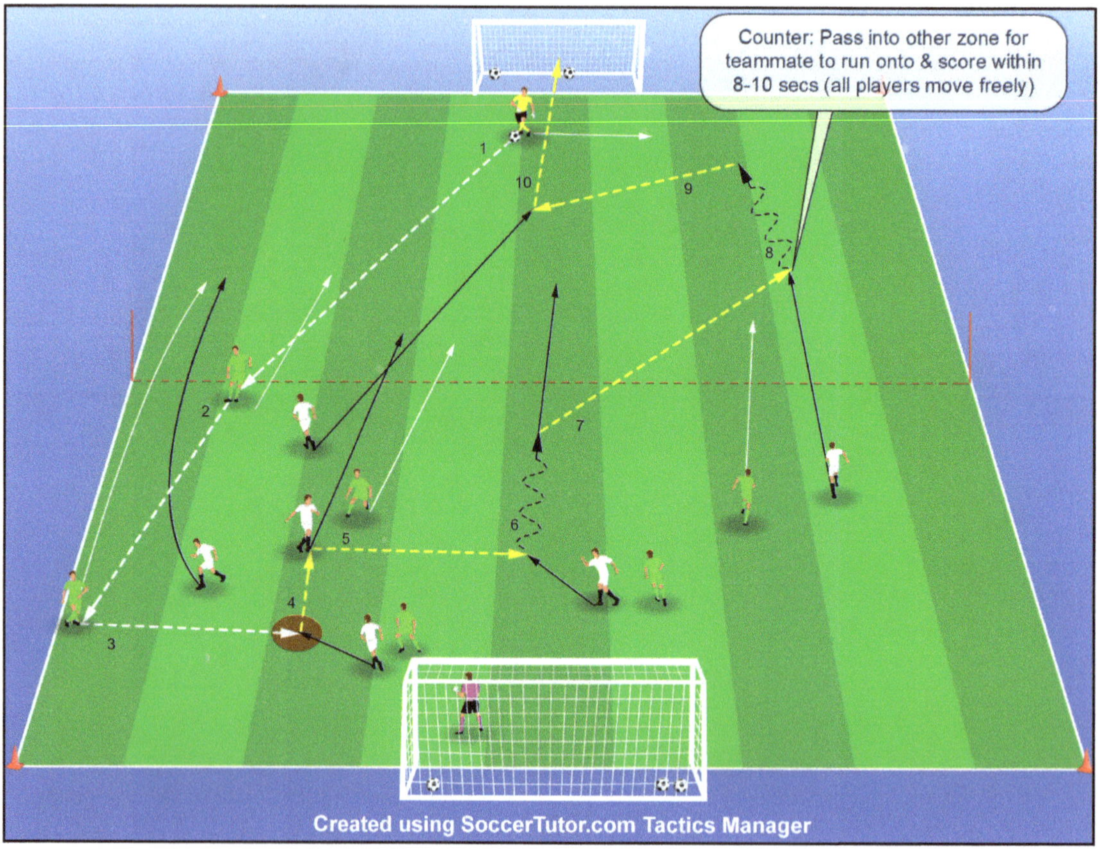

Counter: Pass into other zone for teammate to run onto & score within 8-10 secs (all players move freely)

Objective: Fast and direct counter attacking (play forward quickly) with driving supporting runs.

Description

In a 40 x 60 yard area, we have 2 equal halves. Two teams have 6 outfield players each who start in one half. There are also 2 goalkeepers in large goals. The practice starts with an uncontested pass from the goalkeeper in the other half or a pass inside from the coach. The team in possession (greens in diagram) try to score.

The defending team (whites) try to apply collective pressing and win the ball. If they are successful, their aim is then to launch a fast and direct counter attack. They must do this by playing a well weighted pass into the other zone for a player to run onto, and the other players make fast supporting runs to try and score.

Once the defending team win the ball, all players from both teams are free to move across to attack/defend. If the whites score within 8-10 seconds of winning the ball, the goal counts double. After the attack finishes, the 2 teams change roles and the practice starts from the other half.

Session to Practice **JORGE SAMPAOLI** Tactics - Transition from Defence to Attack (Middle Zone)

PROGRESSION

4. Direct Counter Attacks with Driving Support Runs in a Dynamic "5-5-5 Rule Game" (3-4-3 vs 4-2-3-1)

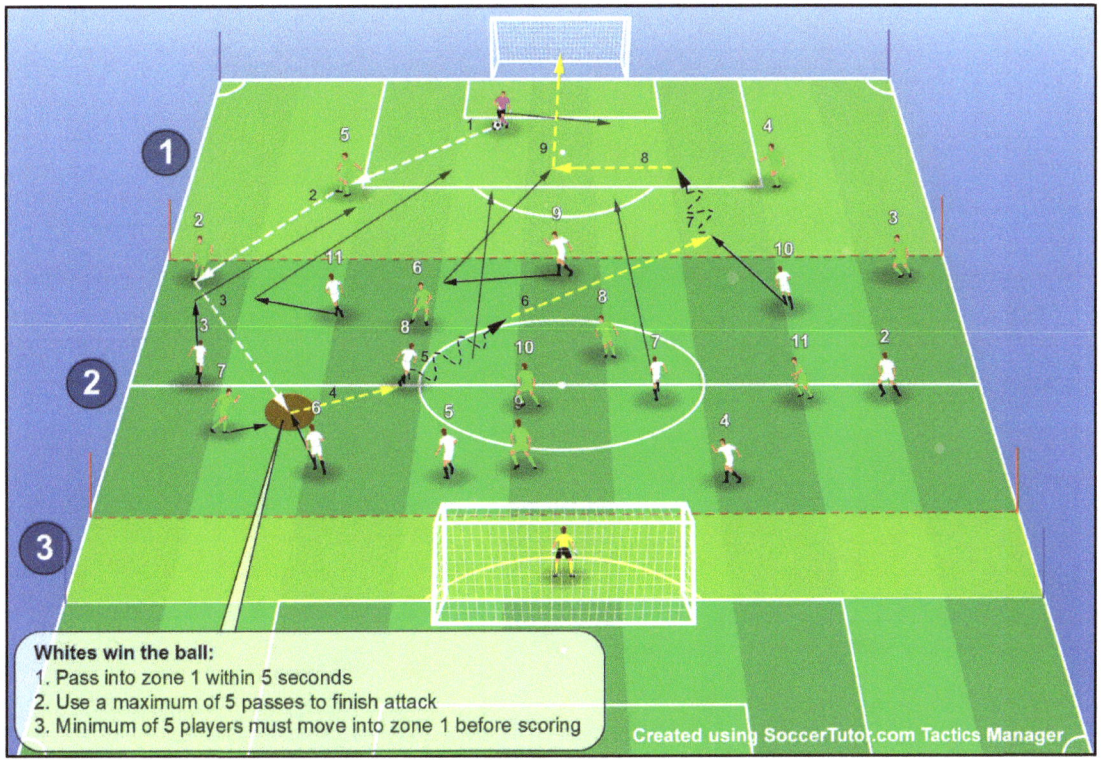

Whites win the ball:
1. Pass into zone 1 within 5 seconds
2. Use a maximum of 5 passes to finish attack
3. Minimum of 5 players must move into zone 1 before scoring

Description

Using a full pitch, we mark out 3 zones. The white team are using the 3-4-3 formation and the greens are using the 4-2-3-1. In zone 1, we have 2 green centre backs and their goalkeeper. In zone 2, we have the rest of the outfield players and in zone 3, we have the white team's goalkeeper.

The practice always starts from the green team's goalkeeper. He passes to one of the centre backs, who then passes into the middle zone. They aim to break through the white team's pressing, build up play, pass into zone 3 and score.

The white team aim to press collectively within the middle zone and win the ball. From this point, all players are free to move across all zones to attack/defend and the following conditions apply:

1. Pass the ball into zone 1 within 5 seconds.
2. Use a maximum of 5 passes to finish their attack.
3. A minimum of 5 players must run into zone 1 before the team can score.

Progression: Extra "5-5-5 Rule": If the greens pass into zone 3, the whites have 5 seconds to win the ball back, a maximum of 5 passes to move the ball into zone 1 and a minimum of 5 players must run into zone 1 before they can score.

TACTICAL SITUATION 3

MAURIZIO SARRI TACTICS

Fast Break Attack when the Opposition is Disorganised

Content taken from Analysis of Napoli during the 2016/2017 season

The analysis is based on recurring patterns of play observed within the Napoli team. Once the same phase of play occurred a number of times (at least 10) the tactics would be seen as a pattern. The analysis on the next page is an example of the team's tactics being used effectively, taken from a specific game.

Each action, pass, individual movement with or without the ball, and the positioning of each player on the pitch including their body shape, are presented.

The analysis is then used to create a full progressive session to coach this specific tactical situation.

Tactical Analysis of MAURIZIO SARRI - Transition from Defence to Attack (Middle Zone)

Analysis Taken from 'Napoli vs Fiorentina - 24th Jan 2017 (Coppa Italia)'
Fast Break Attack when the Opposition is Disorganised

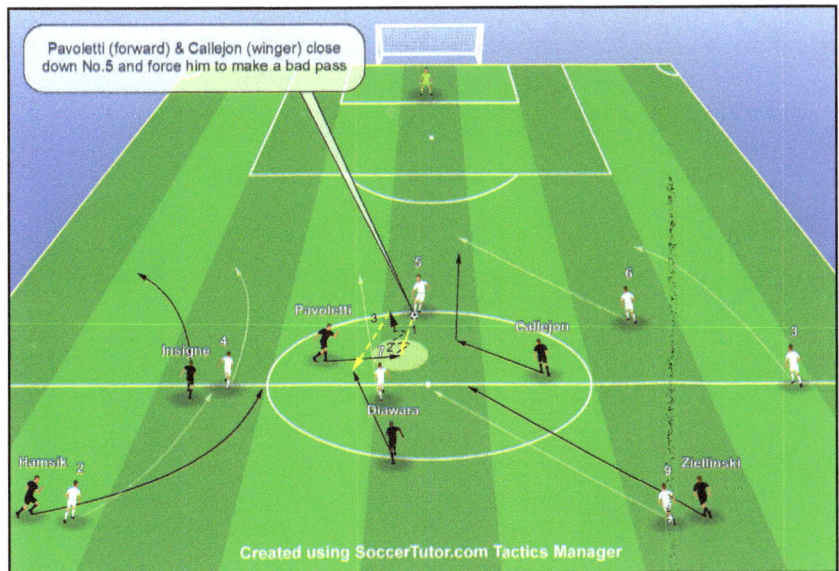

In this situation, Napoli goalkeeper Reina was put under pressure from a forward and clears the ball long.

The Fiorentina centre back (5) controls the ball and tries to pass over the Napoli forward Pavoletti, who dispossesses him and tries to dribble forward.

The Fiorentina centre back tackles Pavoletti but the ball bounces to oncoming defensive midfielder Diawara.

There is space in behind to exploit for this transition to attack. Diawara passes out wide to left forward Insigne. The central midfielder Hamsik has made a bursting run forward and Insigne is able to receive and pass to him.

The Fiorentina defence is disorganised and their defenders are running back towards their own goal.

The right forward Callejón is able to make a well-timed run into the penalty area and score with a header after a first time cross from Hamsik.

Session to Practice MAURIZIO SARRI Tactics - Transition from Defence to Attack (Middle Zone)

SESSION FOR THIS TACTICAL SITUATION (4 PRACTICES)
1. Fast Transition Play in a 4 (+4) v 4 Possession Game

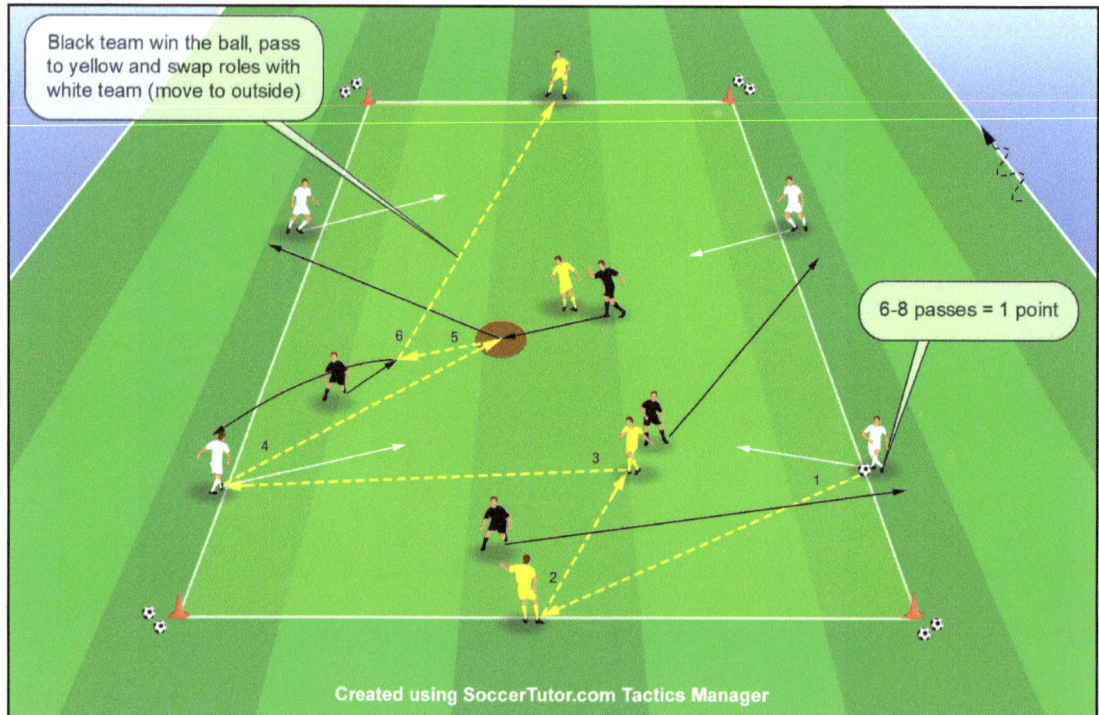

Description

In a 10 x 20 yard area we have 3 teams of 4 players. The black team start inside. The white team have 2 players outside on either side. The third yellow team have 2 players inside and 1 at each end.

The objective for the whites and yellows is to keep possession and complete 6-8 consecutive passes (1 point). The objective for the black team is to win the ball, then make a quick transition to attack.

After winning the ball, they swap roles with the team that lost the ball - in the diagram example the black team swap with the white team and move to the outside positions. The practice continues in the same way with the team roles changed.

Coaching Points

1. Limit the ball carrier to a maximum of 2 passing options, both to players on the outside.
2. Reduce the space available, apply as much collective pressing as possible, to create a strong side and eliminate the numerical disadvantage to win the ball.
3. Transition: Good awareness, quick decision making and high tempo actions to keep possession.
4. Out of Possession = *CLOSE* the Space / In Possession = *OPEN* the Space.

Session to Practice MAURIZIO SARRI Tactics - Transition from Defence to Attack (Middle Zone)

PROGRESSION

2. Fast Break Attack when the Opposition is Disorganised in a 4 (+4) v 4 Dynamic Zonal Game

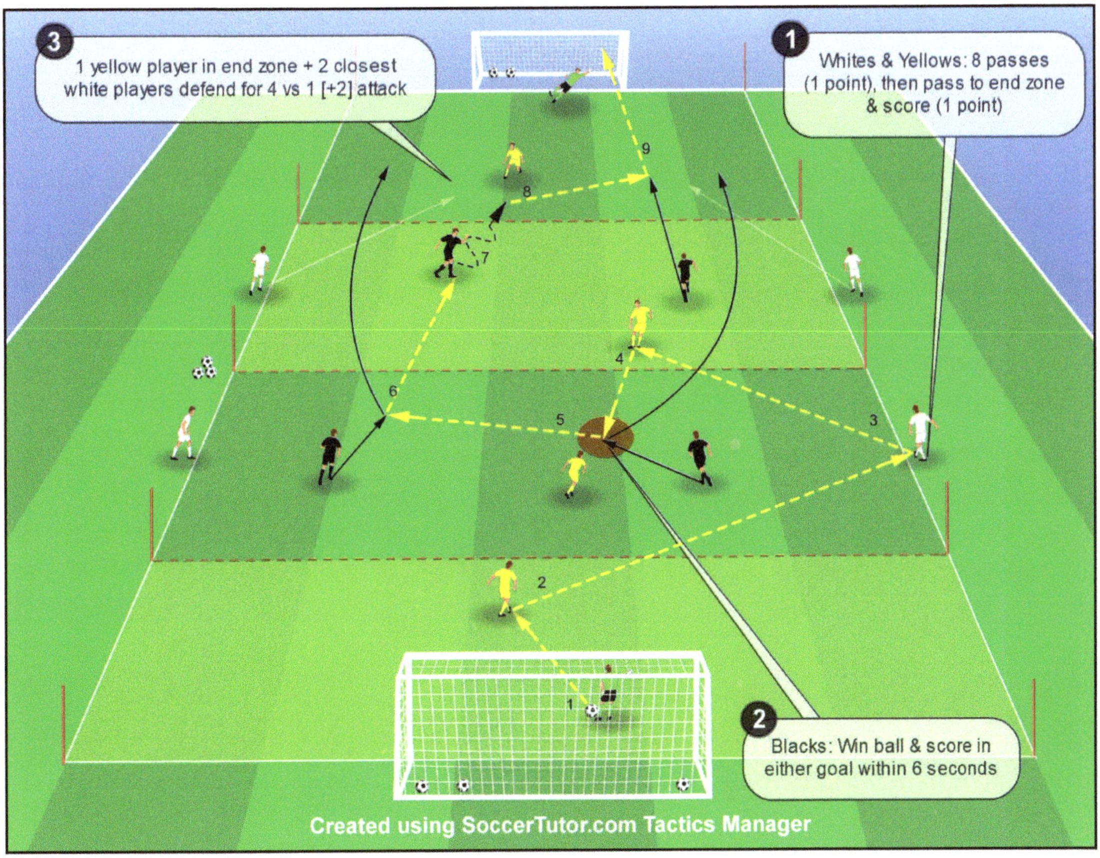

Description

In this progression of the previous practice, we use a 20 x 40 yard area and split the pitch into 4 equal zones. The black team start inside the 2 middle zones (they can move freely). The white team have 2 players outside on both sides. The third team (yellow) have 2 players inside the 2 middle zones and 1 player in each end zone.

The objective for the whites and yellows is to keep possession and complete 8 consecutive passes with help from the neutral players (1 point). They can then pass to one of the 2 yellow players in an end zone to try and score a goal (1 point).

Rules when whites and yellows are in possession:

1. White and yellow players have a limited amount of touches e.g. 2 or 3 touches.
2. After completing 8 passes, the 2 most advanced white side players can move inside to support the yellow players and help finish the attack with fast combination play.

COACHING TRANSITION PLAY - VOL. 2

Session to Practice MAURIZIO SARRI **Tactics - Transition from Defence to Attack (Middle Zone)**

The objective for the black team is to win the ball, then make a quick transition to attack to try and score in either goal. Only the yellow player in that end zone and the 2 outside white players on that side can defend the attack, as shown with the 4 v 1 (+2) attack in the diagram example.

The black team should try and finish their attack within 6 seconds, finishing before the 2 white outside players can get in position to help defend. Change the team roles often.

Coaching Points

1. The defending team (blacks in diagram) need to have maximum concentration to defend well as a unit, limit the time and space the opposition have and press to win the ball.
2. In the transition from defence to attack, the players need to react very quickly, demonstrating good awareness and decisive decision making.
3. The players need to use quality synchronised movements to finish the fast break attacks effectively.
4. Quick combination play is needed with one-touch passing and well weighted passes into space.
5. Run forward from deep to support teammates in the end zone, ask for the ball to be played into the space and finish with one touch.
6. Look to put the defender under pressure and act according to the decision he makes.
7. If the defender moves towards the ball carrier? Pass to a supporting teammate in space (2 v 1).
8. If the defender keeps a balanced position? Run at him in a 1 v 1 attack, beat him and finish.

Session to Practice MAURIZIO SARRI Tactics - Transition from Defence to Attack (Middle Zone)

PROGRESSION

3. Fast Supporting Runs to Finish in an 8 v 8 (+3) Dynamic Zonal Game

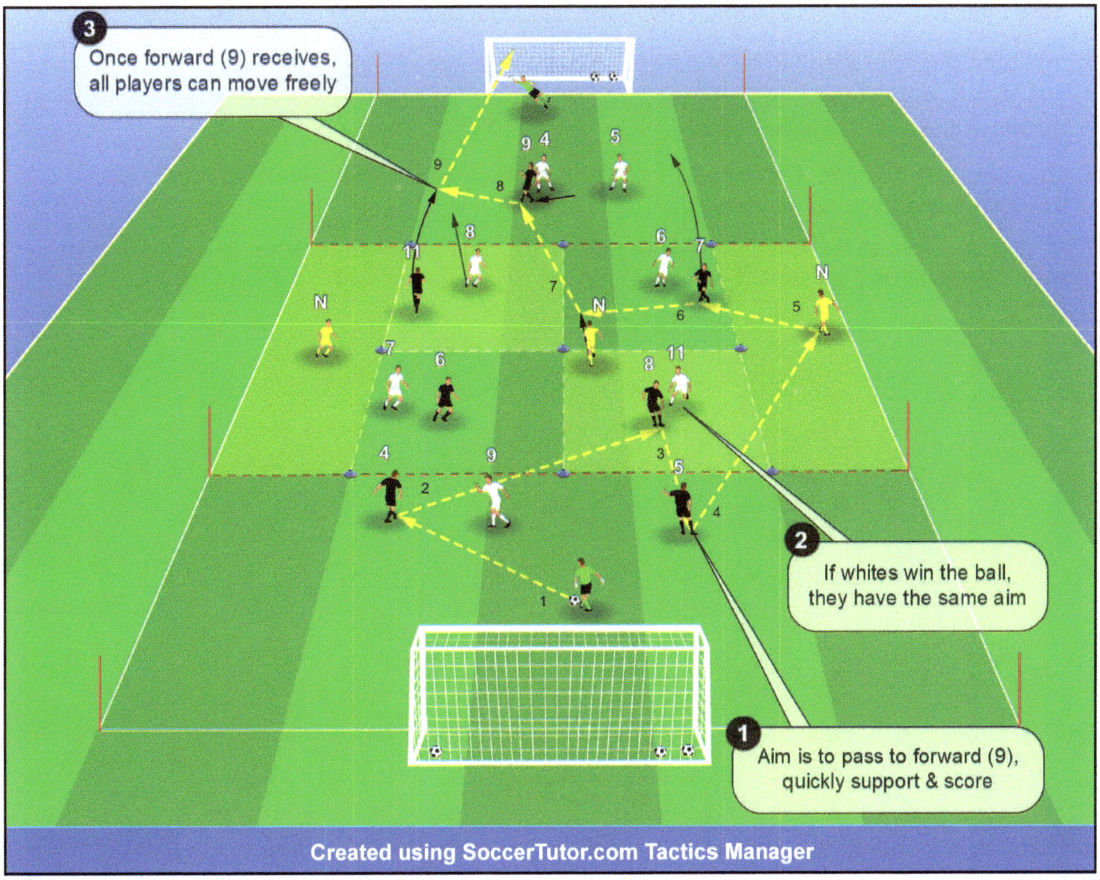

(3) Once forward (9) receives, all players can move freely

(2) If whites win the ball, they have the same aim

(1) Aim is to pass to forward (9), quickly support & score

Description

In a 25 x 45 yard area, we mark out 4 equal 7.5 yard square zones in the middle. In each of the 4 middle zones, we have a central midfielder (6 or 8) vs a winger (7 or 11). In each end zone, we have 2 centre backs (4 & 5) vs 1 forward (9) and a large goal with a goalkeeper.

We have 1 yellow neutral player on each side and 1 in the centre who can move freely across the 4 middle zones to create 2 v 1 situations. The neutral players play with the team in possession.

The practice starts with a goalkeeper and the team in possession (blacks in diagram) have help from the 3 neutral players. Their aim is to pass to the forward (9) and then quickly support him (forward runs to receive) to score. Once the forward (9) receives, all players can move freely to defend/attack.

If the white team win the ball, they then have the same aim. They must use their numerical advantage with the neutral players to pass to their forward, and then provide fast supporting runs to finish their attack quickly.

Session to Practice MAURIZIO SARRI Tactics - Transition from Defence to Attack (Middle Zone)

Coaching Points

1. The players need to use quick combination play with a high tempo and rhythm, as well as use the correct distances and angles of support.

2. Players need to check away from their markers to create space.

3. Utilise the neutral players to exploit the numerical advantage (10 v 7).

4. Monitor the quality of the passes (accuracy and weight) and decision making.

5. The players need to communicate and use synchronised movements to run into space, receive on the move and quickly finish (1 touch).

6. The correct body shape is needed to protect the ball in 1 v 1 situations (getting your body in between the opponent and the ball).

7. Players also need to make a good directional first touch to prevent the defending players from winning the ball in 1 v 1 situations.

Session to Practice MAURIZIO SARRI Tactics - Transition from Defence to Attack (Middle Zone)

PROGRESSION

4. Fast Break Attack when the Opposition is Disorganised in a Dynamic Tactical Game

Description

In this final practice of the session, we use a full pitch and all 22 players (+ 1 extra neutral player). We create a middle zone and 2 side zones, as shown. Both teams use a 4-3-3 formation. In each end zone, we have 2 centre backs (4 & 5) vs 1 forward (9). In the side zones, we have the wingers (7 & 11). In the middle zone, we have the full backs (2 & 3) and central midfielders (6, 8 & 10). In the middle zone, we have a 5 v 5 situation + 1 neutral player who plays with the team in possession.

The practice starts from a goalkeeper and with one team in possession (whites in diagram) trying to build up play and score. The objective of the practice is for the defending team (blacks in diagram) is to try and win the ball, then make a fast transition from defence to attack. All players can enter the end zone to attack/defend once the ball has been played in there. The aim should be to pass to the forward (9) in there and then make forward supporting runs to finish quickly.

Rules 1) Attacking Phase: All players are limited to 2-3 touches.
2) Transition: Unlimited touches, but they must finish counter attack within 10-12 seconds.

TACTICAL SITUATION 4

POCHETTINO TACTICS

High Intensity Pressing and Fast Break Attack from the Middle Zone

Content taken from Analysis of Tottenham Hotspur during the 2016/2017 season

The analysis is based on recurring patterns of play observed within the Tottenham team. Once the same phase of play occurred a number of times (at least 10) the tactics would be seen as a pattern. The analysis on the next page is an example of the team's tactics being used effectively, taken from a specific game.

Each action, pass, individual movement with or without the ball, and the positioning of each player on the pitch including their body shape, are presented.

The analysis is then used to create a full progressive session to coach this specific tactical situation.

Tactical Analysis of POCHETTINO - Transition from Defence to Attack (Middle Zone)

Analysis Taken from 'Hull vs Tottenham - 21st May 2017 (Premier League)'

High Intensity Pressing and Fast Break Attack from the Middle Zone (4-2-3-1 vs 3-4-2-1)

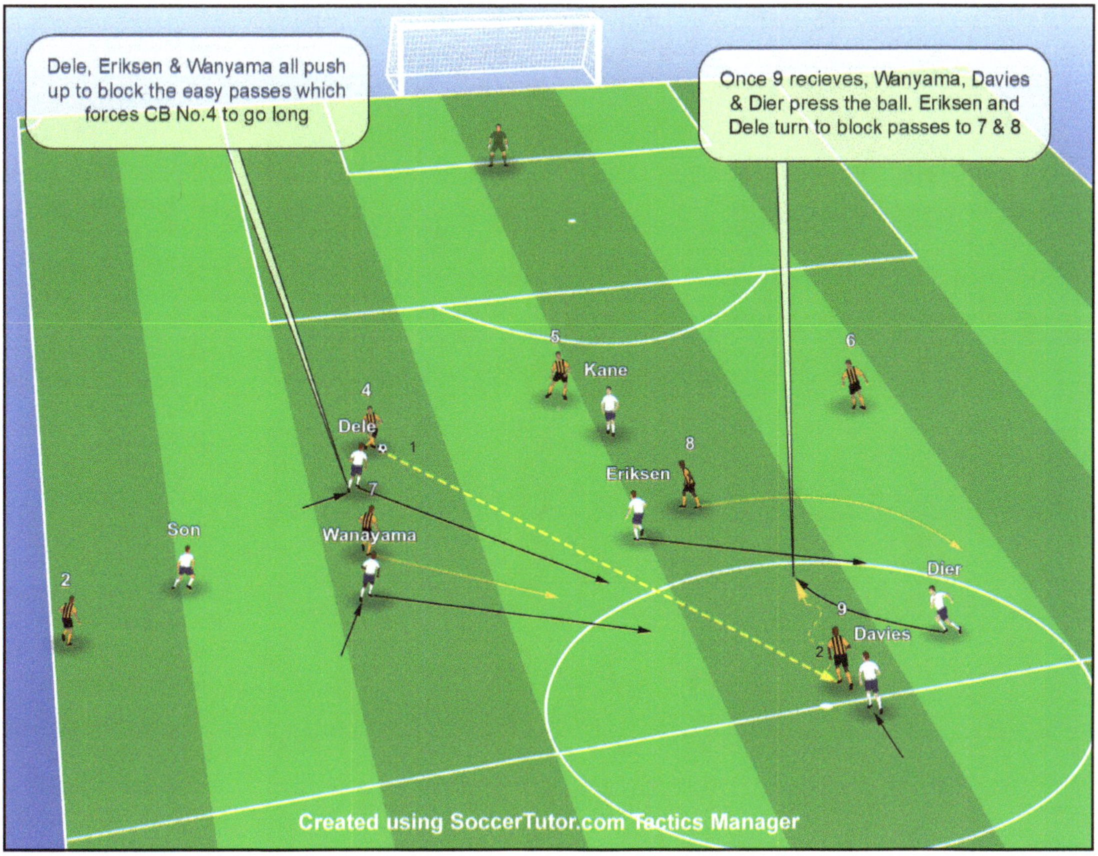

In this situation, the Hull centre back (4) is in possession. The attacking midfielder (Dele Alli), the right winger (Eriksen) and the defensive midfielder (Wanyama) all move up or across to apply pressure to the ball carrier and mark the potential receivers near the ball zone (7 & 8).

The forward Kane blocks the passing options to the other centre back (5) and left back (3), while the left winger Son blocks the pass towards the right back (2).

The defensive movements and positions explained above force the Hull centre back (4) to play a longer pass towards the forward (9). The ball travels a long way and gives defensive midfielder Dier time to react and step up.

The Hull forward (9) receives but is unable to turn - he is put under pressure by Dier, Davies and Eriksen. Eriksen also blocks the pass to No.8 and Dele Alli blocks the pass to No.7.

Without a passing option, No.9 holds the ball too long and is dispossessed by Dier.

Tactical Analysis of POCHETTINO - Transition from Defence to Attack (Middle Zone)

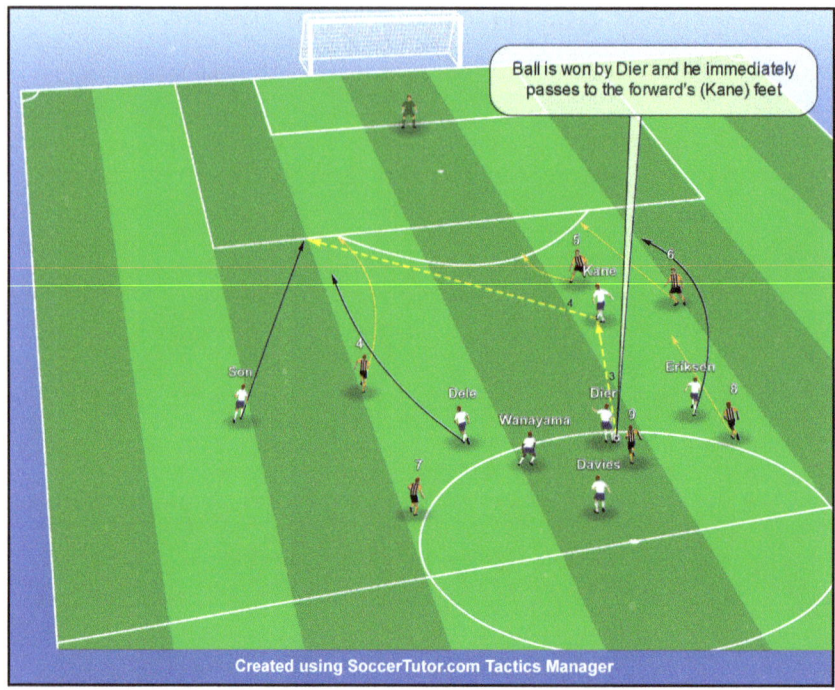

After good pressing from Tottenham in the middle zone, the defensive midfielder Dier is able to win the ball.

Dier launches a fast break attack by passing to the centre forward Kane immediately.

The Hull defence is trying to track back but they are disorganised. The left winger Son makes a well-timed run in behind and Kane finds him with a good pass.

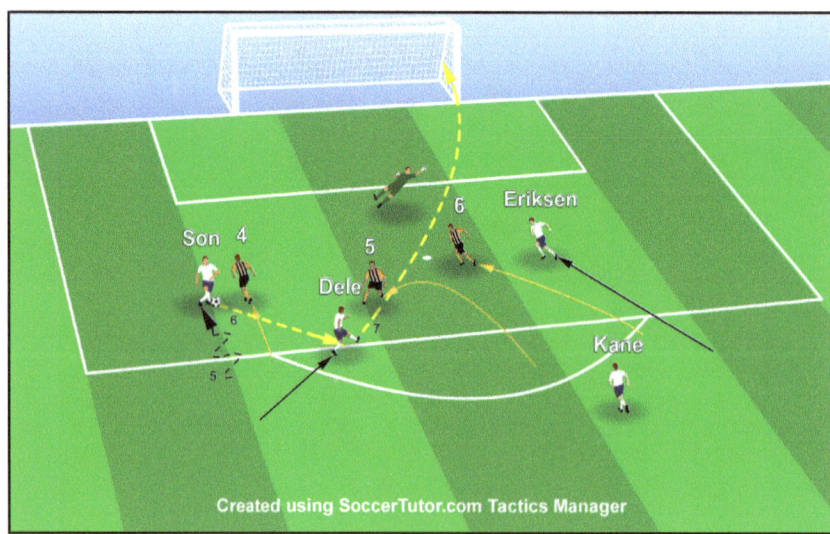

Son dribbles into the box and is tracked well by the Hull centre back (4).

Son stops and passes back to attacking midfielder Dele Alli who has made a forward run.

Dele Alli takes a touch, opens up his body and slots the ball home into the far corner.

Session to Practice POCHETTINO Tactics - Transition from Defence to Attack (Middle Zone)

SESSION FOR THIS TACTICAL SITUATION (5 PRACTICES)
1. One-Touch Combination Play in a Continuous Short Passing Circuit (1)

Objective: One-touch passing combination play - well weighted passes and timing of movements.

Description
In a 20 x 30 yard area, we have 12 players (split into 2 groups - A & B) and mark out 8 cones. We play with 2 balls simultaneously from A1 and B1.

The practice starts with 1 playing a one-two with 2 and then passing to 3. Player 3 passes to 4 from the other group (A3 passes to B4 / B3 passes to A4). The sequence is completed with player 4 dribbling the ball to the start position.

All players move to the next position, with the fourth player dribbling to the back of the other group. This way, the players get to work from both sides.

Coaching Points
1. The accuracy and weight of the pass needs to be correct.
2. The key is the rhythm and timing of the movement, together with the pass.
3. Make sure the players communicate with their teammates and heads are up.
4. Players need to make sure their first touch is made on the move to maintain the fluency of the drill.
5. Passes need to be weighted well and aimed just in front of their teammates to step forward up to.
6. The practice should be done at a high tempo throughout.

Session to Practice POCHETTINO Tactics - Transition from Defence to Attack (Middle Zone)

VARIATION

2. One-Touch Combination Play in a Continuous Short Passing Circuit (2)

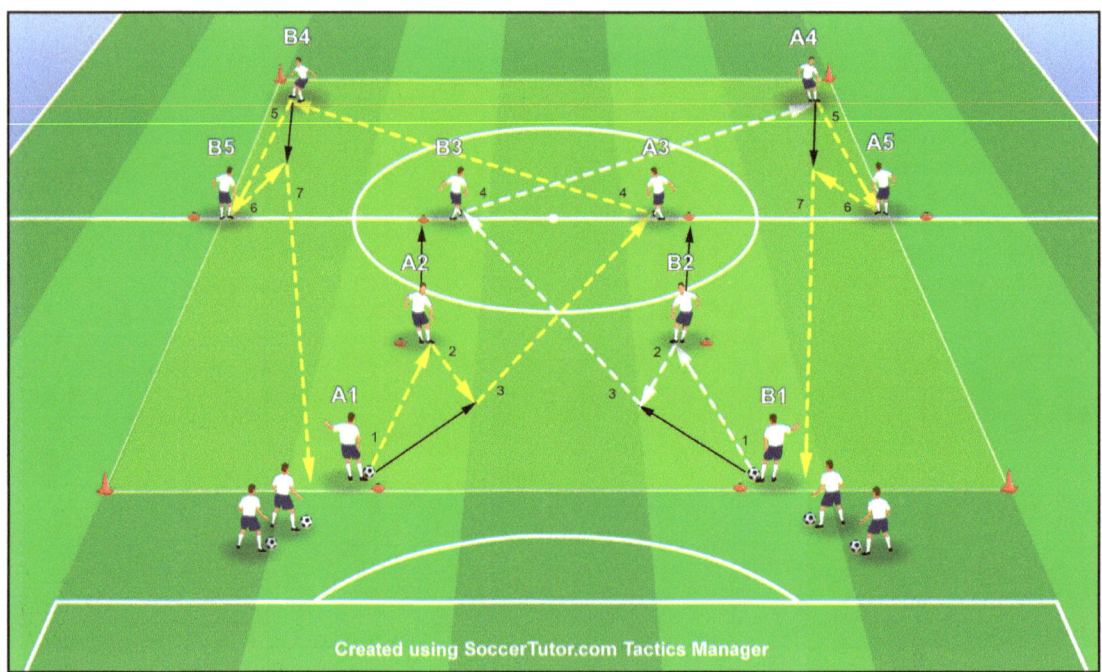

Description

This is a variation of the previous practice - it works in exactly the same way but now we add a player 5 to both groups.

Now, when the ball is passed to 4, instead of dribbling the ball to the start position (1), he plays a one-two with 5 and then passes to the start position.

Player 4 moves to position 5 and player 5 moves to the start position of the opposite group (B5 to A1 / A5 to B1).

Session to Practice POCHETTINO Tactics - Transition from Defence to Attack (Middle Zone)

3. Collective Pressing and Transition to Attack with Fast Break

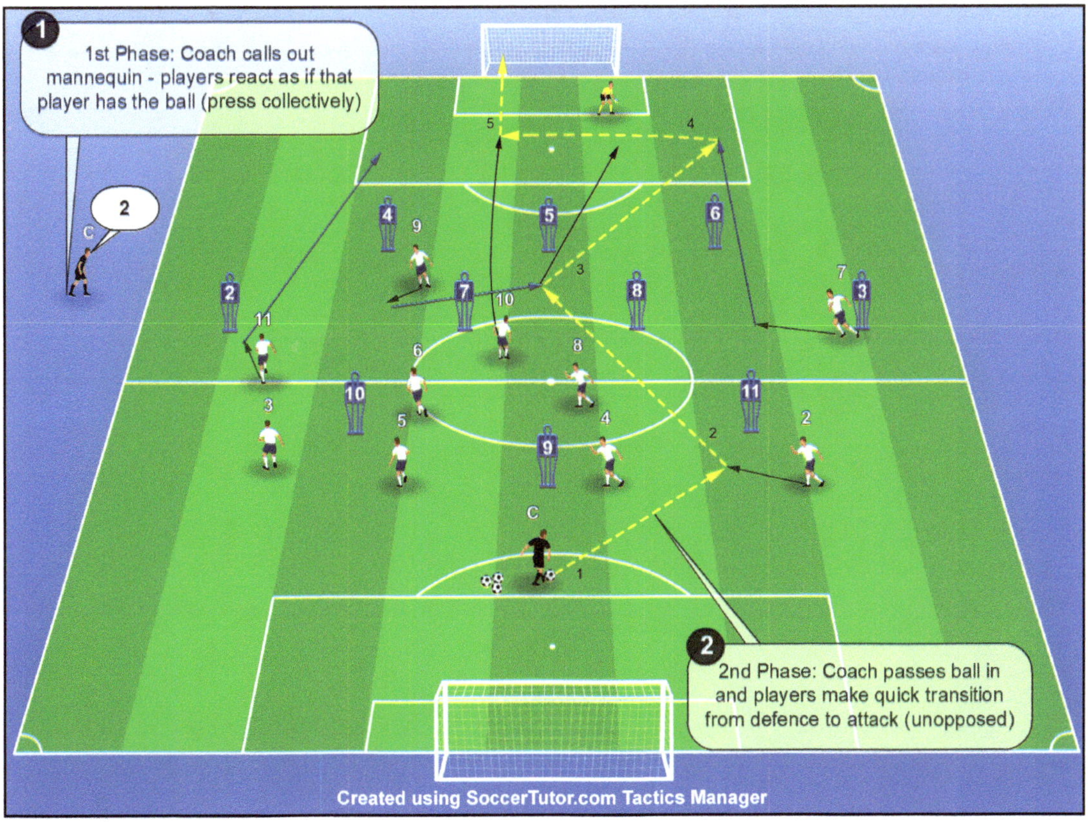

Description
The 9 mannequins are in the positions shown to represent the opposition in a 3-4-2-1 formation. Each mannequin is numbered 2-11 and we start without a ball - the players simply take up the correct defensive positions based on the number that the coach calls out. The practice continues like this until a coach gives a signal - the coach then passes a ball in and the players must make a very fast transition to attack using combination play and tactical movements/cooperation we want as a team.

Coaching Points
1. Quick reactions in transition to offer support movements for the ball carrier.
2. Apply quick and quality combination play with an emphasis on the accuracy and power of the pass (to feet, back passes and passes into space).
3. The final pass and the run into the space behind the defensive line need to be timed perfectly.
4. Players need to use quick forward support runs and synchronised movements inside the box to create space and finish from crosses.
5. Quick (one touch) and quality finishing.

Session to Practice POCHETTINO Tactics - Transition from Defence to Attack (Middle Zone)

PROGRESSION

4. High Intensity Pressing in the Middle Zone and Fast Break Attack in a Tactical Practice

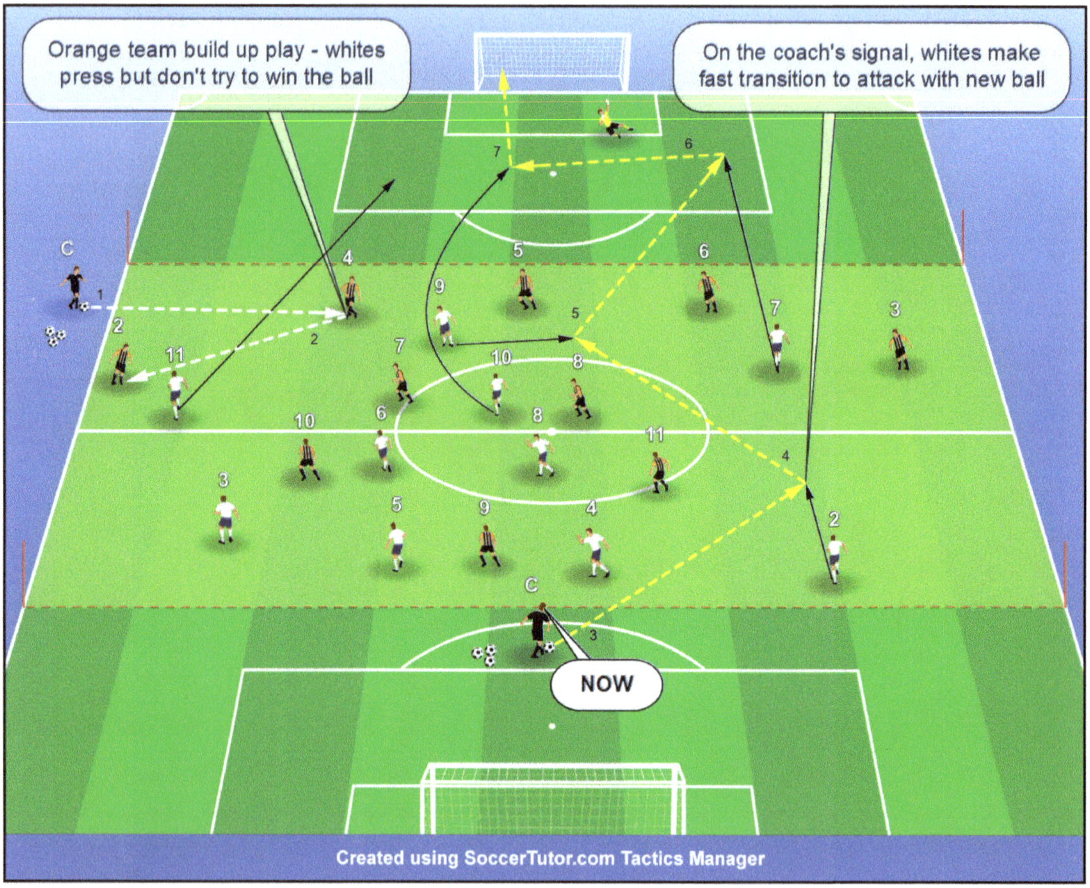

Orange team build up play - whites press but don't try to win the ball

On the coach's signal, whites make fast transition to attack with new ball

NOW

Description

In this progression of the previous practice, we replace the mannequins with active opponents in a 3-4-2-1 formation and mark out a middle zone, as shown in the diagram.

The practice starts with the orange/black team who try to build up play. The white team must apply energetic pressing in the middle zone but they do not try to win the ball.

The practice continues like this until a coach gives a signal - the coach then passes a new ball in and the players must make a very fast transition to attack (opposed).

The orange/black team are not allowed to defend in the final zone until the ball has been played in there. The offside rule is applied throughout.

Coaching Points: The coaching points are the same as the previous practice.

Session to Practice **POCHETTINO** Tactics - Transition from Defence to Attack (Middle Zone)

PROGRESSION

5. High Intensity Pressing in the Middle Zone and Fast Break Attack in a 3 Zone Game

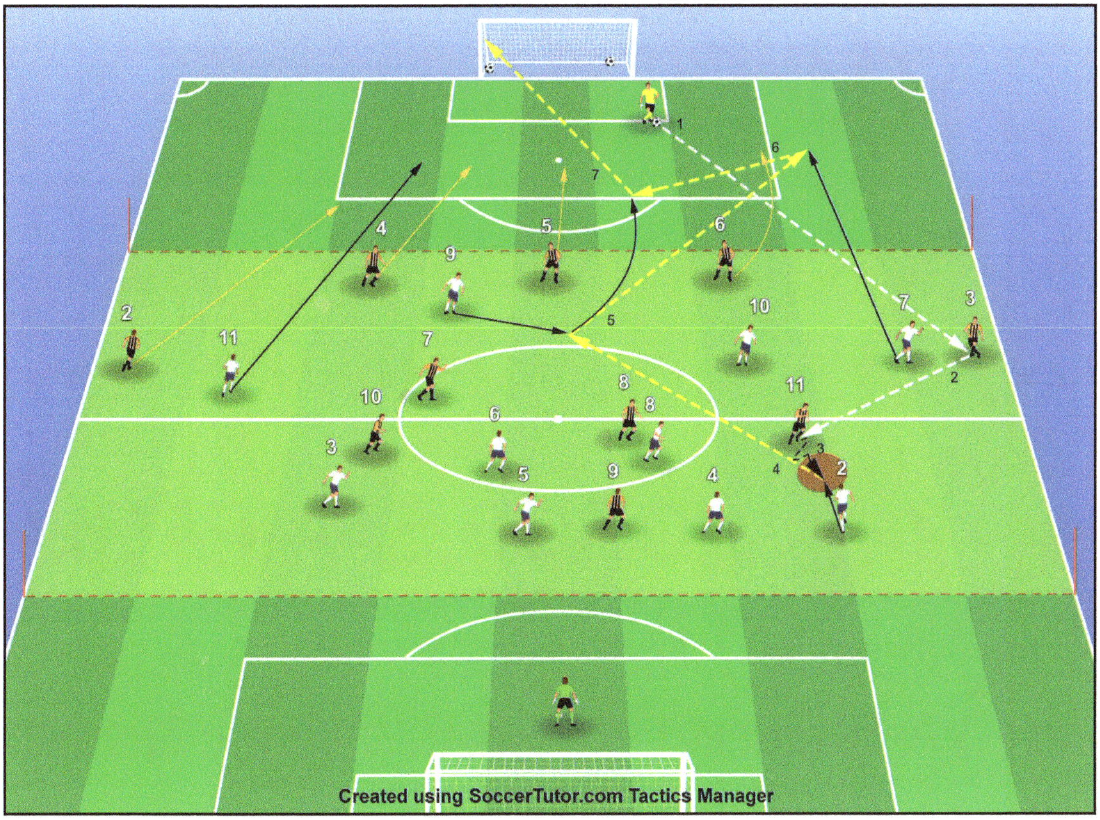

Description

In this progression, we divide a full pitch into 3 zones as shown. The white team are in a 4-2-3-1 formation and the orange/blacks are in a 3-4-2-1 formation.

The practice always starts with the orange/black team's goalkeeper - he has a free pass to one of the defenders. The orange/black team try to build up play, move the ball into the final zone and score.

The white team apply energetic and aggressive pressing within the middle zone to try and win the ball. If they do, they then launch a fast break attack to try and score themselves. The defending team's players are not allowed in the final zone until the ball has been played in there. The offside rule is applied throughout.

Coaching Points

1. The white team must defend well, making sure to keep small distances between their players and consistency in their lines to apply collective pressing around the ball area.
2. Also refer to the coaching points for the previous 2 practices, which still apply.

COACHING TRANSITION PLAY - VOL. 2

TACTICAL SITUATION 5

JORGE SAMPAOLI TACTICS

Fast Break Attacking Overload from the Middle Zone

Content taken from Analysis of Sevilla during the 2016/2017 season

The analysis is based on recurring patterns of play observed within the Sevilla team. Once the same phase of play occurred a number of times (at least 10) the tactics would be seen as a pattern. The analysis on the next page is an example of the team's tactics being used effectively, taken from a specific game.

Each action, pass, individual movement with or without the ball, and the positioning of each player on the pitch including their body shape, are presented.

The analysis is then used to create a full progressive session to coach this specific tactical situation.

Tactical Analysis of JORGE SAMPAOLI - Transition from Defence to Attack (Middle Zone)

Analysis Taken from 'Sevilla vs Espanyol - 20th Aug 2016 (La Liga)'
Fast Break Attacking Overload from the Middle Zone

In this example, Sevilla's defensive midfielder N'Zonzi is able to close down the opposition No.10. He moves in to tackle him and the ball breaks loose.

Sevilla's central midfield player Sarabia is able to get to the ball and play it forward for N'Zonzi to run onto.

N'Zonzi is able to break away by dribbling forward with the ball.

Sevilla attack and hope to create an overload.

N'Zonzi's pass inside to central midfielder Vazquez takes the opposition No.6 and No.8 out of the game.

Sevilla now have an attacking overload with a 4 v 3 situation.

Vazquez is able to dribble forward and commits the centre back (5).

The right wing back Kiyotake makes a very well-timed overlapping run to receive the final pass in behind and score past the goalkeeper.

Session to Practice **JORGE SAMPAOLI** Tactics - Transition from Defence to Attack (Middle Zone)

SESSION FOR THIS TACTICAL SITUATION (4 PRACTICES)
1. Fast Break Attack 1 v 0 (+1) to 4 v 3 (+1) Overload Game

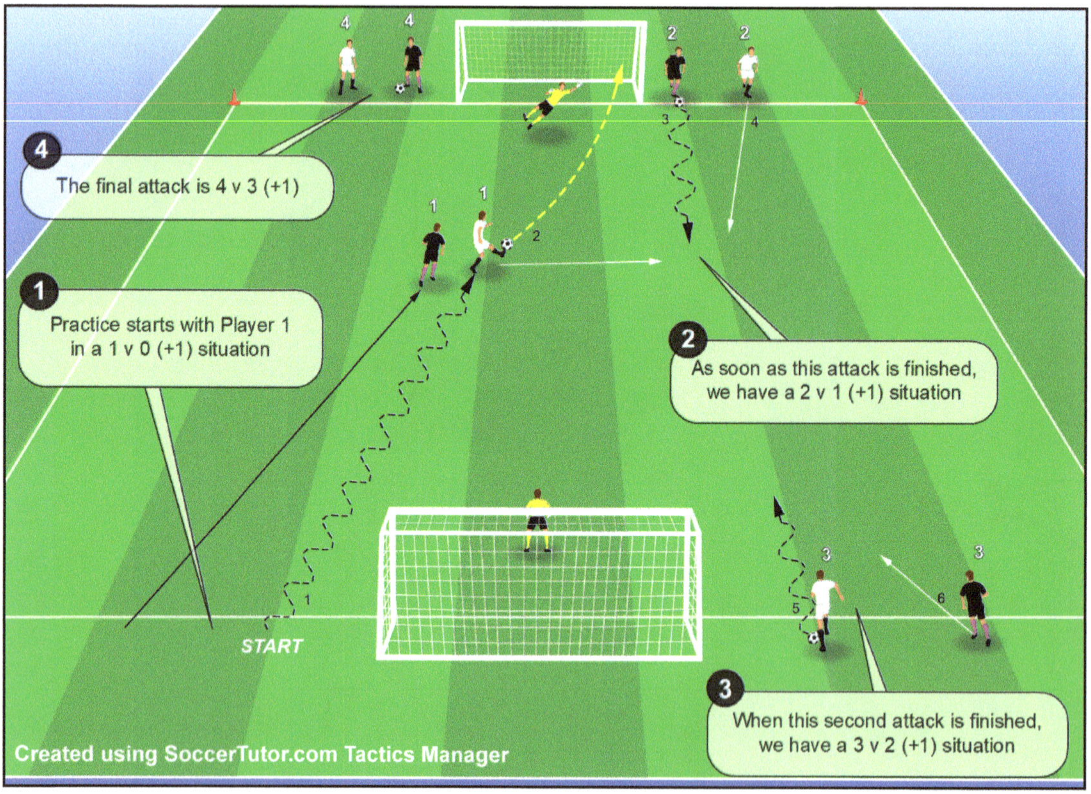

Description

In a 25 x 25 yard area, we have 2 large goals with goalkeepers at either end. We play with 2 teams of 4 - they each have 2 players with balls at one end and 2 players without balls at the other end.

The practice works with the steps explained below:

* After finishing one step, the players remain inside the area ready for the next step.

1. One player starts the practice (white in diagram) and dribbles quickly forward to contest the goalkeeper and try to score. At the same time, a black player tracks the white attacker so there is a 1 v 0 (+1) situation.

2. As soon as this attack is finished, a new black player runs onto the pitch to try and score at the other end - a white player tracks the run to defend and we have a 2 v 1 (+1) situation.

3. When this second attack is finished, a new white player enters with a ball and so does a black player without a ball. We now have a 3 v 2 (+1) overload attack.

4. For the final attack, we have a 4 v 3 (+1) situation. We then start the practice again with the other team (black) starting the first attack with a 1 v 0 (+1) situation.

Session to Practice **JORGE SAMPAOLI** Tactics - Transition from Defence to Attack (Middle Zone)

Progression
Each team has 2 players at the ends and 2 players at the sides, so that we vary the point/angle at which the attacks starts.

Coaching Points
1. Players must show creativity, aggression, high intensity and rhythm to finish their attacks as quickly and effectively as they can.
2. Show good awareness and decision making in relation to the tactical and numerical situation (superiority or equality of numbers), the positions and the actions of the defenders.
3. Very good dribbling and control of the ball under pressure.
4. Quality pass accuracy and weight for teammates' runs, so they can finish with one touch.
5. In a 2 v 1 situation, the ball carrier should try to draw the first defender towards him. If this happens, he can then easily pass to his teammate in space. If the defender decides instead to cover the second attacker, the first attacker attacks the goal and tries to score himself.
6. In a 3 v 2 situation, the player with the ball should run forward with the ball at speed, drawing opponents in and beating them to create space for teammates to run into and then pass to them.

Session to Practice **JORGE SAMPAOLI** Tactics - Transition from Defence to Attack (Middle Zone)

PROGRESSION

2. Fast Break Attack Overload Game with Crossing and Finishing

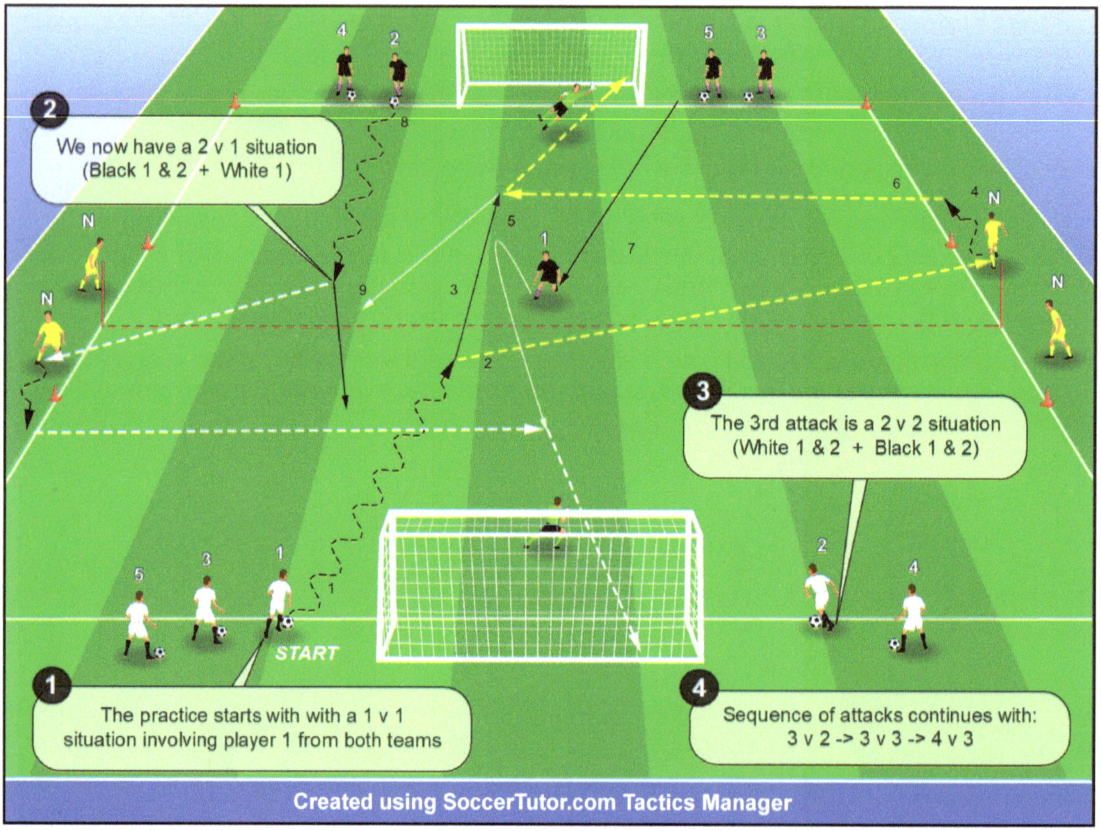

2 We now have a 2 v 1 situation (Black 1 & 2 + White 1)

3 The 3rd attack is a 2 v 2 situation (White 1 & 2 + Black 1 & 2)

1 The practice starts with with a 1 v 1 situation involving player 1 from both teams

4 Sequence of attacks continues with: 3 v 2 -> 3 v 3 -> 4 v 3

Created using SoccerTutor.com Tactics Manager

Description

In this progression, we have the same objectives as the previous practices, but we now have 4 yellow neutral players at the sides who play with the team in possession and receive out wide to deliver crosses. Both teams have 5 or 6 players, all standing at opposite ends as shown.

* After finishing one step, the players remain inside the area ready for the next step.

Sequence of attacks: 1 v 1 -> 2 v 1 -> 2 v 2 -> 3 v 2 -> 3 v 3 -> 4 v 3.

In addition to the numerical situations above, the team that attack can use an extra neutral player out wide. Each time a team is in transition from defence to attack, they should pass to one of the neutral outside players, who then deliver a cross.

The players need to communicate, cooperate and use synchronised movements near the goal to create space. After the 4 v 3, the practice begins immediately again with the player waiting (No.5) with a 1 v 1, then 2 v 1 etc. This practice can be adapted to any numerical situation of the coach's choosing.

Session to Practice JORGE SAMPAOLI Tactics - Transition from Defence to Attack (Middle Zone)

PROGRESSION

3. Fast Break Attacking Overloads in a Position Specific Zonal Game

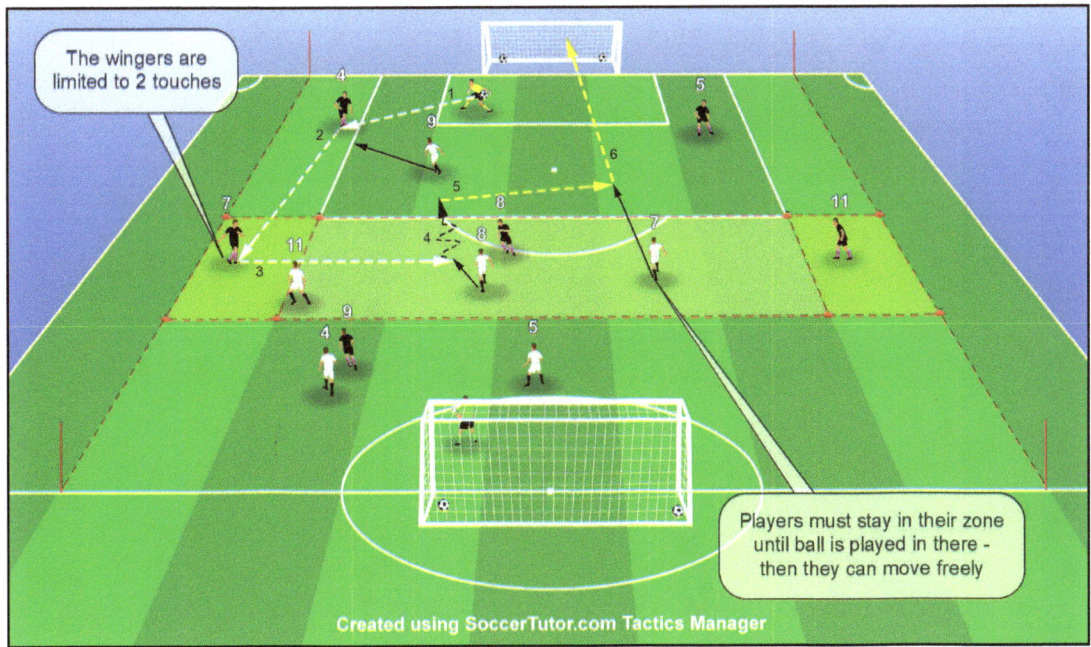

Description

We play a 7 v 7 game using half a pitch (narrower) and also mark out 3 zones in the middle, as shown. Both teams are in a 2-3-1 formation with 2 centre backs (4 & 5), 1 central midfielder (8), 2 wingers (7 & 11) and 1 forward (9).

In both end zones there is a 2 v 1 situation, in the middle zone there is a 3 v 1 situation and the team in possession have their wingers (7 & 11) in their own wide zones.

We play a normal game starting from the goalkeeper, with the team in possession (blacks in diagram) trying to work the ball into the end zone to the forward (9) and score.

The white team aim to guide their opponents to play into the middle zone where they have a 3 v 1 numerical advantage. They try to win the ball and then make a fast transition from defence to attack. From this point, they can easily create an overload and score, as shown in the diagram example.

The players in the end zones stay there throughout. The players in the middle zones can move forward as soon as the ball has been played into the end zone. Restart with the other team's goalkeeper.

Coaching Points

1. All players have unlimited touches but the attack must be finished in a limited time
2. All players have 3 touches and the attack must be finished in a limited time.
3. Stress the importance of the wingers (7 & 11) making forward runs to score.

Session to Practice **JORGE SAMPAOLI** Tactics - Transition from Defence to Attack (Middle Zone)

PROGRESSION

4. Fast Break Attacking Overloads in a Position Specific 9 v 9 Tactical Game

Description

In this progression and final practice of this session, we increase the size of the area and add 3 players to each team.

Both teams are in a 2-4-2 formation with 2 centre backs (4 & 5), 2 central midfielders (6 & 8), 2 wingers (7 & 11) and 2 forwards (9 & 10).

We have a 2 v 2 situation in both end zones a 4 v 4 situation in the middle zone.

We play a normal game starting from the goalkeeper, with the team in possession (blacks in diagram) trying to work the ball into the end zone to their forwards and score.

The white team aim to win the ball in the middle zone and then launch a fast break attack. As soon as they win the ball, the players from the middle zone move forward to create an overload in the end zone and score, as shown in the diagram example.

The players in the end zones stay there throughout. The players in the middle zones can move forward as soon as the ball has been played into the end zone.

Restart with the other team's goalkeeper.

TACTICAL SITUATION 6

LEONARDO JARDIM TACTICS

Fast Break Attacks with Many Support Players

Content taken from Analysis of Monaco during the Ligue 1 Title Winning 2016/2017 season

The analysis is based on recurring patterns of play observed within the Monaco team. Once the same phase of play occurred a number of times (at least 10) the tactics would be seen as a pattern. The analysis on the next page is an example of the team's tactics being used effectively, taken from a specific game.

Each action, pass, individual movement with or without the ball, and the positioning of each player on the pitch including their body shape, are presented.

The analysis is then used to create a full progressive session to coach this specific tactical situation.

Tactical Analysis of LEONARDO JARDIM - Transition from Defence to Attack (Middle Zone)

Analysis Taken from 'AS Monaco vs Lille - 14th May 2017 (Ligue 1)'

Fast Break Attacks with Many Support Players (4-4-2 vs 4-2-3-1)

In this situation, the Lille left back (3) attempts to pass inside to the left winger (11), but plays a poor pass.

The Monaco central midfielder Bakayoko is able to collect the ball, dribble forward and then switch the play to the left winger Lemar, as shown.

Lemar receives the pass in lots of space, so is able to dribble forward. The 2 forwards Mbappe and Falcao + the right winger Bernardo Silva are all able to make forward supporting runs.

The Lille right back (2) is able to put pressure on Lemar but he is able to play a perfect diagonal ball over the top for the forward Mbappe to run onto.

Mbappe plays a first time volley cross into the centre, perfectly weighted and timed for Falcao's run, ahead of the defenders tracking back.

Falcao finishes with a first time left footed volley into the corner.

Tactical Analysis of LEONARDO JARDIM - Transition from Defence to Attack (Middle Zone)

Analysis Taken from 'Bordeaux vs AS Monaco - 10th Dec 2016'
Fast Break Attacks with Many Support Players (4-4-2 vs 4-4-2)

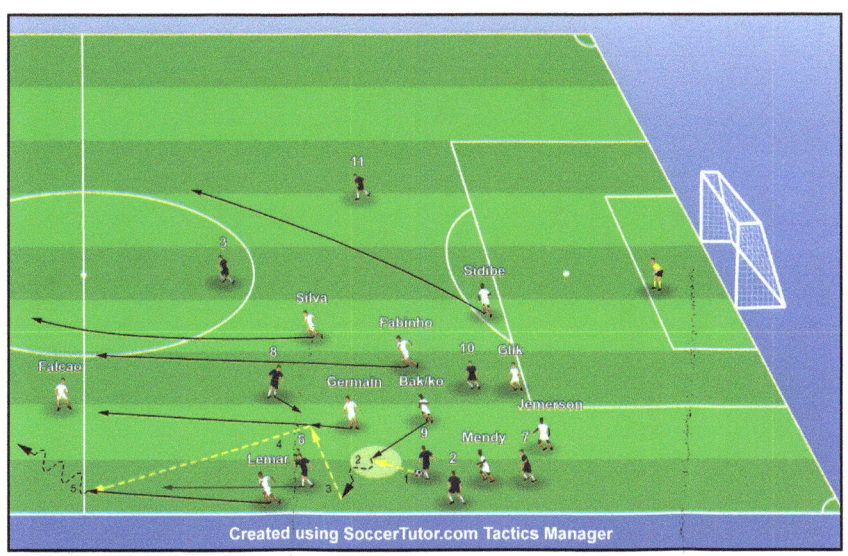

In this situation, the Bordeaux forward (9) is in a very deep position and plays a poor pass, which gives the ball to Monaco central midfielder Bakayoko.

Bakayoko passes inside to the forward Germain, who then plays a first time pass into the space for the winger Lemar to receive and dribble forward.

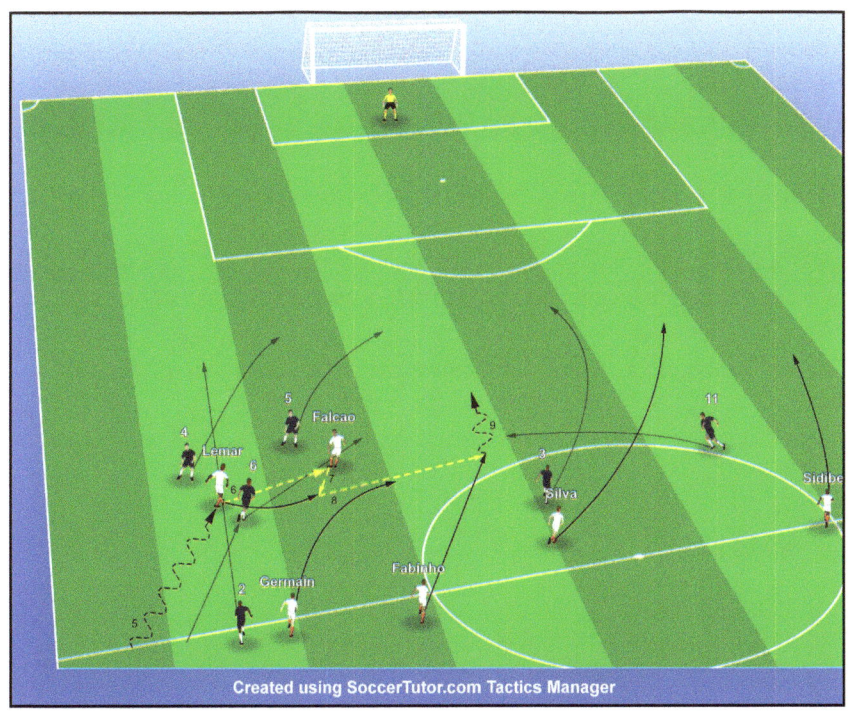

Lemar dribbles inside, plays a one-two with the forward Falcao and then passes inside for central midfielder Fabinho, who has made a supporting run.

Fabinho has space to run into and Monaco have a 6 v 6 situation for their attack.

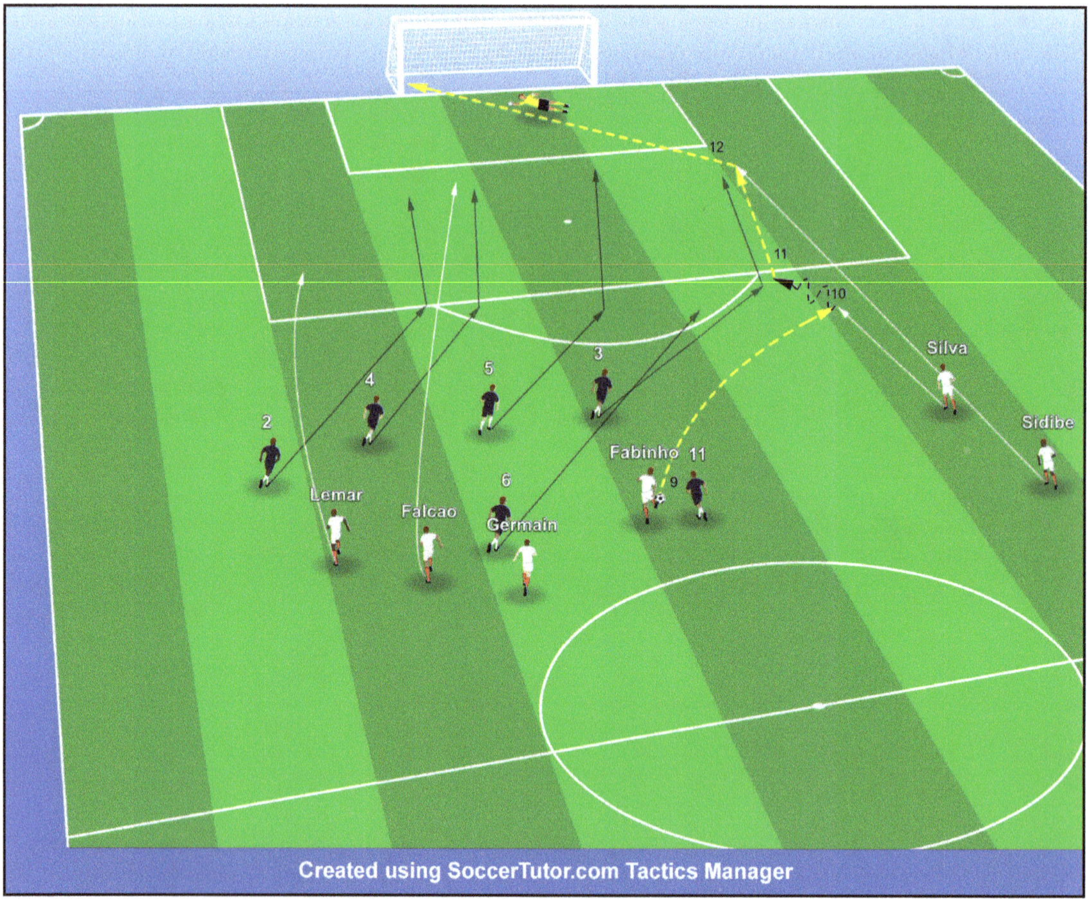

Tactical Analysis of LEONARDO JARDIM - Transition from Defence to Attack (Middle Zone)

The right winger Bernardo Silva has space to run into out wide and Fabinho passes for him to run onto the ball.

Bernardo Silva cuts inside and is tracked by the Bordeaux left back (3). The Monaco right back Sidibe has made a bursting forward run to create an overlap and Bernado Silva passes ahead of him and into the penalty area, as shown.

Sidibe is able to control the ball with one touch and then score into the far corner with his second.

Session to Practice **LEONARDO JARDIM** Tactics - Transition from Defence to Attack (Middle Zone)

SESSION FOR THIS TACTICAL SITUATION (4 PRACTICES)
1. Continuous One-Touch Combination Play in a Passing Practice

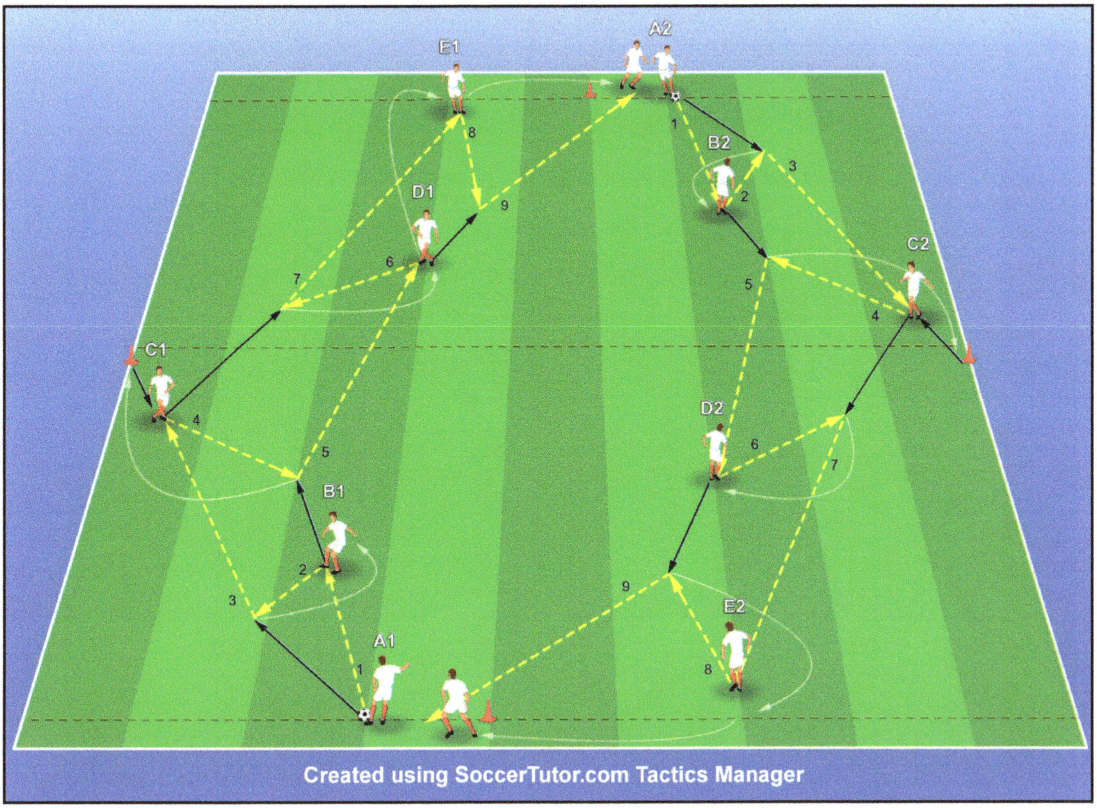

Description
In a 20 x 30 yard area, we have 12 players in the starting positions shown. The practice starts with 2 balls simultaneously at positions A1 and A2, and the same pattern is played on both sides.

- A plays a one-two with B and passes to C.
- C passes back and inside for B, who passes forward to D.
- D passes back for C, who passes forward to E.
- E passes back for D, who passes to the next start position.

All players move to the next position (A -> B -> C -> D -> E) - there is always a spare player at the start.

Coaching Points
1. The rhythm and timing of the movement, together with the accuracy and weight of pass, is key.
2. Players need to make their first touch on the move to maintain the fluency of the practice.
3. The players must play at a high tempo, communicate with teammates and keep their heads up.

Session to Practice **LEONARDO JARDIM** Tactics - Transition from Defence to Attack (Middle Zone)

PROGRESSION

2. Possession and Fast Support Play in a Dynamic 2 Zone Transition Game

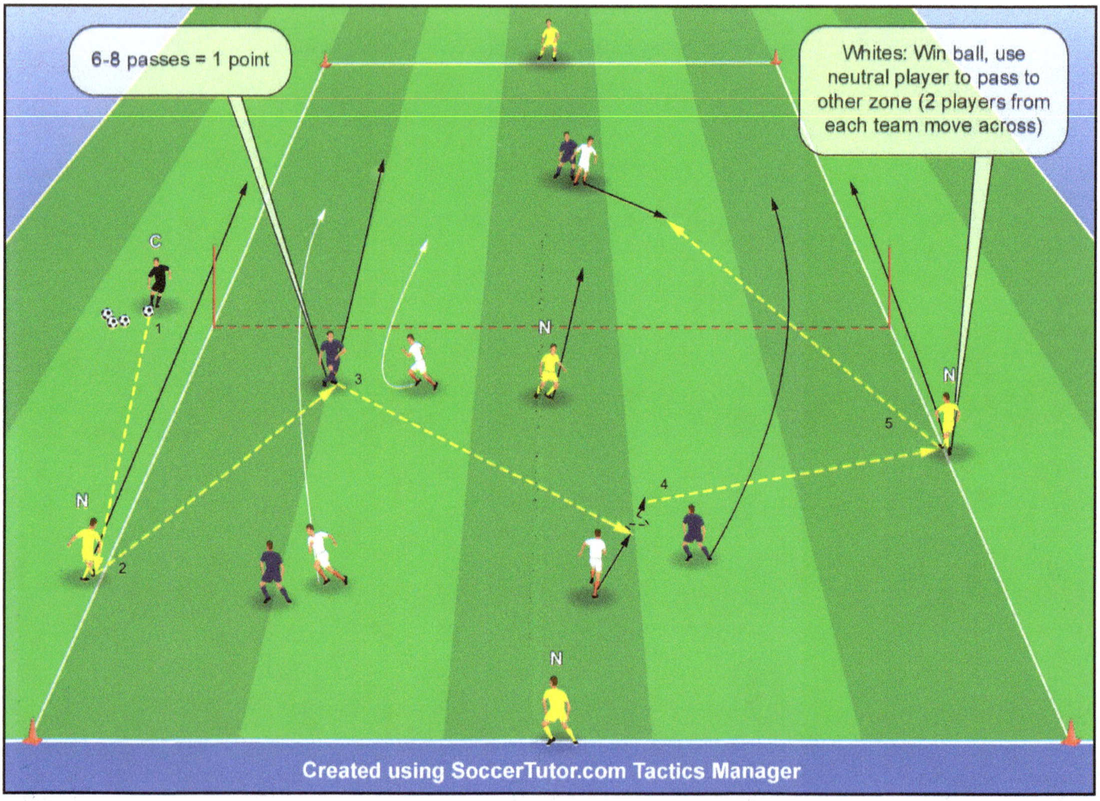

Description

In a 15 x 30 yard area, we have 2 equal zones. In the first zone, we play 3 v 3 + 4 neutral players (3 at the sides and 1 inside). In the second zone, we have 1 player from each team and 1 neutral player. The practice starts with one team in possession (navy in diagram) and their objective is to utilise their numerical advantage with the neutral players to complete 6-8 passes = 1 point.

The white team's objective is to press collectively, win the ball and then utilise the neutral players to pass the ball very quickly to the second zone - from this point, 2 players move across very quickly to support their teammate and maintain possession for their team within this zone. 2 navy players also move across to help their teammate defend. We have the same 3 v 3 (+4) situation with roles reversed.

Coaching Points

1. Reduce the space and apply collective pressing to win the ball with a numerical disadvantage.
2. In the transition to attack, the reactions and the supporting runs must be fast.
3. After making fast supporting runs, offer a passing option at the correct angles and distances.
4. The timing, weight and accuracy of the passes is key to maintain possession.

Session to Practice **LEONARDO JARDIM** Tactics - Transition from Defence to Attack (Middle Zone)

PROGRESSION

3. Fast Break Attacks with Support Players in a Position Specific Small Sided Game

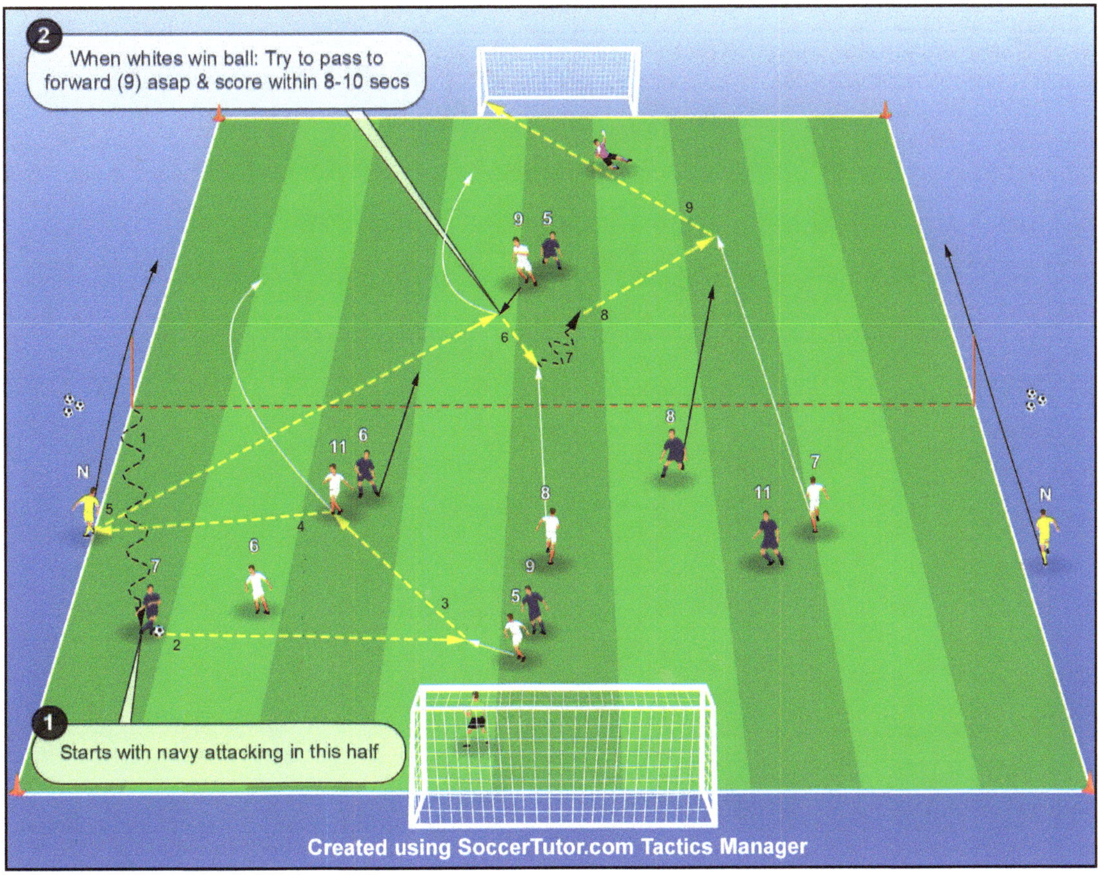

[Diagram: When whites win ball: Try to pass to forward (9) asap & score within 8-10 secs. Starts with navy attacking in this half.]

Description

In a 40 x 60 yard area, we split the pitch into 2 equal zones. We play a 7 v 7 game with 2 extra neutral players on the sides, who play with the team in possession. Each team has 1 centre back (5), 2 central midfielders (6 & 8), 2 wingers (7 & 11) and 1 forward (9) from the 4-4-2 (or 4-2-3-1) formation.

The practice starts with one team (navy) attacking in one zone with a 5 (+2) v 5 situation, as they try to score a goal. In the other zone, we have 1 navy defender and 1 white forward (9).

If the white defending team win the ball, they then quickly make a transition from defence to attack with help from the neutral players in a 6 (+2) v 6 situation. As soon as they win the ball, all players are free to move into the other zone.

The counter attacking team (whites in diagram) should try to pass to the forward (9) as quickly as possible, make fast supporting runs and combine with him to score within 8-10 seconds - if they achieve this, the goal counts double.

Session to Practice LEONARDO JARDIM Tactics - Transition from Defence to Attack (Middle Zone)

PROGRESSION

4. Fast Break Attacks with Many Support Players in an 11 v 11 Tactical Game (4-4-2 vs 4-2-3-1 or 4-4-2)

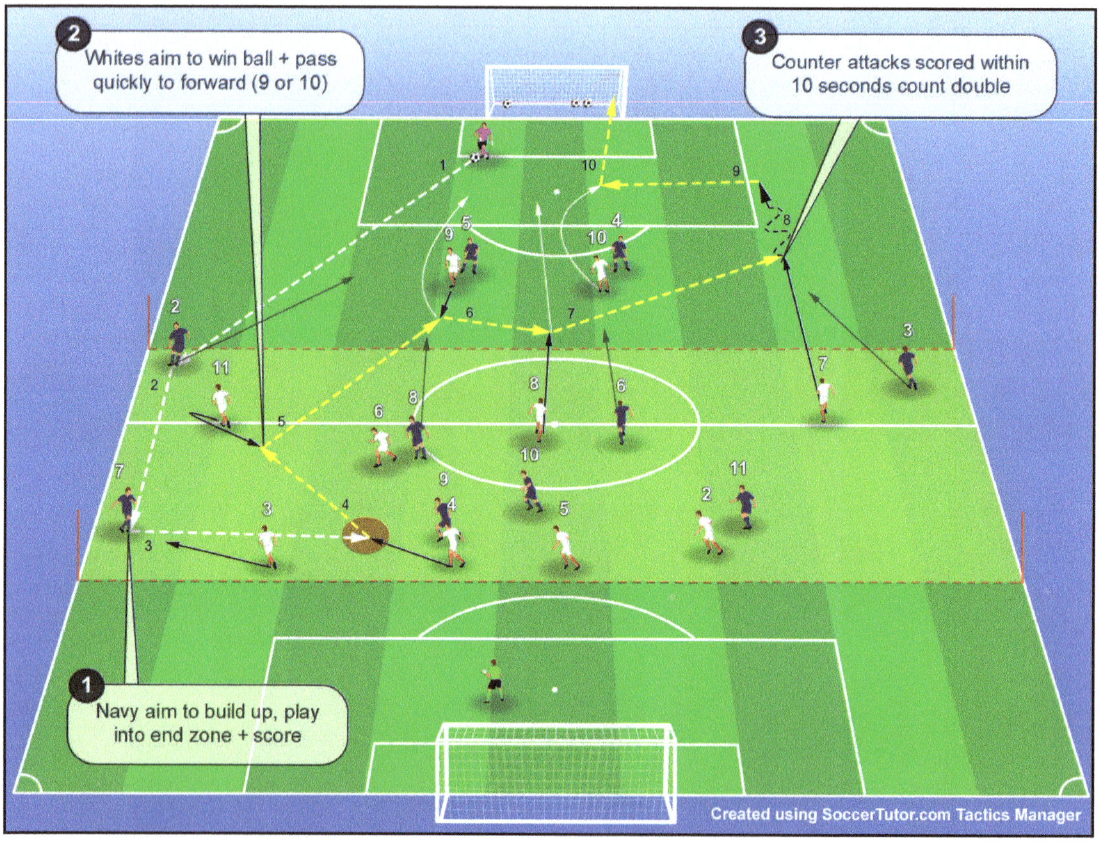

Description

In this progression, we now use a full pitch and mark out a middle zone as shown. We play an 11 v 11 game, with all the outfield players except for 2 white forwards and 2 navy centre backs starting within the middle zone. The white team are in a 4-4-2 formation and the navy team are in a 4-2-3-1.

The practice starts with a pass into the middle zone from the navy team's goalkeeper. The navy team try to break through the pressing, build up play, pass into the end zone and score.

The defending team (whites) apply collective pressing to try and win the ball. If they are successful, their aim is then to launch a fast and direct counter attack. They must do this by quickly passing to one of their forwards (9 or 10) in the end zone.

From the point the whites win the ball, all players are free to move across the zones to attack/defend. The white players' aim is to run forward quickly to support their 2 forwards and finish the counter attack as quickly as possible. If the whites score within 10 seconds of winning the ball, the goal counts double.

CHAPTER 6

TRANSITION FROM DEFENCE TO ATTACK IN THE HIGH ZONE

TRANSITION FROM DEFENCE TO ATTACK IN THE HIGH ZONE

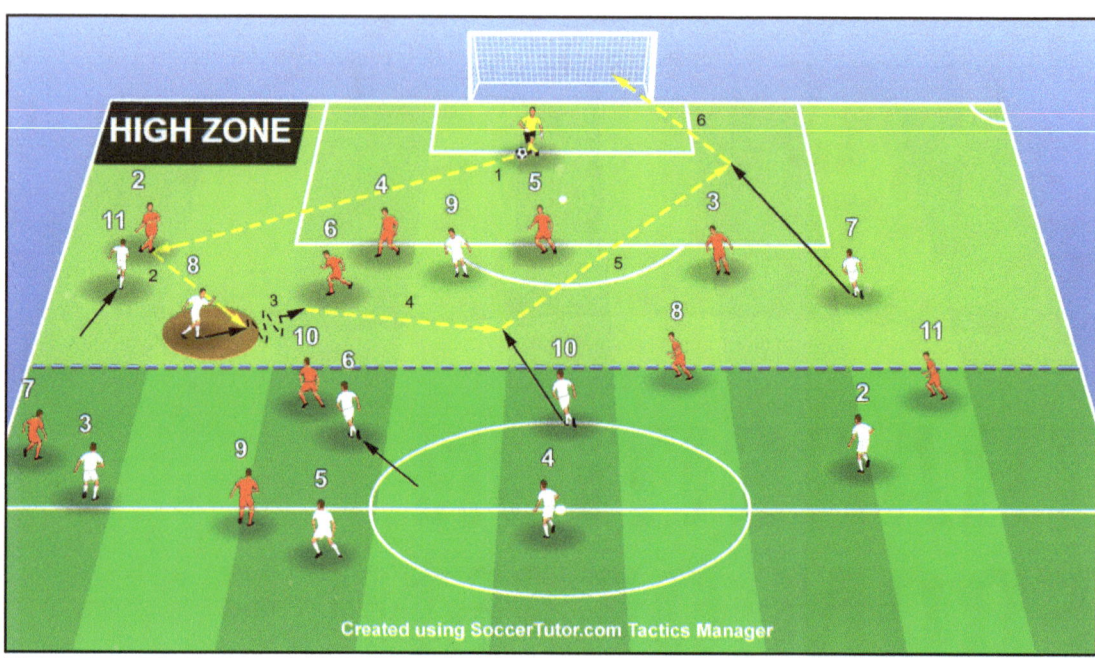

For this book, we have divided the chapters by which zone the transition starts in. There are 3 zones:

1. **Low Zone**
2. **Middle Zone**
3. **High Zone**

This diagram shows an example of a team that has won the ball in the high zone.

In this situation, the white team have players behind the ball when defending. To win the ball, they need to implement high pressing, close down the ball carrier, limit the opponent's time/space and block potential passing lanes with tight marking and good positioning.

In this example, the goalkeeper passes out wide to the red right back (2). As the white team are using a high press, there are limited passing options and limited time for the ball carrier to make a decision. The right back attempts a pass into the No.10, but it is intercepted by the white No.8 in an advanced position.

The white No.8 moves inside with the ball which draws in the white defensive midfielder (6). This creates space for the white No.10 to move forward and receive in space near the edge of the penalty area.

The white No.10 plays a good diagonal pass in between the red centre back (5) and left back (3). The right winger (7) makes a well-timed run and scores with a first time shot.

The team in transition from defence to attack have limited time and space. The key to attacking in this situation from the high zone is to quickly pass into the opponent's box before other players are able to track back and recover. This requires good synchronisation between the weight of pass and the run in behind.

TRANSITION FROM DEFENCE TO ATTACK IN THE HIGH ZONE

What is the Tactical Situation?

- Our team is high up the pitch and defending with many players in the opponent's half.

- We have a lot of space in behind our defensive line and often only have 2 players at the back.

- There is a short distance to the opponent's goal.

- We have many attacking options if we win the ball, but we have limited time and space.

- The opposition have many players in their own half of the pitch.

- There is little space to exploit in behind the opponent's defensive line.

- This tactical situation normally occurs with an equality in numbers.

What Objectives Should We Have?

- The basic aim is to win the ball by pressing the ball carrier and blocking off potential passing lanes.

- We must apply a high press and limit the opposition's space and time. We want to avoid our opponents playing a long pass in behind our defensive line or dribbling forward with the ball.

- Fast and quality attacking combinations are needed with good cooperation under pressure of time and space.

- We need to be aggressive and creative.

- Quickly pass into the opponent's penalty area with players making good runs.

- Synchronised movements in and around the penalty area to finish our attacks effectively and efficiently.

- To complete our attack within 4-8 seconds.

What Practices/Sessions Can We Create for this Tactical Situation?

- Defensive organisation and synchronised movements with an emphasis on high pressing within the high zone.

- Fast break attacks - we need to practice making the transition from defence to attack as quickly as possible. You should emphasise that the players should look to finish their attacks within a maximum time of 8 seconds.

TACTICAL SITUATION 1

POCHETTINO TACTICS

High Press to Win the Ball + Fast Attack

Content taken from Analysis of Tottenham Hotspur during the 2016/2017 season

The analysis is based on recurring patterns of play observed within the Tottenham team. Once the same phase of play occurred a number of times (at least 10) the tactics would be seen as a pattern. The analysis on the next page is an example of the team's tactics being used effectively, taken from a specific game.

Each action, pass, individual movement with or without the ball, and the positioning of each player on the pitch including their body shape, are presented.

The analysis is then used to create a full progressive session to coach this specific tactical situation.

Tactical Analysis of POCHETTINO - Transition from Defence to Attack (High Zone)

Analysis Taken from 'Watford vs Tottenham - 1st Jan 2017 (Premier League)'

High Press to Win the Ball + Fast Attack
(3-4-2-1 vs 3-1-4-2)

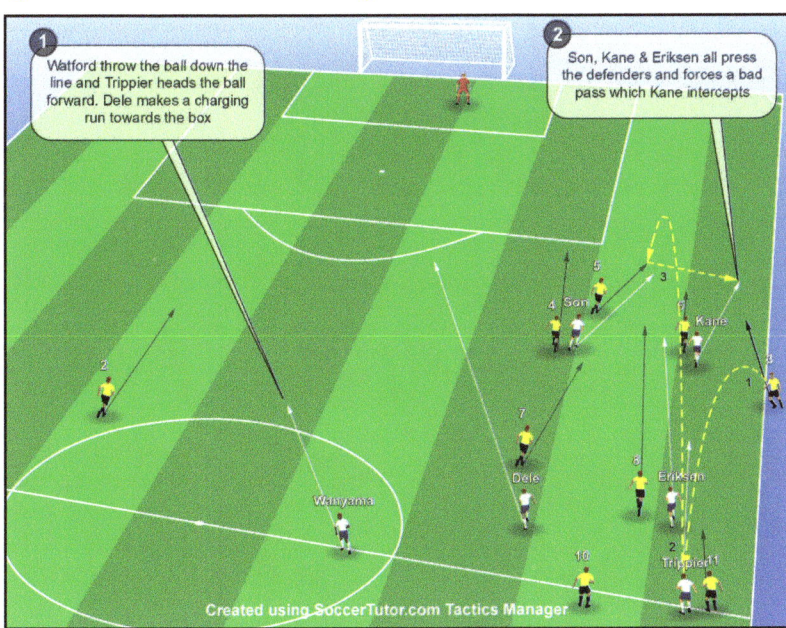

The Watford left back (3) has taken a throw-in up the line which the Tottenham right back Trippier has forcefully headed long and high over the opposition's defence. From this point, Tottenham apply a high press (squeeze) with Kane, Son, Eriksen, Trippier and Dele.

The Watford centre back (5) is running back towards his own goal. He miss-hits his clearance straight to Tottenham forward Harry Kane, who is able to control the ball.

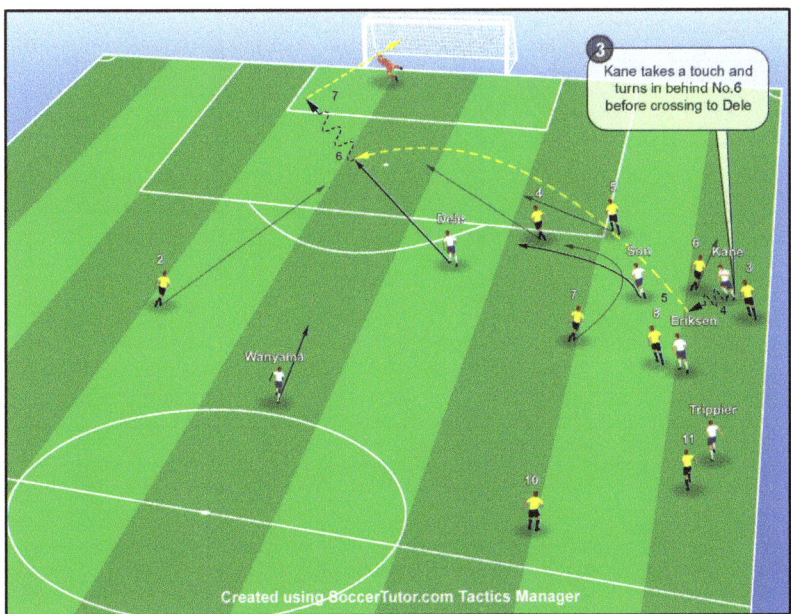

Tottenham's aim here is to take advantage of their opponent's temporarily disorganised defence. They want to create a scoring opportunity as quickly as possible.

Harry Kane turns inside the Watford centre back (6) and delivers a cross into the box.

Attacking midfielder Dele Alli has made a good run into the penalty area. Dele has time to control the ball and then finish past the keeper at the far post.

Tactical Analysis of POCHETTINO - Transition from Defence to Attack (High Zone)

Analysis Taken from 'Tottenham vs Everton - 5th Mar 2017 (Premier League)'

High Press to Win the Ball + Fast Attack (3-4-2-1 vs 4-3-2-1)

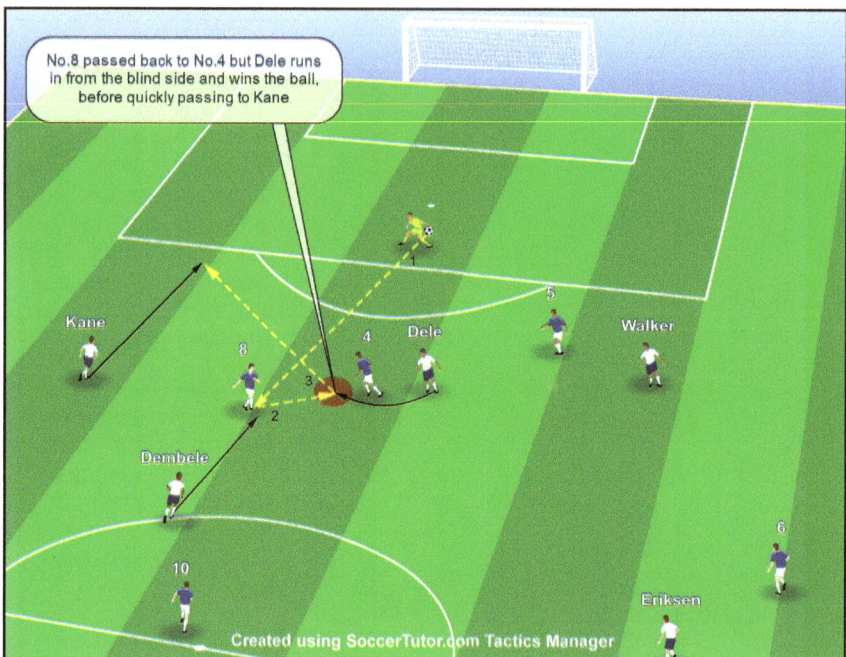

In this situation, the goalkeeper rolls the ball out to the defensive midfielder Schneiderlin (6), who drops deep to receive.

Tottenham see this as an opportunity to press high and win the ball. As soon as the ball is rolled out, central midfielder Dembele and attacking midfielder Dele sprint towards Schneiderlin. Dele is able to win the ball and quickly pass to the forward Kane, who is free in space.

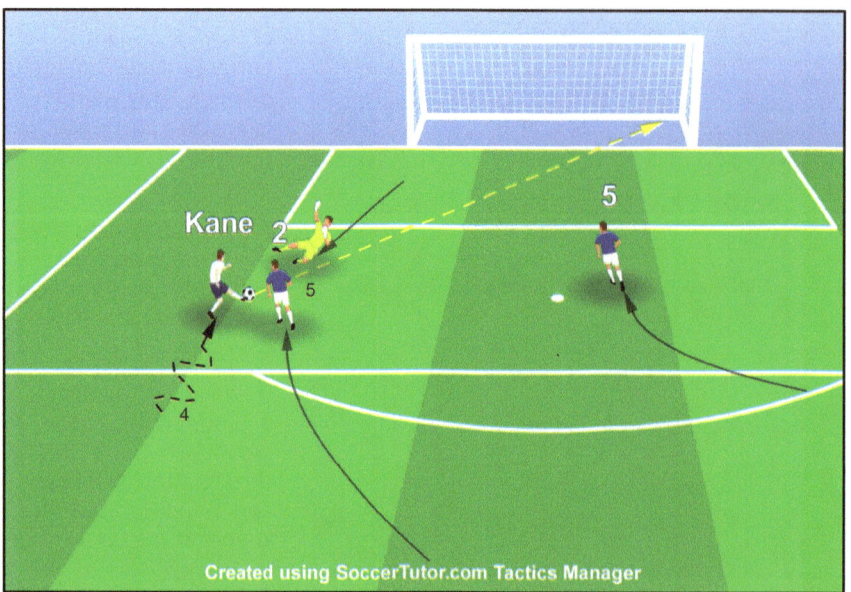

The Tottenham forward Harry Kane has time to take a touch and slot the ball past the oncoming goalkeeper.

This is a very good example of Tottenham pressing high up the pitch, winning the ball and then scoring very quickly, which has been a trait for them under Pochettino.

Session to Practice POCHETTINO Tactics - Transition from Defence to Attack (High Zone)

SESSION FOR THIS TACTICAL SITUATION (4 PRACTICES)
1. High Press to Win the Ball + Keep Possession in a Dynamic 2 Zone Transition Game

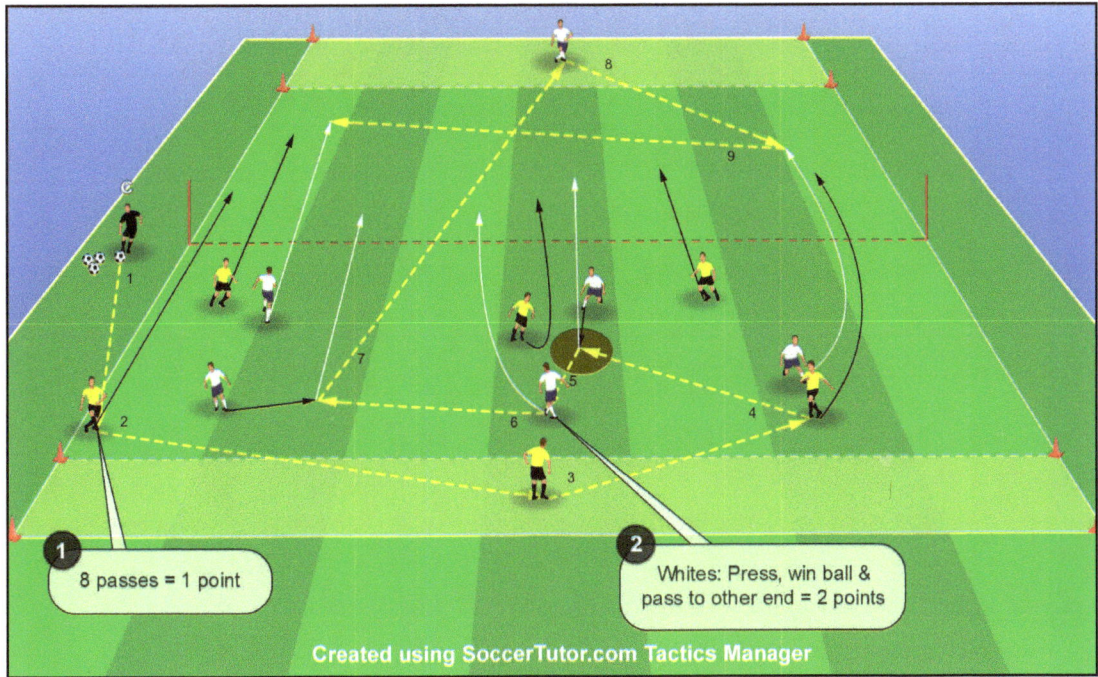

1 8 passes = 1 point

2 Whites: Press, win ball & pass to other end = 2 points

Description

In a 30 x 40 yard area, we divide the pitch into 2 equal sized main zones and also mark out 2 end zones (30 x 5 yards). We have 5 v 5 starting in one zone, with each team having an extra player in an end zone.

The practice starts with the coach's pass and the team in possession (yellows in diagram) try to complete 8 passes to score 1 point. They have a 6 v 5 numerical advantage with the extra player in the end zone who plays with them.

The aim for the defending team (white) is to press collectively, win the ball and then pass to their teammate in the end zone on the opposite side (2 points).

If this happens, all the players from both teams (except the player in the end zone) run to the other zone and we have the same 5 (+1) v 5 situation with the team roles reversed.

Rules

1. Inside players cannot enter the end zones.
2. End zone players must not leave their zone.
3. Inside players have unlimited (or 3) touches.
4. End zone players are limited to 1 or 2 touches.

Session to Practice **POCHETTINO** Tactics - Transition from Defence to Attack (High Zone)

PROGRESSION

2. High Press to Win the Ball + Fast Attack in a Dynamic 2 Zone Small Sided Game

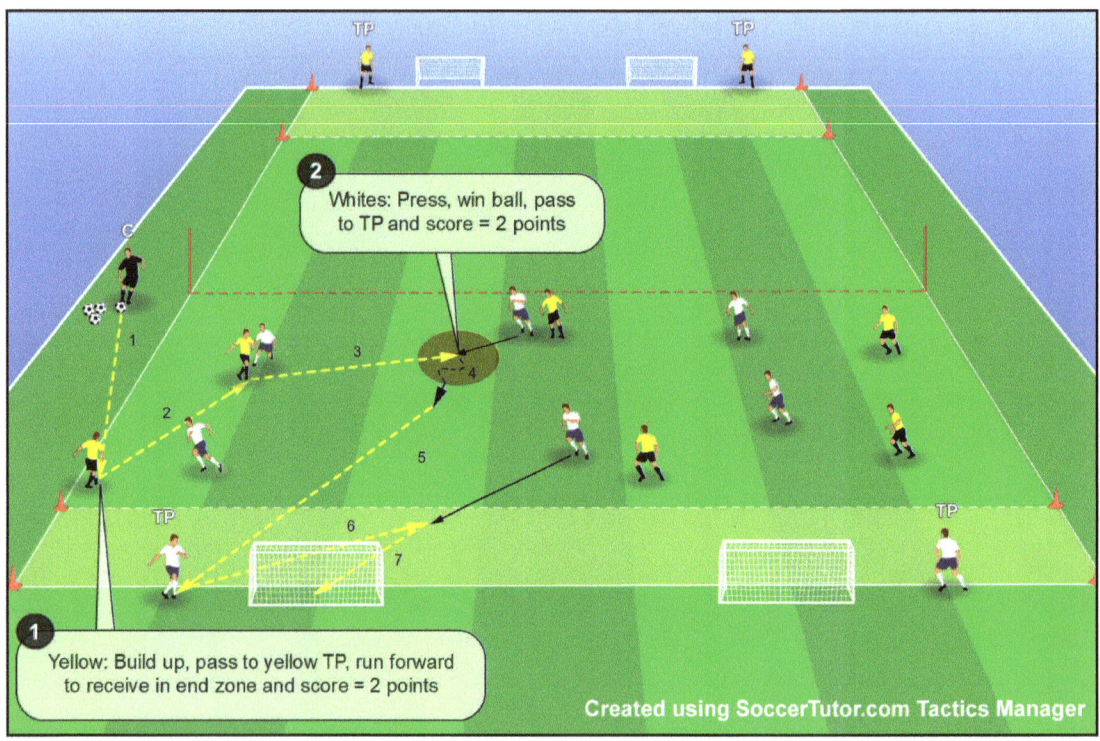

Description

In this progression of the previous practice, we remove the end zone player and each team now has 2 Target Players outside at the ends, as shown. We also now play 6 v 6 inside instead of 5 v 5 and there are 2 mini goals at each end.

The practice starts with the coach's pass and the team in possession (yellows in diagram) trying to break through their opponent's pressing and pass to a Target Player (TP) at the other end. They then quickly run forward to support the Target Players, receive back and try to score a goal (2 points).

The defending team (white) aim to press collectively to block the passing lines towards the Target Players and win the ball. As soon as they win the ball, they look to pass to one of their Target Players, receive back and score (1 point - this example is shown in the diagram).

When an attack is finished, the practice always starts from the other side and the teams change roles.

Rules: These are the same as the previous practice + the Target Players cannot move inside.

Session to Practice **POCHETTINO** Tactics - Transition from Defence to Attack (High Zone)

PROGRESSION

3. High Press to Win the Ball + Fast Attack in a Dynamic Game with Target Players

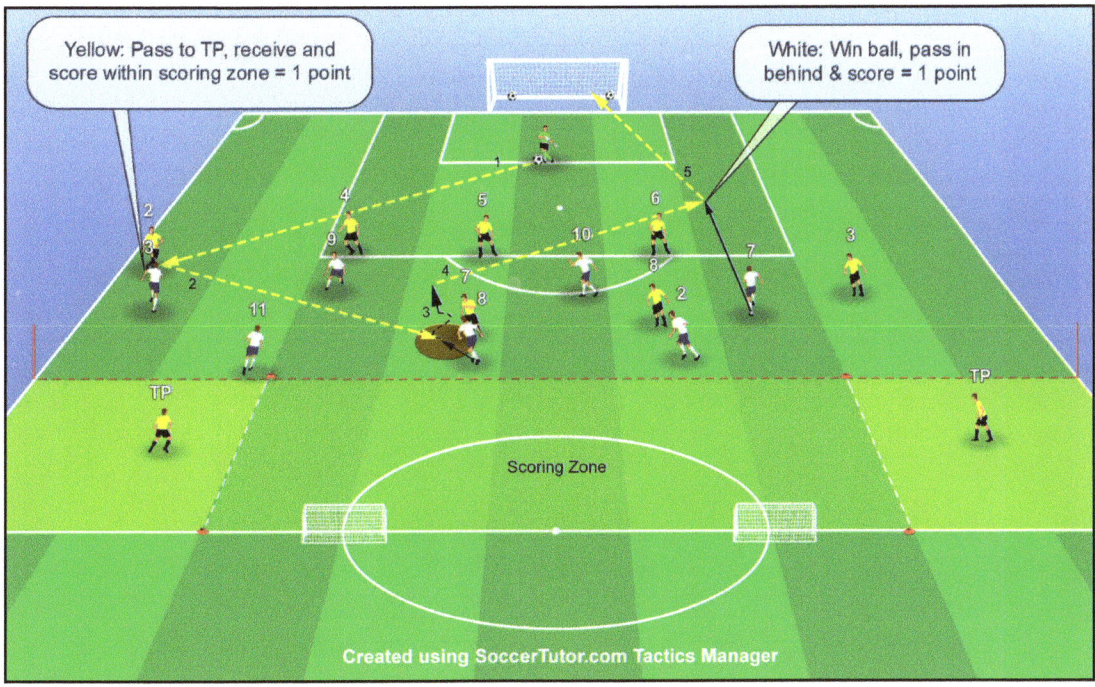

Objective: Collective pressing high up the pitch and a very fast transition to attack, trying to score as quickly as possible.

Description

Using the area shown, we mark out 2 small zones for the Target Players (TP) and a "Scoring Zone" for the yellow team, as shown

The yellow team are using a 3-4 formation (from 3-4-2-1) and the white team are using a 1-4-2 formation (from 3-1-4-2).

The practice starts from the yellow team's goalkeeper. The aim for the yellows is to break through the pressing of the white team to build up play and pass to a Target Player. The Target player passes into the "Scoring Zone" for a yellow player who runs forward to receive and score in a mini goal (1 point).

The defending team (white) aim to press collectively in the high zone to block the passing lines toward the Target Players and win the ball. As soon as the whites win the ball, they immediately look to exploit the space in behind the defensive line with a final pass and score a goal (1 point).

Rule: The white team are not allowed to enter the "Scoring Zone" until the ball is played in there.

Session to Practice POCHETTINO Tactics - Transition from Defence to Attack (High Zone)

PROGRESSION

4. High Press to Win the Ball + Fast Attack in a Tactical 2 Zone Game (3-1-4-2 vs 3-4-2-1)

Description

To finish the session, we play an 11 v 11 game. The pitch is divided into 2 zones and all players are in the high zone. The white team are in a 3-1-4-2 formation and the yellows are in a 3-4-2-1 formation.

The practice starts with the yellow team's goalkeeper - their aim is to break through the white team's pressing, play the ball beyond the halfway line into the other zone and then score a goal (2 points).

The white team aim to press collectively high up the pitch, block the passing lanes and win the ball. They then launch a fast break attack, trying to score a goal (1 point). If they are able to score a goal within 6-8 seconds of winning the ball, they get 2 points.

Rule: The white team are not allowed to enter the low zone until the ball is played in there.

Coaching Points

1. Players need to synchronise their pressing movements with short distances between each other.
2. Quickly press the ball carrier to stop him passing or dribbling forward, forcing him to play under pressure of time and space.
3. Mark the players around the ball zone very tightly and block off potential passing lanes.

TACTICAL SITUATION 2

MAURIZIO SARRI TACTICS

High Press and Fast Attack with Third Man Run

Content taken from Analysis of Napoli during the 2016/2017 season

The analysis is based on recurring patterns of play observed within the Napoli team. Once the same phase of play occurred a number of times (at least 10) the tactics would be seen as a pattern. The analysis on the next page is an example of the team's tactics being used effectively, taken from a specific game.

Each action, pass, individual movement with or without the ball, and the positioning of each player on the pitch including their body shape, are presented.

The analysis is then used to create a full progressive session to coach this specific tactical situation.

Tactical Analysis of MAURIZIO SARRI - Transition from Defence to Attack (High Zone)

Analysis Taken from 'Napoli vs Fiorentina - 20th May 2017 (Serie A)'

High Press and Fast Attack with Third Man Run (4-3-3 vs 4-2-3-1)

In this situation, the Fiorentina central midfielder (8) is dribbling out from the back. The Napoli players shift across collectively. Red No.8 plays a short pass to the left winger (11) but he is quickly closed down by Napoli right back Hysaj, who bursts forward.

The Napoli central midfielder Zieliński is able to tackle the Fiorentina left winger (11) and the ball goes straight to Napoli's winger Callejón who receives and turns (see second diagram below).

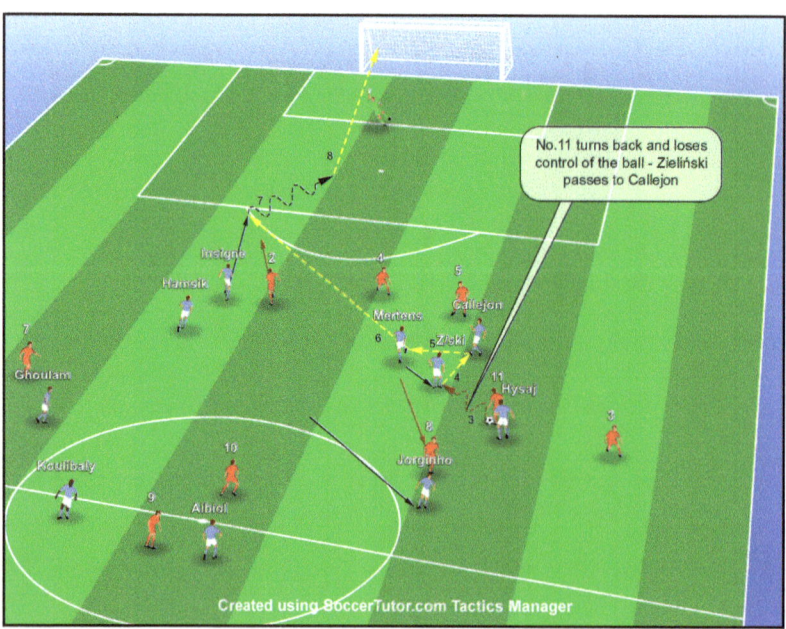

Callejón plays a short pass inside to the forward Mertens.

Although the Fiorentina centre backs have regained effective positions, both full backs are out of position and there is lots of space to exploit in behind.

Mertens shows good awareness to finish the attack quickly - he gets his head up and spots the run from the left winger Insigne and plays it in behind for him to run onto. Insigne receives, dribbles inside and scores.

Session to Practice MAURIZIO SARRI Tactics - Transition from Defence to Attack (High Zone)

SESSION FOR THIS TACTICAL SITUATION (5 PRACTICES)
1. Quick Passing Combination, Third Man Run, Final Ball and Finish

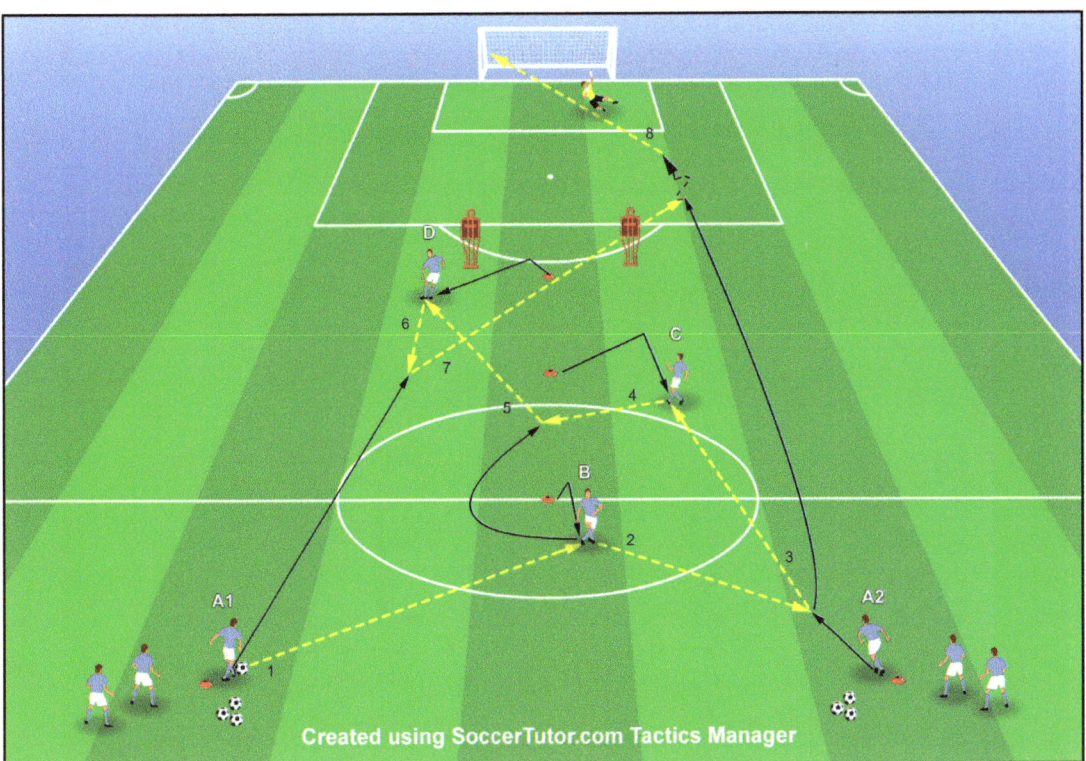

Description
1. A1 passes to B and B passes to A2, who moves forward off the cone.
2. A2 passes to C who moves off of his cone to that side. B turns and C lays the ball off to him.
3. In the meantime, A1 and A2 have both made forward runs. B passes to D who moves off his cone and lays the ball back for A1.
4. For the final pass, A1 plays the ball in between the 2 mannequins (defenders) for A2 to receive on the move and finish. The offside rule is applied.
5. We start again from A2. C and D make their movements in the opposite direction so we complete a mirrored sequence on the other side with A1 receiving the final pass and finishing.

Coaching Points
1. The rhythm and timing of the movement, together with the accuracy and weight of pass, is key.
2. C and D check away from their marker (cone) and move to meet the ball.
3. Make sure the first touch is made on the move to maintain the fluency of the practice.
4. Communicate with teammates and make sure heads are up.
5. The practice should be done at a high tempo throughout.

Session to Practice MAURIZIO SARRI Tactics - Transition from Defence to Attack (High Zone)

PROGRESSION

2. Possession Play and Pressing to Win the Ball in a Dynamic 2 Zone Transition Game

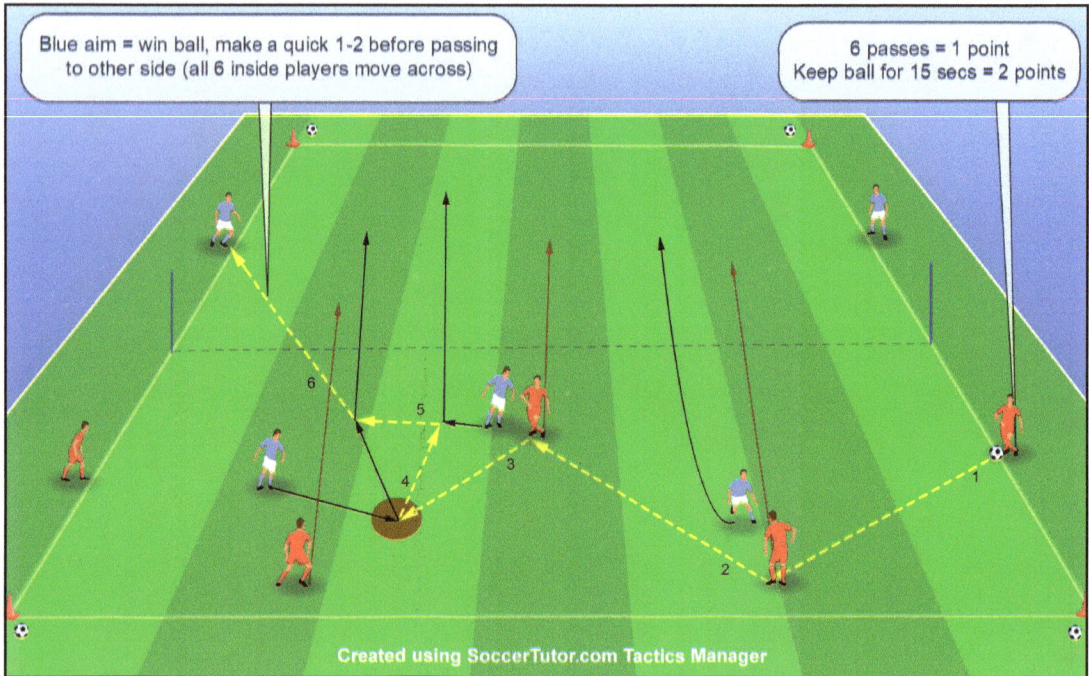

Description

In a 20 x 20 yard area, we have 2 equal sized zones. Each team has 5 players with 3 inside and 2 players at the sides of their own zone, as shown.

The practice starts in one zone with one team in possession (reds) with a 5 v 3 numerical advantage. The aim for the reds is to maintain possession - if they complete 6 passes they score 1 point and if they keep the ball for 15 seconds, they score 2 points.

The aim for the 3 blue players is to press high and force the reds into a wrong decision/mistake so that they can win the ball. When this happens, they play a quick 1-2 and pass to a teammate in the other zone. All players move across to the other zone and the practice continues with the same 5 v 3 situation, with the team roles reversed.

Rules

1. Inside players have unlimited (or 3) touches and the outside players are limited to 1 or 2 touches.
2. Each time a team wins the ball, they score get 1 point.

Coaching Points

1. Defenders must reduce the space for their opponents, limiting the time and options available.
2. Transition: Good awareness, quick and accurate first pass, fast support play (angles/distances) and the players need to spread out and use all the space available to maintain possession.

Session to Practice MAURIZIO SARRI Tactics - Transition from Defence to Attack (High Zone)

PROGRESSION

3. High Press and Fast Attack with Third Man Run in a Position Specific Game

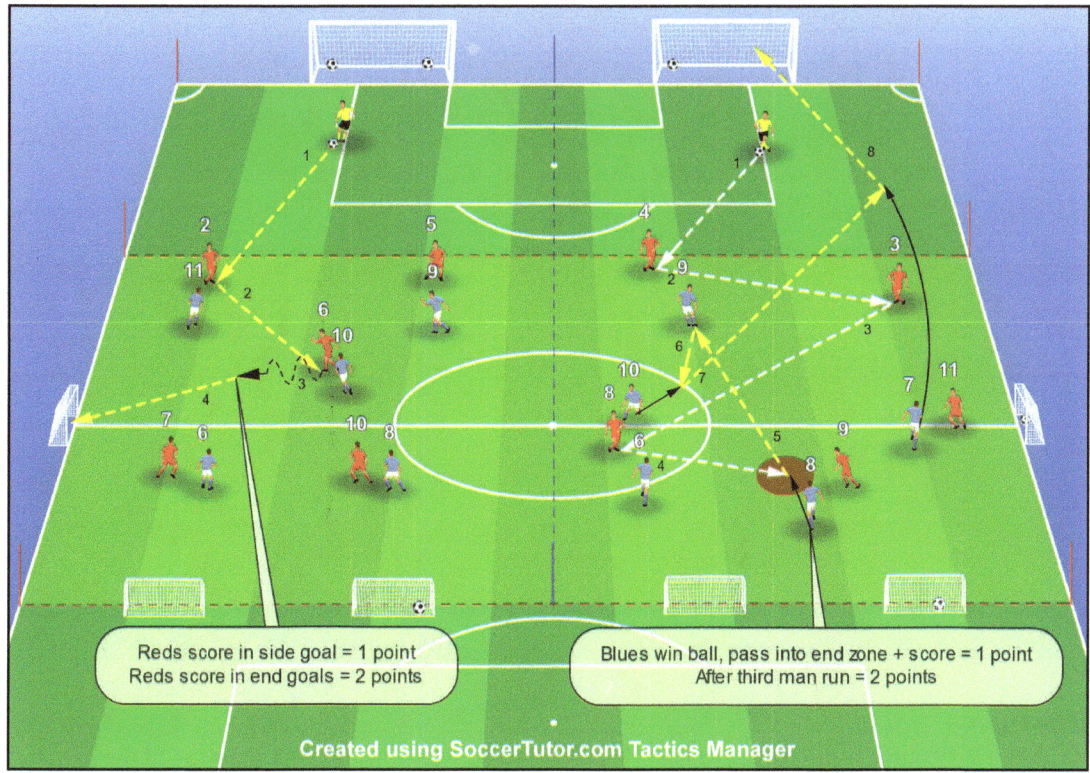

Description

Using 3/4 of a full pitch, we divide the area in half vertically as shown. Each side has an end zone which is 20-25 yards in depth. We work with 2 groups of 10 outfield players.

The reds have their full 4-2-3-1 formation across both sides. The blues have 3 central midfielders (6, 8 & 10), a winger (7 or 11) and the forward (9) from the 4-3-3 formation on each side.

Both sides play at the same time with their own ball. The practice starts from the red team's goalkeeper with the reds building up play and trying to score in the mini goal at the side (1 point) or one of the 2 mini goals at the end (2 points).

The aim for the blues is to apply a high press, squeeze the space to force a mistake and win the ball. From this point, they make a fast transition to attack and play a pass into the end zone to score (1 point). If they are able to score after a third man run, they score 2 points.

Rules

1. After winning the ball, the blues must finish their attack within 8 seconds.
2. The red players are not allowed in the end zone until the ball has been played in there.

Session to Practice **MAURIZIO SARRI** Tactics - Transition from Defence to Attack (High Zone)

PROGRESSION

4. High Press and Fast Attack with Third Man Run in a 9 v 9 Small Sided Game

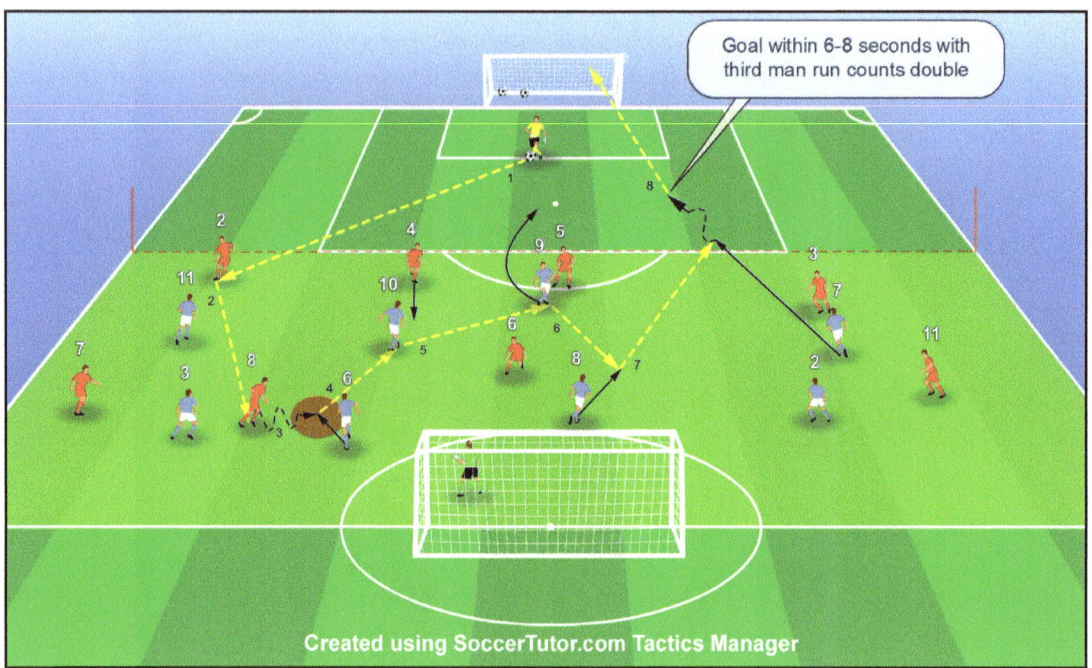

Description

We play a 9 v 9 game using half a pitch and mark out an end zone in line with the edge of the penalty area. The red team are in a 4-2-2 formation (from 4-2-3-1) and the blues are in a 2-3-3 (from 4-3-3). The practice starts with the red team's goalkeeper and the reds build up play and try to score a goal.

The blue team apply a high press and try to win the ball. If this happens, they try to score with a fast break attack within 6-8 seconds. If they achieve this with a final ball for a third man run (see diagram example), the goal counts double.

Rules

1. The blue players are limited to 2 touches.
2. The red players are not allowed in the end zone at any point.
3. Only 2 blue players are allowed to make runs into the end zone to try and score (11 & 9 in diagram).

Coaching Points

1. The weight, angle and accuracy of the final pass is important, so that the player making the third man run can receive on the move in the space behind the defensive line.
2. The players should show good anticipation, decision making + quick and quality finishing.

Progression: Once the ball goes into the end zone, all players are free to attack/defend in there.

Session to Practice MAURIZIO SARRI Tactics - Transition from Defence to Attack (High Zone)

PROGRESSION

5. High Press and Fast Attack with Third Man Run in a Tactical Transition Game (4-3-3 vs 4-2-3-1)

Description

The blue team are in a 4-3-3 formation and the red team are in a 4-2-3-1.

1. The practice starts with the blues building up play and trying to score. In this phase, the blue players are limited to 2 or 3 touches.

2. If the reds win the ball and keep possession for 6-8 seconds, they score 1 point. If they complete 6 passes, they score 1 point. If they move the ball into the "Attacking Zone", they score 2 points and if they score a goal, they get 3 points.

3. All of these rules and chances for the reds to score force the blue team to press very high up the pitch to win the ball back. If they do, they make a very fast transition to attack. They score 1 point for a normal goal, 2 points for a goal within 6 seconds of winning the ball and 3 points if it is also scored using a third man run. - *Steps 2 & 3 are not shown in the diagram because the ball goes out of play before the reds can counter attack, and therefore before the blues can recover the ball.*

4. After the blue team's second attack finishes, the coach passes a new ball to the red team. The blues again make a quick transition from attack to defence with a high press, try to win the ball and then score, as shown in the diagram with No.10's goal.

5. Once step 4 is finished, start the practice from the beginning again.

THE TRANSITION FROM ATTACK TO DEFENCE

CHAPTER 7

TECHNICAL & TACTICAL REQUIREMENTS IN THE TRANSITION FROM ATTACK TO DEFENCE

COACHING THE TRANSITION FROM ATTACK TO DEFENCE

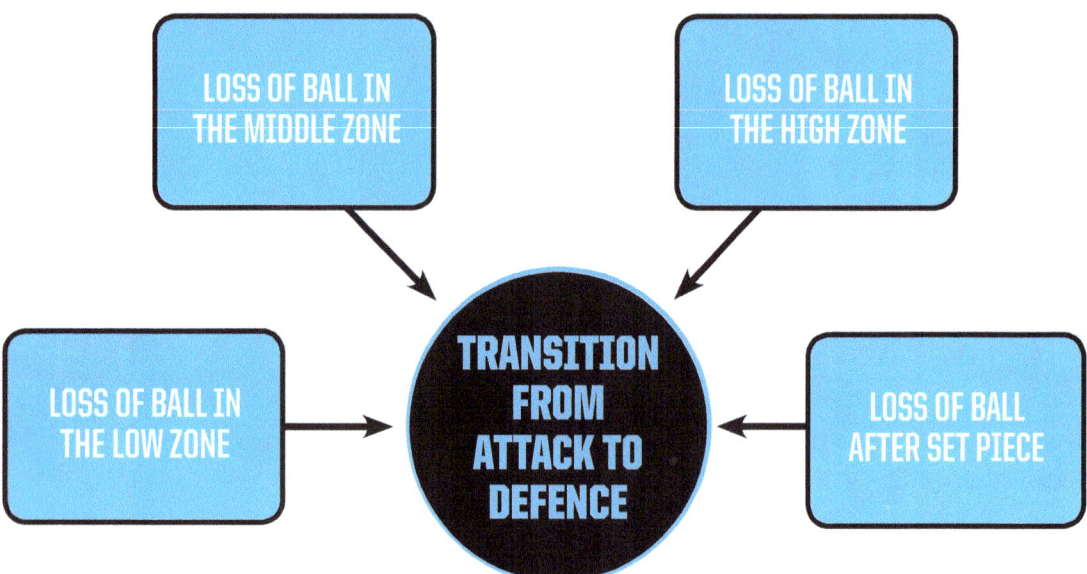

In this phase of the game we should first and foremost think about where and how we start our attack and what attacking style we want to implement.

We can then determine what positioning and reactions we will need for the transition from attack to defence.

We must then work on all the possible tactical situations in the transition from attack to defence repeatedly in training, so we are ready for all potential tactical situations in our competitive matches.

Based on this, every coach should be targeting his team's training on the possible loss of the ball in all zones of the pitch (low, middle and high zones).

We then work on how we want to defend, based on what kind of players we have in our team and what kind of players the opposition have. We must utilise the individual strengths of our players and as a group, against the weaknesses of our opponents.

TECHNICAL & TACTICAL REQUIREMENTS IN THE TRANSITION FROM ATTACK TO DEFENCE

TRANSITION FROM ATTACK TO DEFENCE FLOW CHART

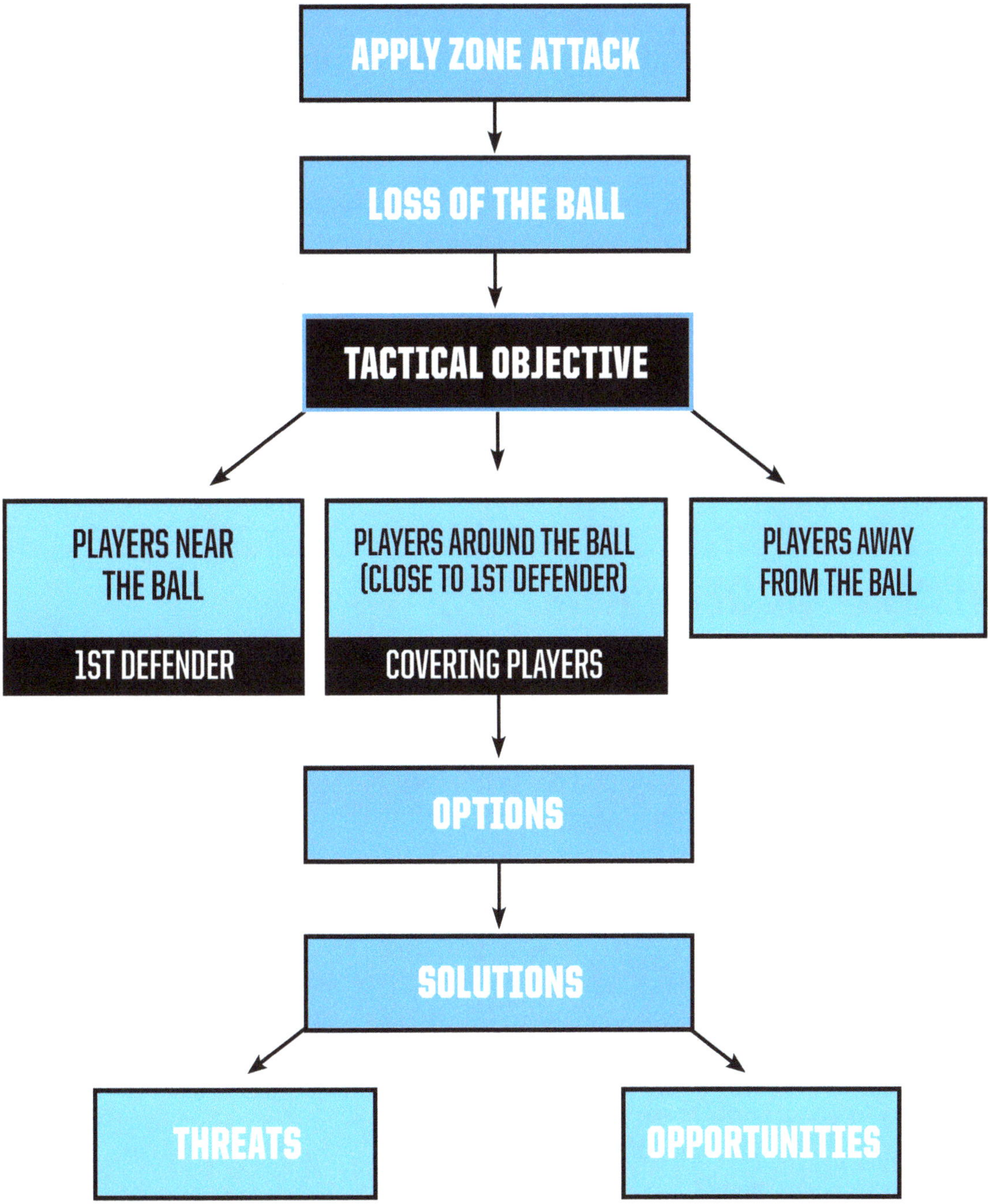

```
         APPLY ZONE ATTACK
                │
                ▼
         LOSS OF THE BALL
                │
                ▼
         TACTICAL OBJECTIVE
        ┌───────┼───────┐
        ▼       ▼       ▼
   PLAYERS   PLAYERS AROUND   PLAYERS AWAY
   NEAR THE  THE BALL (CLOSE  FROM THE BALL
   BALL      TO 1ST DEFENDER)

   1ST       COVERING
   DEFENDER  PLAYERS
                │
                ▼
             OPTIONS
                │
                ▼
            SOLUTIONS
           ┌─────┴─────┐
           ▼           ▼
        THREATS   OPPORTUNITIES
```

COACHING TRANSITION PLAY - VOL. 2

TECHNICAL & TACTICAL REQUIREMENTS IN THE TRANSITION FROM ATTACK TO DEFENCE

Apply Zone Attack: We must decide which zone to build up our attacking game. Where and how do we consolidate possession of the ball, how do we penetrate the opposition defence and how do we finish our attack as a team?
The zone we decide to attack from depends on our tactical/technical characteristics and formation against our opponent.

Loss of the Ball: We must decide which zone and area of the pitch our team can afford to lose the ball. This requires having good positioning while in possession, to prepare for the negative transition.

Tactical Objective

What are the tactical objectives that we have in this situation as individuals, as a group and as a whole team?

Decision Making

- The player nearest to the ball when we lose it must press the new ball carrier - where, how, when?
- The other players closest to the ball - should they press the ball, mark the potential receivers tightly or cover space?
- The players away from the ball - what movements should they make? - Where, how, when?

Options: What are the basic objectives and options in all of these situations and how can we work to avoid our opponents taking advantage when we lose the ball?

Solutions: What solutions do we have and how can we be most effective in this situation? (We can provide the players with solutions for each situation in training).

Opportunities: What are the opportunities in these tactical situations and how can we exploit them to get the best results?

Threats: What are the threats we must pay attention to which the opposition may be able to exploit?

TECHNICAL REQUIREMENTS

- When defending, use a staggered stance, alternating front and back foot.
- Feet shoulder width apart, legs bent, arched over, on your toes (don't get flat-footed).
- Feints and stabs but do not fully commit until the ball carrier makes a mistake.
- Concentrate on the player, not the ball, and look at his hips, not his feet or upper body.
- Keep an eye on the space between the ball and the ball carrier. If the ball gets away from their feet, step in to win possession.
- Close the distance between yourself and the ball carrier. Get close enough to force him to alter his course of attack and to force his head down to concentrate on not losing possession of the ball.
- Choose the angle of approach to guide/force the ball carrier away from dangerous areas and spaces.
- Deny the player space to run into and penetrate.
- Prevent the player from shooting at goal. Block any attempted shot.
- If the ball carrier allows the ball to get in between his feet then step in to make a tackle.
- Tackles should be fully committed through the centre of the ball.

TECHNICAL & TACTICAL REQUIREMENTS IN THE TRANSITION FROM ATTACK TO DEFENCE

TACTICAL REQUIREMENTS

- Balanced positioning in the possession phase with small distances between the players and the midfield and defensive lines.

- The transition from attack to defence comes after we are in possession, so we will usually have at least 3 players around the ball.

- The goal is to win the ball back, not just force the ball carrier back.

- The whole team presses aggressively and in unison to win the ball back. Players step towards the ball.

- Move quickly to close down opponents with well-rehearsed, coordinated pressing by 2 or more players.

- Limit the ball carrier's time, space and options to pass or dribble the ball forward.

- Force the ball to be played in a specific direction (wide) to create and exploit a numerical advantage around the ball area.

- Get compact in width and depth. Intelligent positioning is needed to restrict space for the opposition to pass and move into.

- The player nearest the ball is **"The 1st Defender"**. Their role is to slow down the attack, not necessarily win the ball. They should prevent the ball being played forward. This pressure will cause the ball carrier's head down, making him concentrate on keeping control of the ball, so he is unable to look for passing options.

- The player or players further away from the ball get into position to intercept all passing options and provide cover.

- The players can leave the most difficult and longest passing options provided there is good pressure and cover on the ball carrier and his nearest passing options.

- The first defender should not run straight at the ball carrier, but should come in at an angle that would force the ball carrier to pass back or to attack towards our covering defenders or towards the side-line. This makes the opponent's attack predictable and easy to read for covering defenders.

- Once the ball carrier has been contained and delayed, the first defender may move in closer to challenge for the ball, as he has sufficient cover.

- If the first defender can force the ball carrier to go backwards, he must maintain close pressure to prevent him from opening up space.

- The defence should use this opportunity to push forward as well, compressing the attack away from their goal.

- If there is no pressure on the ball carrier, then the defence do not push up as the player will have time and space to find and take advantage of the space in behind the defensive line. The players need to recognise the situation to determine when to press and when to track back to defend behind the ball.

- **"The 2nd Defender"** (the second closest to the ball) marks the player who is the nearest passing option. They must cover the space behind their teammate who is pressuring the ball. However, if there is a numerical advantage, he might decide to risk double teaming the ball carrier to win the ball back quickly.

- **"The 3rd Defender"** provides balance by covering the space (blocking passes) which could be exploited by the opponent to switch their point of attack e.g. by playing a long pass to the opposite wing.

- The team need to work effectively in a situation with a numerical disadvantage or equality in numbers.

- The strong side and the easiest/nearest path to goal needs to be protected.

- The team needs to also protect the weak side with quick reactions and switch the point (direction) of defence if necessary.

CHAPTER 8

TRANSITION FROM ATTACK TO DEFENCE IN THE LOW ZONE

TRANSITION FROM ATTACK TO DEFENCE IN THE LOW ZONE

For this book, we divided the chapters by which zone the transition starts in. There are 3 zones:

1. **Low Zone**
2. **Middle Zone**
3. **High Zone**

In this situation, the white team are building up play from the back and the opposition winger (11) intercepts the pass from the full back (2). The white team are temporarily unbalanced so the players must shift across or track back to close the spaces available (as shown in the diagram).

Pressure is applied to the new ball carrier immediately, before he is able to get his head up to dribble or pass forward. 1 or 2 players should apply direct pressure and the other players converge, block potential passing options and mark other players. This creates a numerical advantage in and around the ball zone.

Once the right back (2) loses the ball, the other 3 defenders all shift across. The left back (3) and one centre back (4) mark their direct opponents and the other centre back (5) moves forward to block off a forward pass and close the space available. The right back (2) and No.8 move to apply direct pressure. No.10 marks the opposing No.10 and the defensive midfielder (6) moves across to block any potential passes inside.

These cohesive movements delay or stop the opposition attacking quickly, allowing time for the team to re-group and get players behind the ball. The red winger (11) can either turn and play a pass back or most likely lose the ball.

TRANSITION FROM ATTACK TO DEFENCE IN THE LOW ZONE

What is the Tactical Situation?

- Our team start the attack from the back and we have at least 7-8 players in our half.

- There are normally a minimum of 3-4 players (midfielders and forwards) in front of the ball.

- In some cases there will be large distances between the wide players and the central players. This is because teams try to utilise the full width of the pitch when building up play from the back.

- The opposition (if they press us) have many players high up the pitch and in our half.

- Our defenders have a numerical advantage or an equality of numbers.

- Our opponents have a short distance to our goal and will use direct attacks once they win the ball.

- The opponent tries to finish their attack within 6-8 seconds (average).

What Objectives Should We Have?

- To make the transition from attack to defence very quickly, defending well in our own half and limiting the space and time available for our opponents - to prevent them from creating goal scoring opportunities.

- Get as many players back and behind the ball as we can, as soon as possible.

- To create a numerical advantage in and around the ball and our penalty area.

- Players need to position themselves in central areas to guard the 'danger zone' in case the opposition are able to pass into the penalty area.

- To quickly close off the passing channels towards our goal and delay the opposition's attack.

- Prevent the opposition from attacking quickly so that they have to play an extra pass, allowing time to re-group and get players behind the ball.

What Practices/Sessions Can We Create for this Tactical Situation?

- We should set out practices with building up play from the back and basic possession games.

- Defensive organisation and movements in our own half after losing possession.

- Transition to defence games against opponents that press high.

- Defending against opponent's fast attacks, trying to block the channels to our goal. The basic aim of these practices is to get players behind the ball and not concede.

- Press the ball and mark players tightly, with the aim of preventing the opposition scoring within 6-8 seconds, before then trying to recover the ball.

TACTICAL SITUATION 1

LEONARDO JARDIM TACTICS

Condensing the Space After Losing Possession in the Low Zone

Content taken from Analysis of Monaco during the Ligue 1 Title Winning 2016/2017 season

The analysis is based on recurring patterns of play observed within the Monaco team. Once the same phase of play occurred a number of times (at least 10) the tactics would be seen as a pattern. The analysis on the next page is an example of the team's tactics being used effectively, taken from a specific game.

Each action, pass, individual movement with or without the ball, and the positioning of each player on the pitch including their body shape, are presented.

The analysis is then used to create a full progressive session to coach this specific tactical situation.

Tactical Analysis of LEONARDO JARDIM - Transition from Attack to Defence (Low Zone)

Analysis Taken from 'Marseille vs AS Monaco - 15th Jan 2017 (Ligue 1)'

Condensing the Space After Losing Possession in the Low Zone (4-4-2 vs 4-3-3)

Monaco's central midfielder Fabinho's pass is intercepted by Marseille's defensive midfielder (6).

The defensive midfielder (6) moves forward, then plays a one-two combination to receive back in space.

Marseille have the opportunity to launch a counter attack as they are not too far from Monaco's goal. The Monaco players must react quickly to condense the space and recover the ball.

Fabinho closes down the ball carrier, while the other central midfielder Bakayoko tracks back. Both full backs (Toure and Sidibe) track back and move inwards to provide balance and cover.

Once white 6 passes to 10, the centre back Jemerson confronts him head on and Glik provides cover. The Monaco defenders condense the space around the ball and the right back Sidibe is able to tackle 10 and win possession back.

Session to Practice **LEONARDO JARDIM** Tactics - Transition from Attack to Defence (Low Zone)

SESSION FOR THIS TACTICAL SITUATION (5 PRACTICES)
1. Condensing the Space After Losing Possession in a 5 v 3 Transition Game

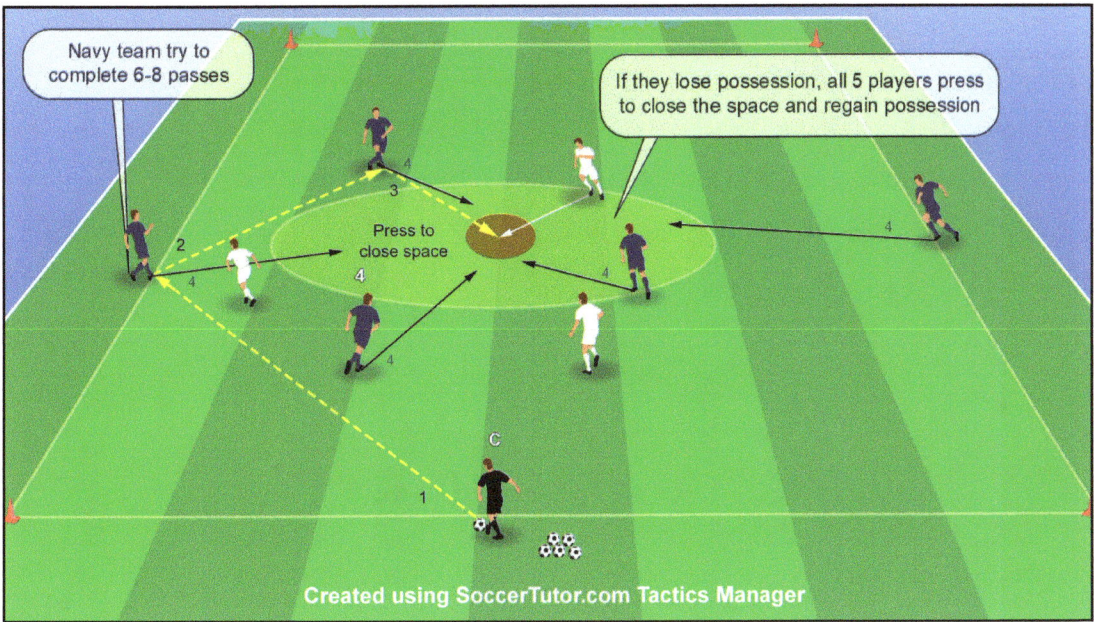

Objective: Fast transitions to defence, condensing the space around the ball to win it back.

Description
In a 10 x 12 yard area, we have one team with 5 players (navy) and another team with 3 players (white). Both teams have 3 players inside and the navy team also have 2 players outside, as shown.

The practice starts with the navy team keeping possession in a 5 v 3 situation, trying to complete 6-8 passes (1 point). The 3 white players try to win the ball - if they do, all 5 navy players must react quickly to press the new ball carrier (condensing the space) and win the ball back.

Rules
1. If the white team win the ball and complete 3-4 passes, they score 1 point.
2. If the white team keep the ball for 8 seconds, they score 2 points and if they are able to dribble the ball out of the area, they score 3 points.

Coaching Points
1. In possession, monitor the timing, weight and accuracy of the passes, the angles and distances of the support players, and the verbal (mainly) and visual communication.
2. Players need very quick reactions for the transition to defence, making sure to limit the time and space available for their opponents.
3. After winning the ball back, the players need to demonstrate quick and intelligent movements to open up and exploit all the space available.

Session to Practice **LEONARDO JARDIM** Tactics - Transition from Attack to Defence (Low Zone)

PROGRESSION

2. Condensing the Space After Losing Possession in a 5 v 3 Transition Game with Goals

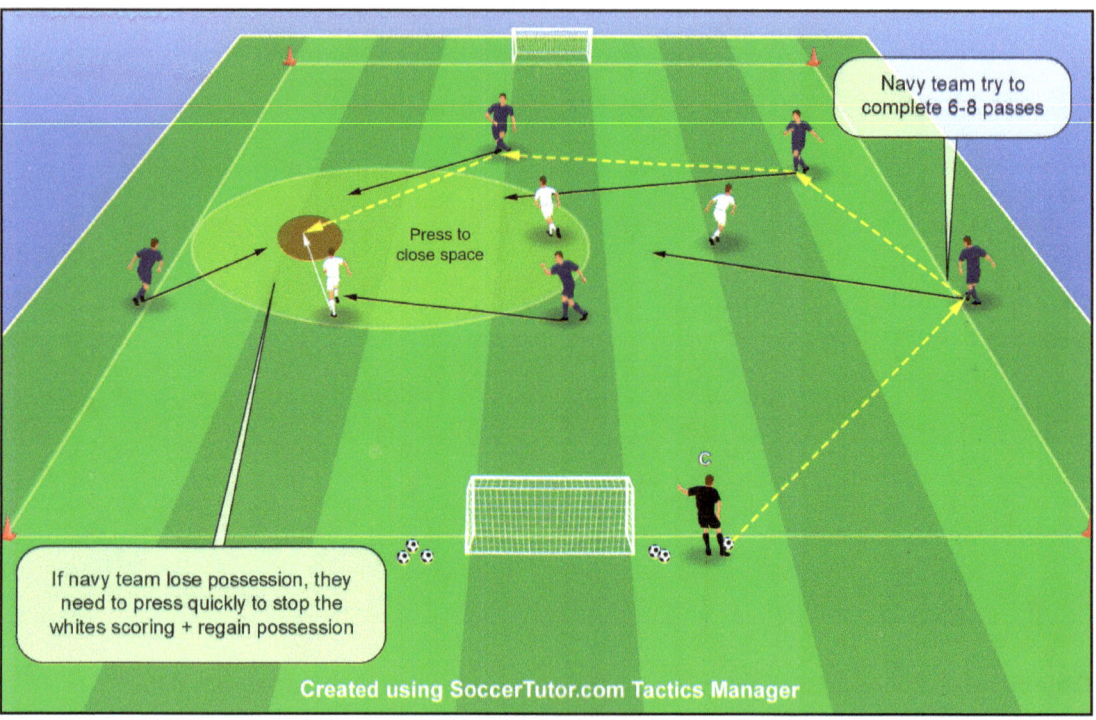

Description

In this progression of the previous practice, we add 2 mini goals.

The objective for the 5 navy players is the same as the previous practice, but now when the white team win the ball, their objective is to score in one of the 2 mini goals (2 points).

The navy team now have to be more intense in their pressing to condense the space around the ball and be aware to close off the angles to goal.

Coaching Points

The coaching points are the same as the previous practice.

Session to Practice **LEONARDO JARDIM** Tactics - Transition from Attack to Defence (Low Zone)

PROGRESSION

3. Condensing the Space After Losing Possession in a Dynamic Possession Practice

Description
The practice starts with the goalkeeper's pass into the main area - the navy team have help from the outside players (8 v 5) and try to complete 6 passes (1 point) or keep the ball for 15 seconds (2 points).

The aim for the defending team (white) is to press collectively, win the ball, move into the penalty area and try to score a goal.

When they lose the ball, all 6 navy players (not the neutrals) must make a fast transition from attack to defence. They must press the ball, provide cover, continuously shift collectively towards the ball (condensing the space) and prevent the opponents dribbling or passing into the penalty area.

The offside rule is applied throughout. If a goal is scored or the ball goes out of play, start again from the goalkeeper.

Different Rules
1. The 4 navy inside players have unlimited touches and all other players have 2 touches.
2. All players are limited to 2 touches.

Session to Practice LEONARDO JARDIM Tactics - Transition from Attack to Defence (Low Zone)

Coaching Points

1. Accuracy / weight of pass to feet is key, with quick support movements at good angles / distances.
2. The players need to use quality directional first touches in this small space.
3. Quick and effective reactions when possession is lost are needed to limit the opportunity for an opponent to shoot at goal.
4. Press the opponents and hurry them, forcing mistakes to win the ball back.

Session to Practice **LEONARDO JARDIM** Tactics - Transition from Attack to Defence (Low Zone)

PROGRESSION

4. Condensing the Space After Losing Possession in the Low Zone in a Dynamic Game

If navy team lose the ball, they make a fast transition to defence

Description

The navy team are in a 4-2 formation and the white team are in a 3-3 formation. The 4 yellow neutral outside players play with the team in possession.

When the navy team have possession, the neutral players take up the roles of wingers and forwards. For the white team, the neutral players take up the roles of the centre backs and full backs.

The practice starts from the goalkeeper and the aim is to build up play and score in one of the 3 mini goals. If the navy team lose the ball, they must make a fast transition from attack to defence by condensing the space and try to stop a successful counter attack from the white team.

Rules

1. All players have unlimited (or 3) touches and the neutrals are limited to 1 or 2 touches.
2. The white team must finish their counter attack within 10-12 seconds of winning the ball.

Coaching Points

1. **Navy team in possession:** Correct positioning and distances between the players, so they are ready to react quickly and effectively if they lose the ball - when in attack, prepare to defend.
2. **Transition from defence to attack:** Good awareness, quick decision making (recognition of the tactical and numerical situation), quick reactions, backward movement to protect the path to goal, synchronisation, cooperation for the defensive press/cover and good communication.

Session to Practice **LEONARDO JARDIM** Tactics - Transition from Attack to Defence (Low Zone)

PROGRESSION

5. Condensing the Space After Losing Possession in the Low Zone with a Numerical Disadvantage (6 v 6 to 4 v 6)

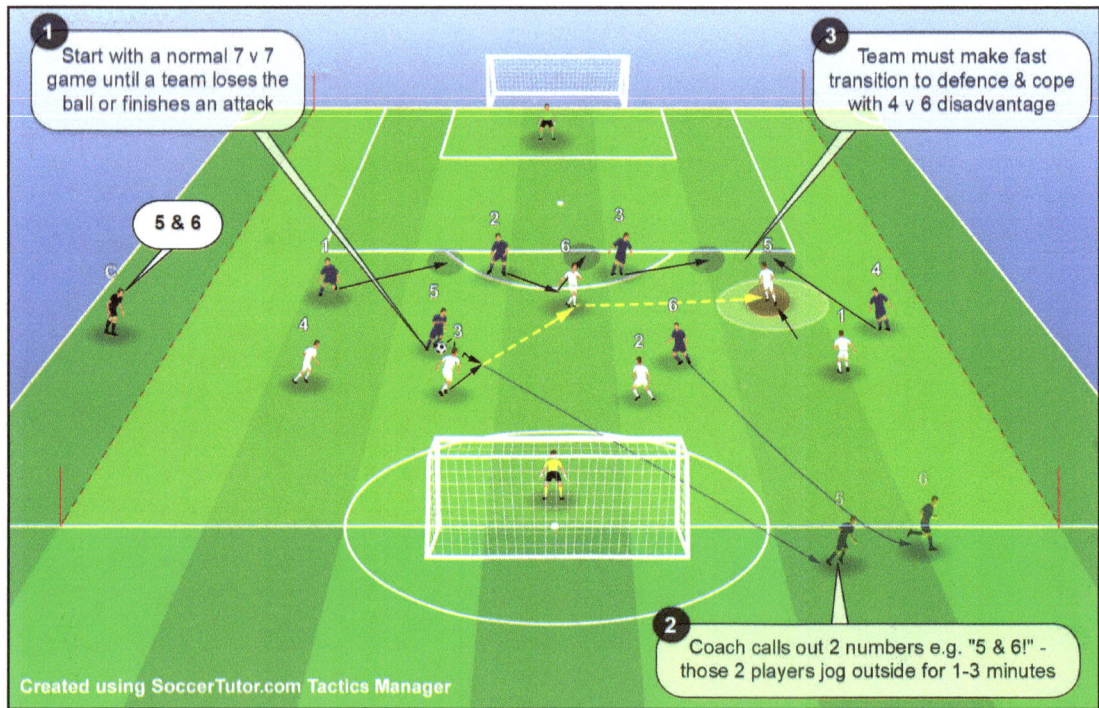

Description

1. We start by playing a normal 7 v 7 game. The outfield players are numbered 1-6.
2. When the coach recognises a tactical situation such as a team losing the ball or a team finishing their attack, he calls out 2 numbers e.g. "Navy 5 & 6!" These 2 players must leave the pitch and jog around the outside for a set amount of time (1-3 minutes) at a specific speed.

This creates a numerical disadvantage of 4 v 6 for one team (navy in diagram example), who must respond and make a very quick transition from attack to defence. They continue to play 4 v 6 for the entire 1-3 minutes, even if they win the ball.

Coaching Points

1. There needs to be a quick recognition of the tactical situation with a numerical disadvantage and the defensive group must operate together with good coordination.
2. Close the space in and around the goal, block channels toward goal and push opponents out wide - this will delay them and make them less likely to be able to exploit their numerical advantage.
3. If the team with the numerical disadvantage wins the ball, they must try to keep it for as long as possible, using the goalkeeper and moving the ball to the corners. This helps change the rhythm of the game, as we would in a 9 v 11 situation.

TACTICAL SITUATION 2

POCHETTINO TACTICS

Defensive Adjustments to Defend a Through Ball in Behind in the Transition to Defence

Content taken from Analysis of Tottenham Hotspur during the 2017/2018 season

The analysis is based on recurring patterns of play observed within the Tottenham team. Once the same phase of play occurred a number of times (at least 10) the tactics would be seen as a pattern. The analysis on the next page is an example of the team's tactics being used effectively, taken from a specific game.

Each action, pass, individual movement with or without the ball, and the positioning of each player on the pitch including their body shape, are presented.

The analysis is then used to create a full progressive session to coach this specific tactical situation.

Tactical Analysis of POCHETTINO - Transition from Attack to Defence (Low Zone)

Analysis Taken from 'Tottenham vs Chelsea - 20th Aug 2017 (Premier League)'

Defensive Adjustments to Defend a Through Ball in Behind in the Transition to Defence (4-3-2-1 vs 3-5-1-1)

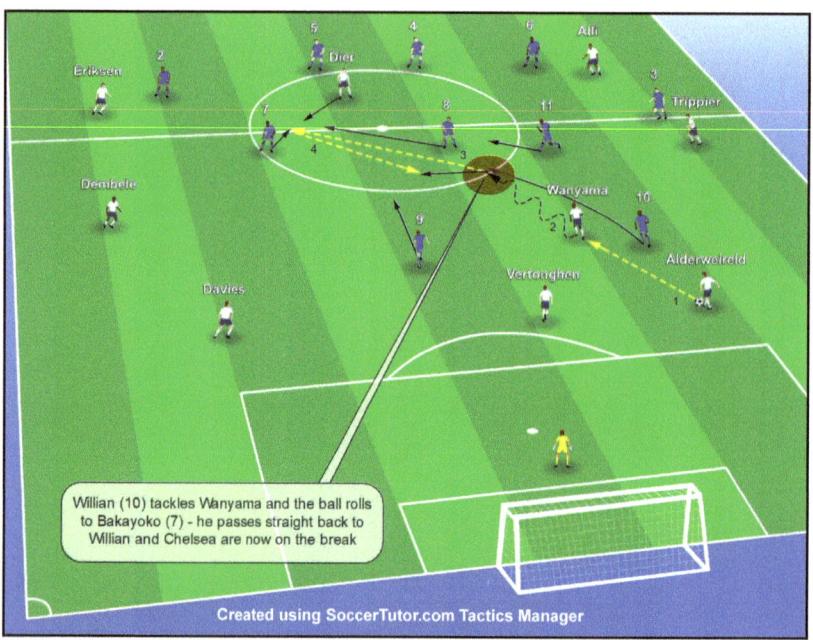

Tottenham centre back Alderweireld passes forward to central midfielder Wanyama, who dribbles the ball forward.

Chelsea No.10 Willian tracks Wanyama and tackles him.

The ball ends up with the Chelsea central midfielder Bakayoko (11), who passes to Willian (10) - he is then able to receive and turn.

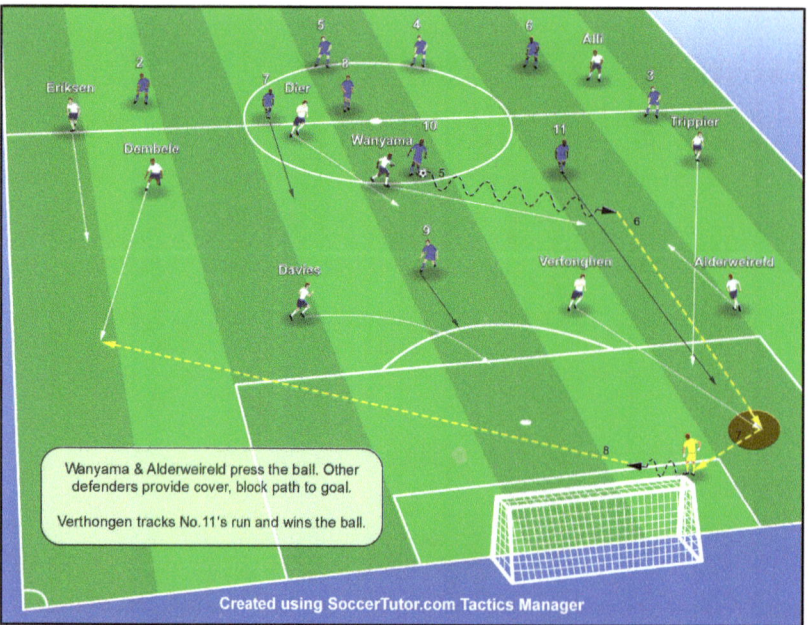

Wanyama and Alderweireld are able to apply pressure to the ball carrier (Willian - No.10).

Both full backs (Davies and Tripper) and the other centre back Verthongen track back to provide cover and block the opposition's path to goal.

As he is under pressure, Willian (10) plays an early through ball which is easily intercepted by Verthongen, as he provides cover and tracks No.11's run.

Session to Practice POCHETTINO Tactics - Transition from Attack to Defence (Low Zone)

SESSION FOR THIS TACTICAL SITUATION (5 PRACTICES)
1. Quick Reactions and Tracking Back in a Dynamic Transition Game

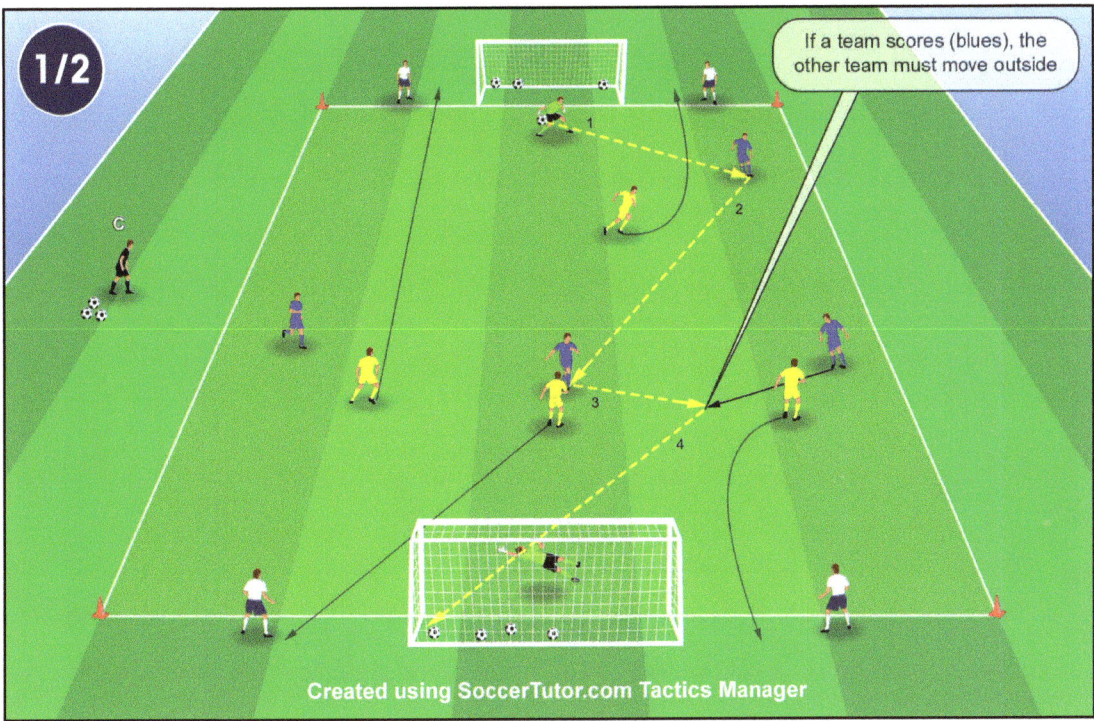

Objective: Fast transitions to defence - delaying the opponent, blocking the path to goal, tracking back and winning the ball.

Description (1/2)

In a 20 x 25 yard area, we have 2 large goals with goalkeepers and 3 teams of 4 players. Two teams start inside the area and the other team (whites) have 2 players outside at each end, as shown.

The practice starts with a goalkeeper and one team (blues in diagram example) who build up play and try to score a goal in a normal 5 v 5 game.

When a team scores a goal or the coach gives a signal, the defending team (yellows in diagram) leave the area and the attacking team (blues) receive a new ball from the other goalkeeper for a new attack (see diagram on the next page).

The practice description continues on the next page...

Session to Practice POCHETTINO Tactics - Transition from Attack to Defence (Low Zone)

Description (2/2)

The goalkeeper passes a new ball to the blue team as shown, and the yellow team have moved to the outside positions.

The white players enter the pitch and must move quickly to defend. We have a 4 v 2 (+2) situation, with the emphasis on the first 2 white players to delay the attack while they have a numerical disadvantage and block the path to goal, giving time for their 2 teammates to run back into good defensive positions.

If the blue team score, the yellows and the whites will swap positions again and we will have another 4 v 2 (+2) attack.

If the white team win the ball from the blues, the game continues with the same aims and objectives.

Coaching Points

1. The 2 players that are tracking back must run as quickly as they can to provide support and take up effective defensive positions.
2. The aim is to prevent the fast attack of the opponents who have the initial advantage, and quickly restore the game to a numerical equality.
3. The first 2 defenders must be intelligent when they are at a 4 v 2 numerical disadvantage, making sure to delay the attackers, using backward steps and defending their goal.

Session to Practice POCHETTINO Tactics - Transition from Attack to Defence (Low Zone)

PROGRESSION

2. Defensive Adjustments to Defend a Through Ball in Behind in the Transition to Defence (4 v 4 Practice)

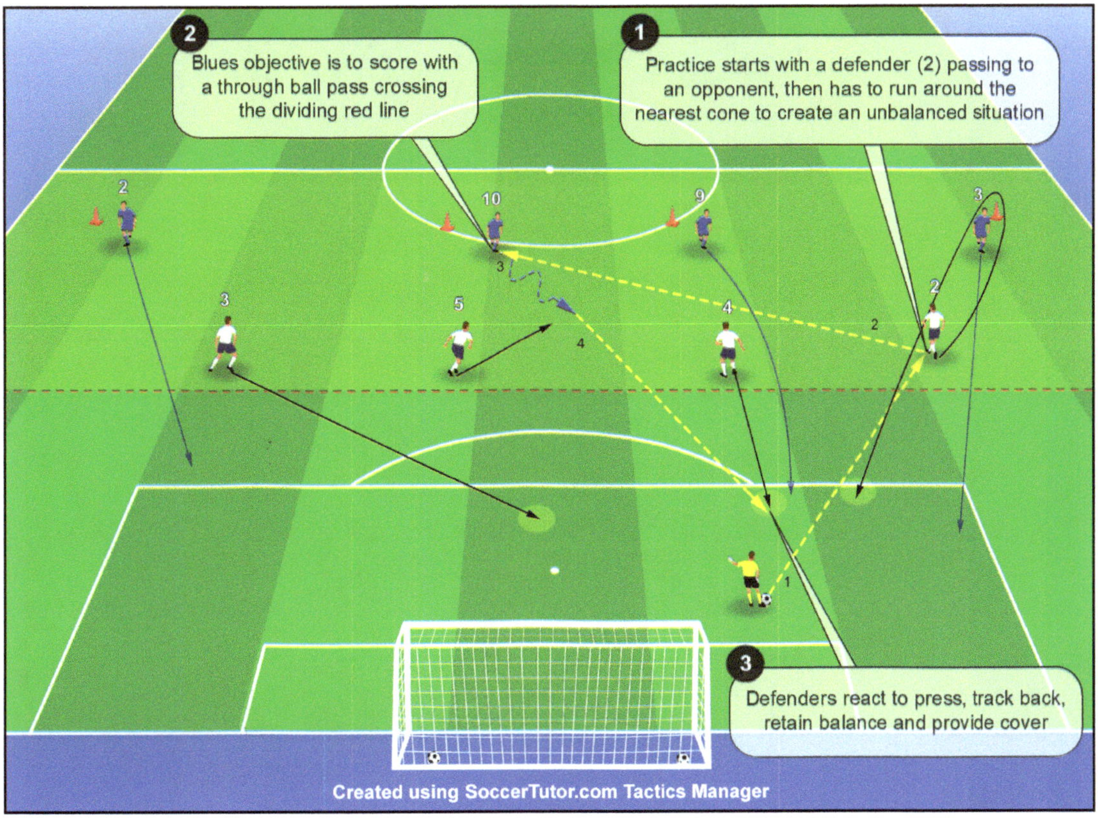

Objective: Fast transition to attack - adjust positioning, track back to provide cover and defend goal.

Description

One team (white) have 4 defenders and the other team (blue) have 4 attackers. We position 4 cones in the starting positions of the blue players. These are the practice objectives:

1. The practice starts with the goalkeeper's pass. The player that receives (No.2 in diagram) passes the ball to a blue opponent and then runs around the nearest cone to create an unbalanced situation.

2. The blues (No.10 in possession) start a 4 v 3 (+1) attack - the white No.2 is the +1 as he has to run round the cone before he is able to help defend for his team. The blues must play a through ball crossing the red line before scoring. If they score within 8 seconds, the goal counts double.

3. The whites try to delay the attack until No.2 can get back into position and prevent the blues from scoring (1 point). One player will press the ball carrier and the others track back to defend the penalty area, intercept the through ball, retain balance and provide cover.

Session to Practice **POCHETTINO** Tactics - Transition from Attack to Defence (Low Zone)

PROGRESSION

3. Defensive Adjustments to Defend a Through Ball in Behind in the Transition to Defence (6 v 6 Practice)

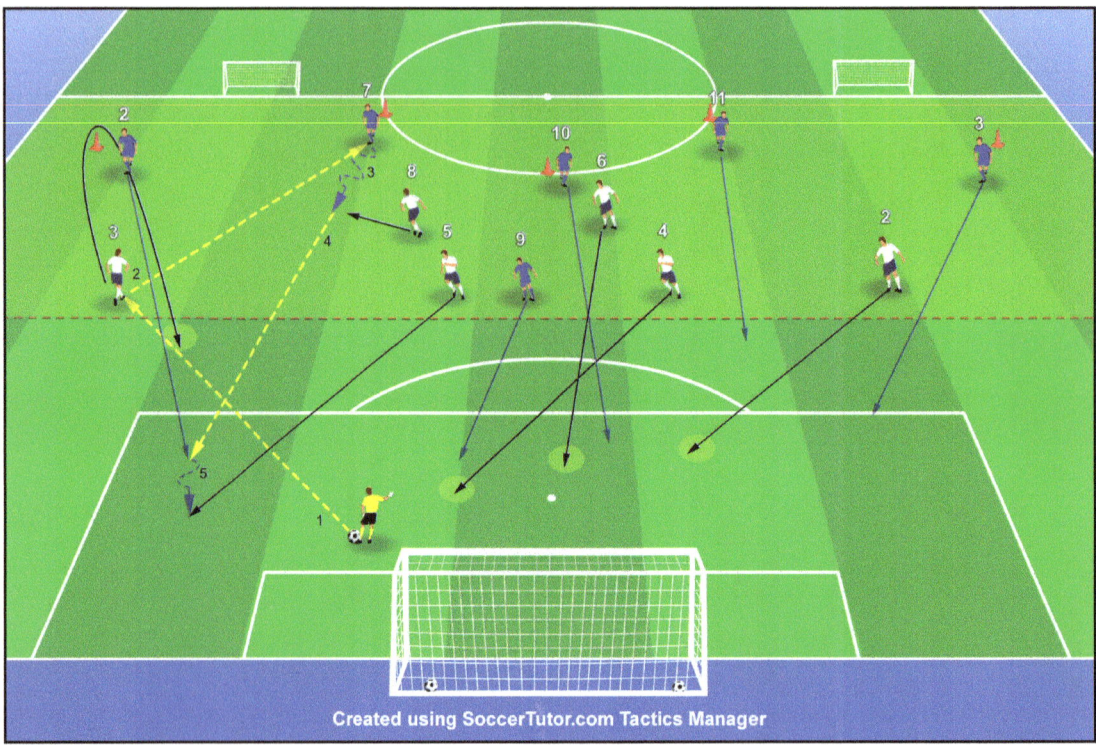

Description

In this progression of the previous practice, we add 2 blue players. The blue team now have 2 central midfielders (7 & 11), the No.10, 2 wing backs (2 & 3) and the forward (9).

We also add 2 central midfielders (6 & 8) for the white team who are now in a 4-2 formation.

The objectives, aims and rules are the same as the previous practice, except that if the white team recover the ball in the second phase, they can now counter attack and try to score in the mini goals on the halfway line.

Coaching Points

1. The white team have a numerical disadvantage for a short period so they must focus on team balance and cohesion, tracking runners into the penalty area, delaying their opponents, closing channels and protecting the goal.

2. The +1 player (No.3 in diagram example) must run back as quickly as possible to provide support for his teammates and return the situation to an equal one (6 v 6), before the blues are able to take advantage.

Session to Practice POCHETTINO Tactics - Transition from Attack to Defence (Low Zone)

PROGRESSION

4. Defensive Adjustments to Defend a Through Ball in Behind in a Positional Game

Scenario 1: The Defending Team Win the Ball in the First Phase

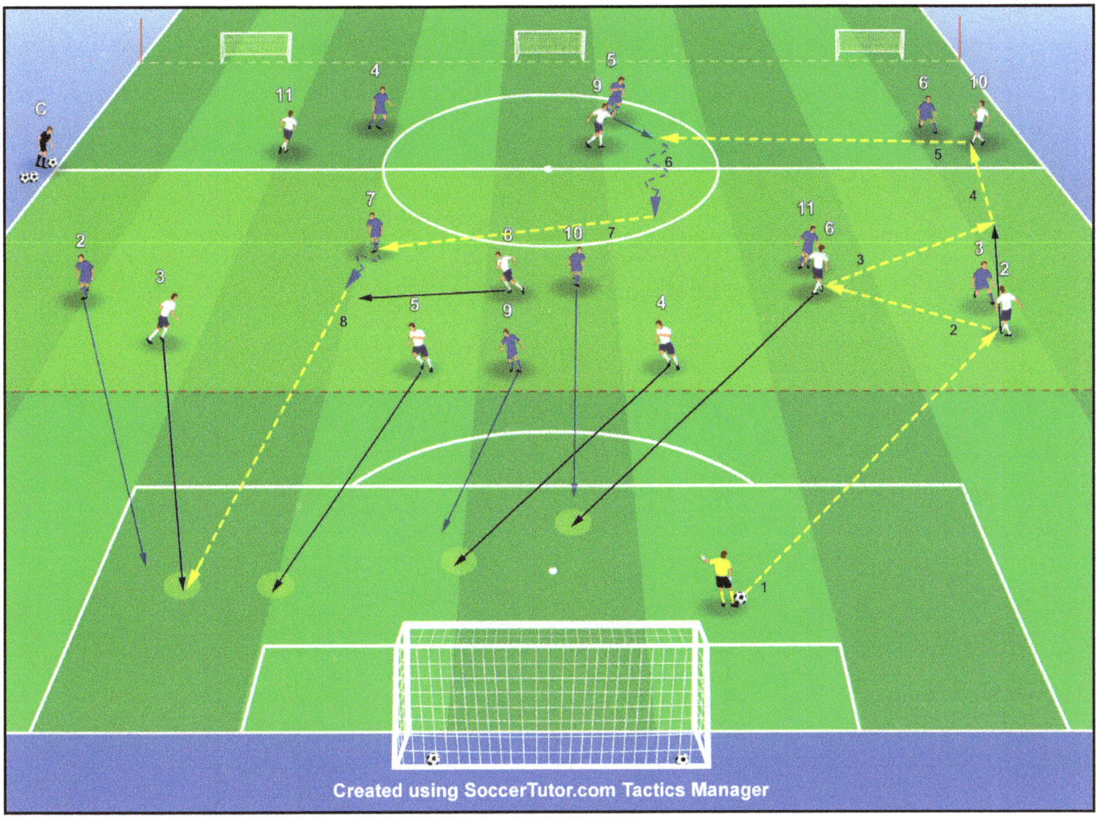

Description (Scenario 1)

We position 3 mini goals 15 yards beyond the halfway line. The white team are in a 4-2-2-1 formation (from 4-3-2-1) and the blues are in a 3-3-1-1 formation (from 3-5-1-1). You can either have a fixed 3 v 3 situation beyond the halfway line or let the players play freely.

1. The practice starts with the goalkeeper - the white team build up play and try to score a goal.
2. If the white team lose the ball, the blues launch a fast counter attack. They must play a through ball crossing the red line before scoring. If they score within 10 seconds, the goal counts double.
3. The white team work together to defend, focusing on team balance and cohesion, tracking runners into the penalty area, delaying their opponents, closing channels and protecting the goal. If the 3 v 3 zone beyond the halfway line is fixed (as mentioned previously), 1 blue player can move out (No.5 in diagram) and the whites are unbalanced with a 6 v 7 numerical disadvantage.

Session to Practice **POCHETTINO** Tactics - Transition from Attack to Defence (Low Zone)

Scenario 2: The Attacking Team Score in the First Phase

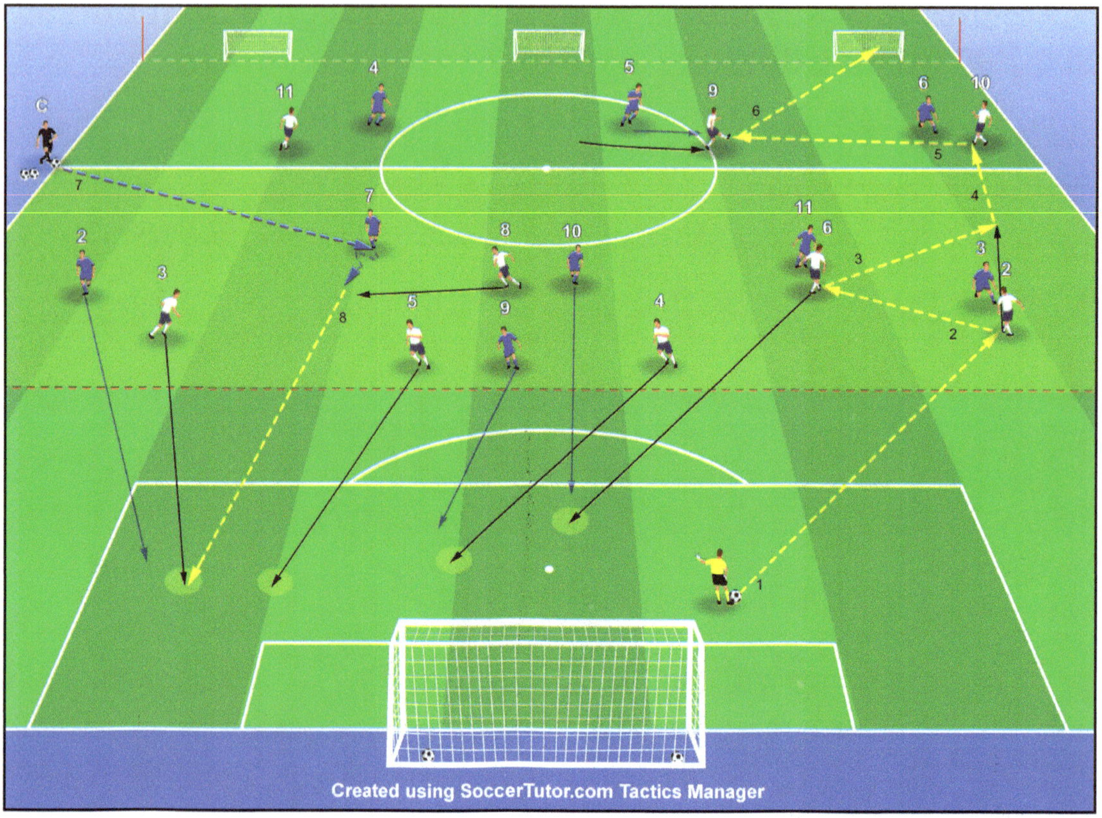

Description (Scenario 2)

This diagram shows what happens if the white team don't lose the ball in the first phase and score a goal instead.

When this happens, the coach plays a new ball to the blues, who then launch a fast break attack. All the white players must make a quick transition from attack to defence.

The blues must still play a through ball crossing the red line before scoring and if they score within 10 seconds, the goal counts double.

Coaching Points

1. One white player should press the ball carrier (No.8 in diagram example) and the other players track back to defend the penalty area, intercept the through ball and retain balance.
2. Keep close distances between each other, provide cover and block all channels to the goal.

Session to Practice **POCHETTINO** Tactics - Transition from Attack to Defence (Low Zone)

PROGRESSION

5. Defensive Adjustments to Defend a Through Ball in Behind in an 11 v 11 Game

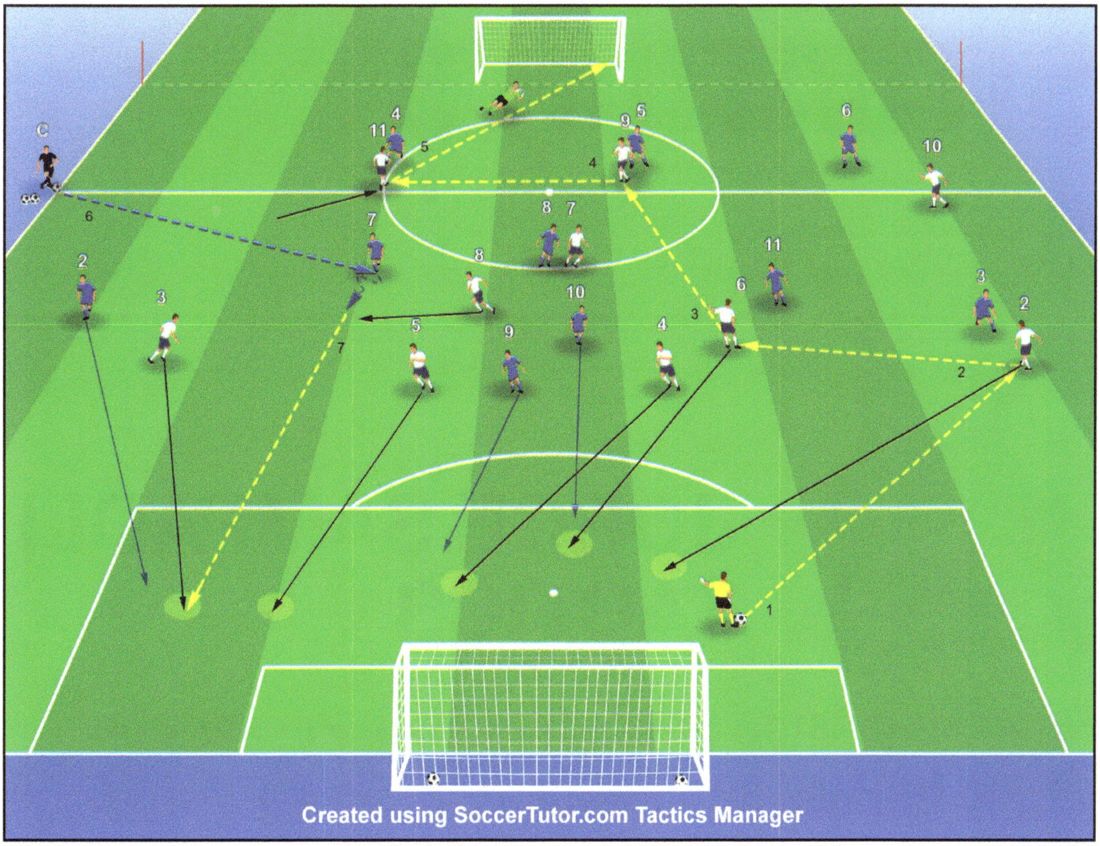

Description

In this final practice of the session, we now have 2 large goals and goalkeepers for both teams. The white team are in a 4-3-2-1 formation and the blues are in a 3-5-1-1 formation.

The objectives and rules are exactly the same as the previous practice. The blues should still try to score as quickly as possible using a through ball.

Coaching Points

1. In the transition to defence, the players need very quick reactions and to be able to change the point of defence depending on the ball position.
2. Players need to quickly recognise the new tactical situation and use the correct decision making. E.g. Numerical disadvantage, unbalanced situation, superiority in numbers etc.
3. The players must quickly run back to defend the penalty area, providing defensive support to limit time/space for their opponents, thus stopping the attack or forcing mistakes.

TACTICAL SITUATION 3

JORGE SAMPAOLI TACTICS

Reactions when Defenders Lose Possession Trying to Pass into Midfield

Content taken from Analysis of Sevilla during the 2016/2017 season

The analysis is based on recurring patterns of play observed within the Sevilla team. Once the same phase of play occurred a number of times (at least 10) the tactics would be seen as a pattern. The analysis on the next page is an example of the team's tactics being used effectively, taken from a specific game.

Each action, pass, individual movement with or without the ball, and the positioning of each player on the pitch including their body shape, are presented.

The analysis is then used to create a full progressive session to coach this specific tactical situation.

Tactical Analysis of JORGE SAMPAOLI - Transition from Attack to Defence (Low Zone)

Analysis Taken from 'Juventus vs Sevilla - 14th Sep 2016 (Champions League)'

Reactions when Defenders Lose Possession Trying to Pass into Midfield

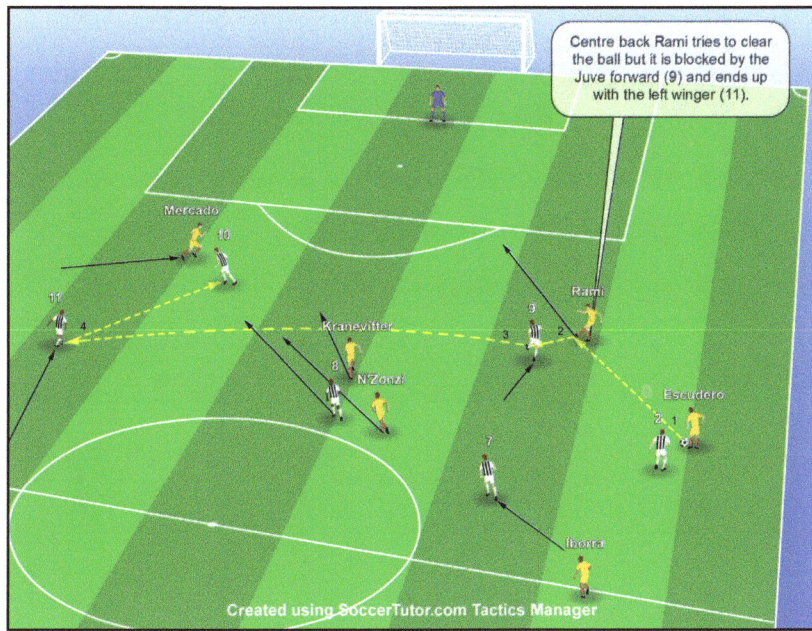

In this example, the Sevilla centre back Rami is closed down well by the opposing forward (9) and attempts to play a pass into midfield.

However, the pass is blocked and the ball bounces to the Juve left winger (11). He passes forward to No.10 and Sevilla must react quickly to defend their goal and recover the ball.

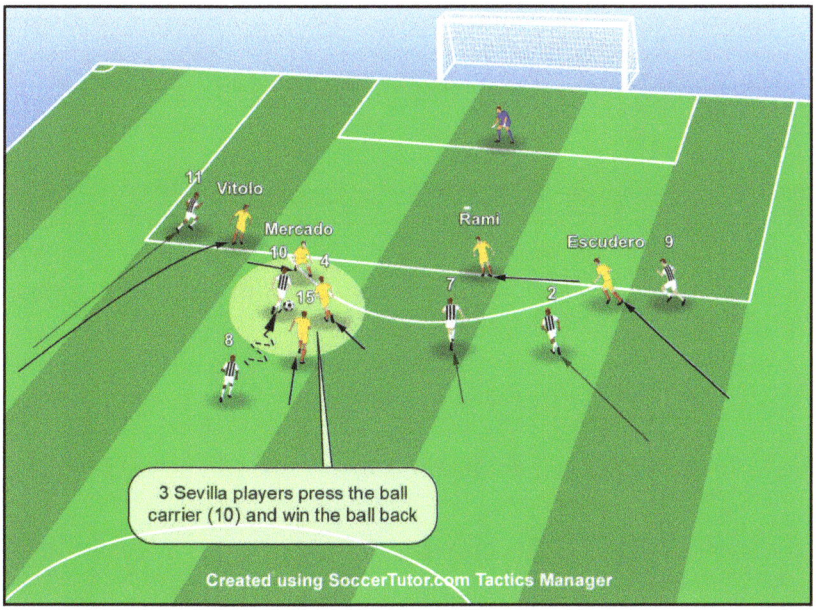

The centre back Mercado moves forward to press the ball carrier (10). He is able to do this because the right back Vitolo and the other centre back Rami are providing cover.

Mercado and 2 central midfielders (Kranevitter - 4 & N'Zonzi - 15) apply triple pressing to the ball carrier (10) and block all options to dribble or pass, which leads to Sevilla winning the ball back.

Session to Practice **JORGE SAMPAOLI** Tactics - Transition from Attack to Defence (Low Zone)

SESSION FOR THIS TACTICAL SITUATION (4 PRACTICES)
1. Reactions when Defenders Lose Possession Trying to Pass into Midfield in a Dynamic 3 Zone Transition Game

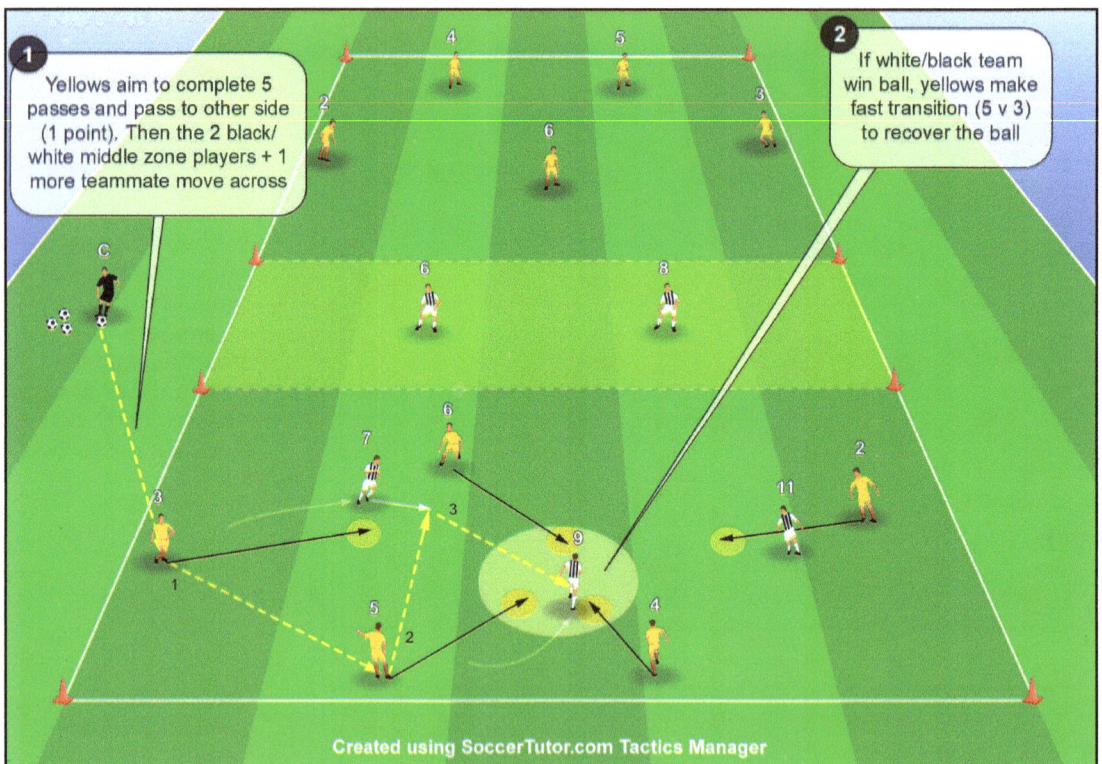

Description

In a 30 x 60 yard area, we mark out a 10 yard middle zone. We start in one end zone with a 5 v 3 situation. There are also 2 white/black players in the middle zone and 5 more yellow players in the opposite end zone.

The yellow players have a back 4 and 1 central midfielder in each end zone. The white/black team take the roles of 3 attackers in the end zone and have 2 central midfielders in the middle zone.

1. The practice starts with the coach and the yellow team aim to complete 5 passes and pass across to the other end zone (1 point). The 2 white/black players in the middle zone (6 & 8) must run across quickly to apply pressure with 1 more teammate, and the practice continues in the same way.

2. The 3 white/black attackers try to win the ball in the end zone initially - if they do, the yellow team make a fast transition to defence with a 5 v 3 numerical advantage, **as shown in the diagram**.

If a pass across to the other zone is intercepted in the middle zone, we then play 5 v 5 in a bigger area which includes the middle zone - the yellows still aim to win the ball back as quickly as possible, this time with equal numbers (5 v 5). The 2 middle zone players (6 & 8) must still stay in their zone, but all the other players are able to move freely across both zones.

Session to Practice **JORGE SAMPAOLI** Tactics - Transition from Attack to Defence (Low Zone)

PROGRESSION

2. Reactions when Defenders Lose Possession Trying to Pass into Midfield in a Positional Transition Game

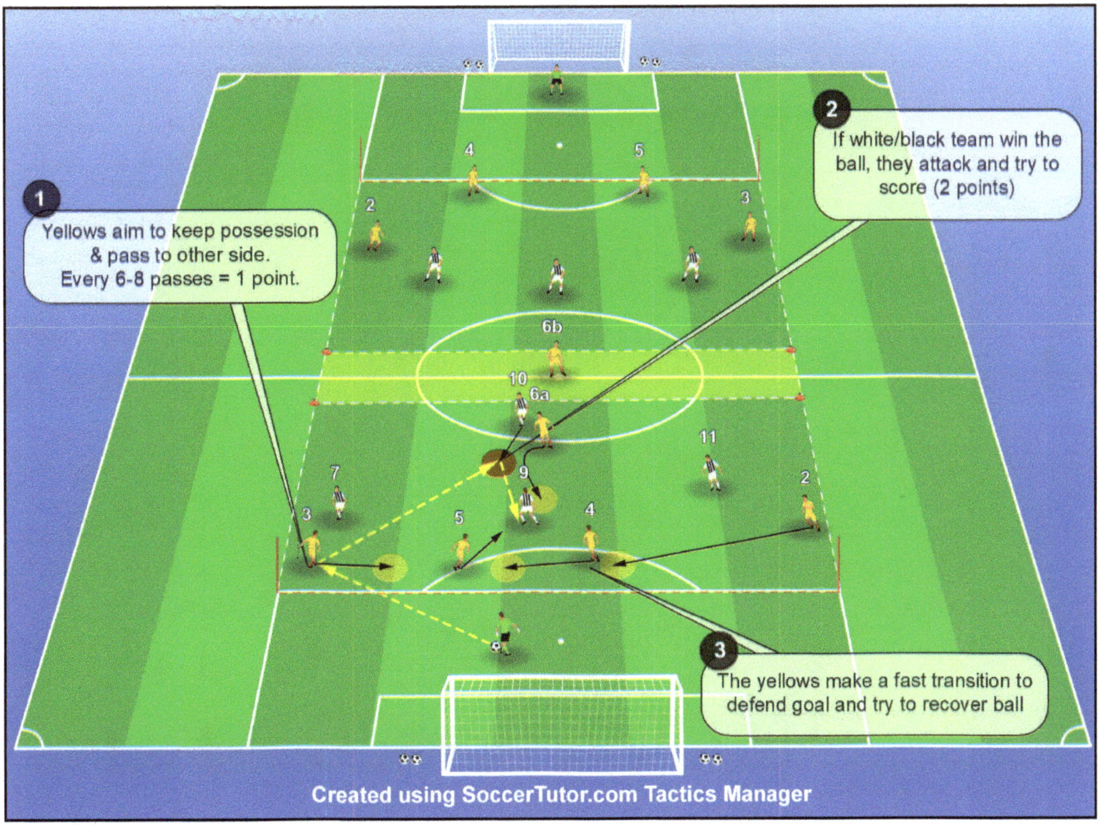

1. Yellows aim to keep possession & pass to other side. Every 6-8 passes = 1 point.

2. If white/black team win the ball, they attack and try to score (2 points)

3. The yellows make a fast transition to defend goal and try to recover ball

Description

The practice starts with a goalkeeper and we have a 5 v 4 situation in the first zone - the yellows are in a 4-1 formation against 4 white/black attackers. There is an extra central midfielder (6b) in the middle zone and there are also 5 yellow players and 3 white/black players in the third zone.

1. The aim for the yellows is to build up play and pass to the other side while keeping possession. When this happens, 6a moves to the middle zone and 6b moves into the third zone. One white/black player must also run across to create the same 5 v 4 situation and the practice continues in the same way. Each time the yellows complete 6-8 passes, they score 1 point.

2. If the white/black team win the ball at any time, their aim is to attack and try to score past the goalkeeper at that end (2 points).

3. The yellows must therefore make a fast transition to defence to stop a goal being scored and try to win the ball back.

Rule: Either all players have unlimited touches or just the yellows are limited to 2-3 touches.

Session to Practice **JORGE SAMPAOLI** Tactics - Transition from Attack to Defence (Low Zone)

PROGRESSION

3. Reactions when Defenders Lose Possession Trying to Pass into Midfield in a 10 (+2) v 8 End to End Possession Game

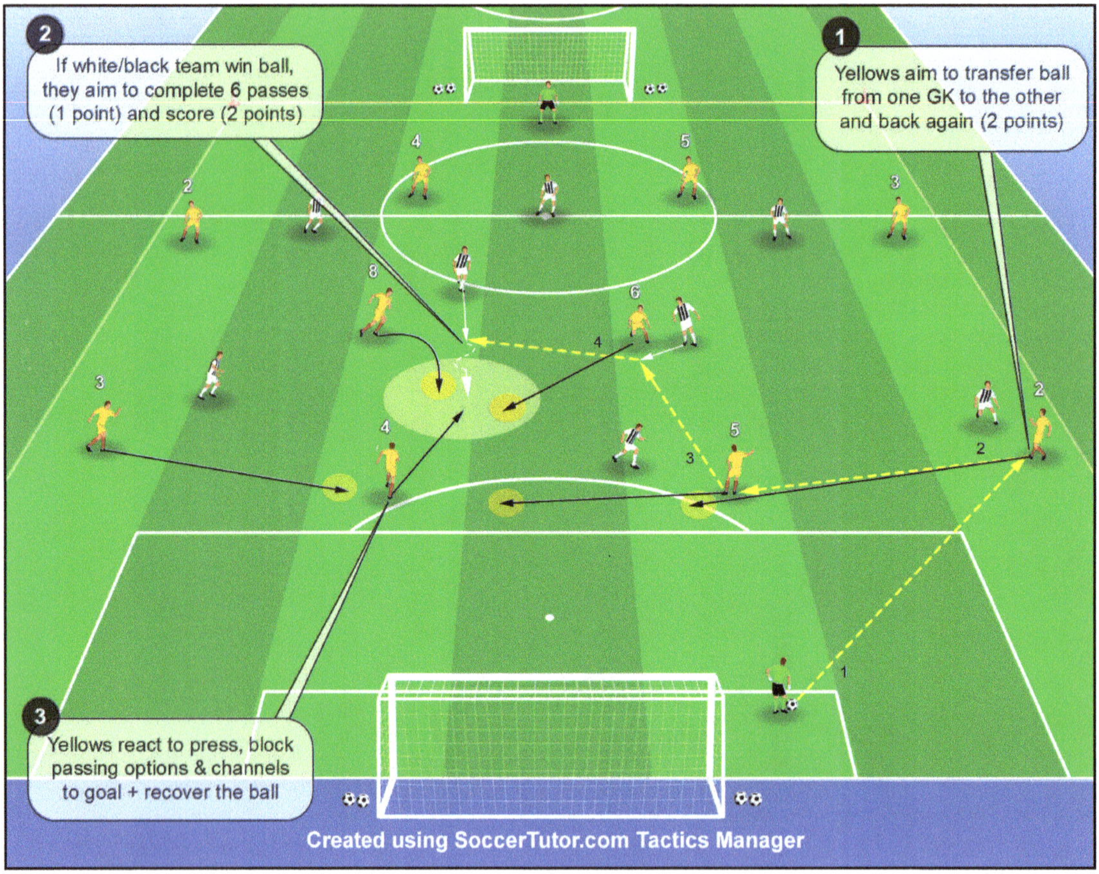

1 Yellows aim to transfer ball from one GK to the other and back again (2 points)

2 If white/black team win ball, they aim to complete 6 passes (1 point) and score (2 points)

3 Yellows react to press, block passing options & channels to goal + recover the ball

Description

The yellows have a back 4 at either end and 2 central midfielders (6 & 8). The white/black team are in a 3-2-3 formation.

1. The practice starts with the goalkeeper and the yellows aim to transfer the ball from one goalkeeper to the other and back again (2 points). They also score 1 point each time they complete 8 passes.

2. The white/black team press collectively to try and win the ball. Their aim from there is to complete 6 passes or keep the ball for 10 seconds (1 point) and try to score a goal at either end (2 points).

3. The yellow team are forced to make a fast transition from attack to defence - press the ball carrier, block passing options and channels to goal, and ultimately recover the ball as soon as possible.

Rule: Either all players have unlimited touches or just the yellows are limited to 2-3 touches.

Session to Practice JORGE SAMPAOLI Tactics - Transition from Attack to Defence (Low Zone)

Progression: If the yellows complete 8 passes, they can then score in either goal too = 1 extra point.

Coaching Points

1. In the transition from attack to defence, there should be direct pressing from the closest player to limit the ball carrier's time, space and choices (shooting, dribbling or passing).
2. The other players that are near should quickly move to mark any possible receivers.
3. The other defenders move towards the ball area to reduce the time and space available for any actions of the opposition's counter attack.
4. Out of Possession = **CLOSE** the Space / In Possession = **OPEN** the Space.

PROGRESSION

4. Fast Transition to Defence in the Low Zone in a Dynamic End to End Possession Game

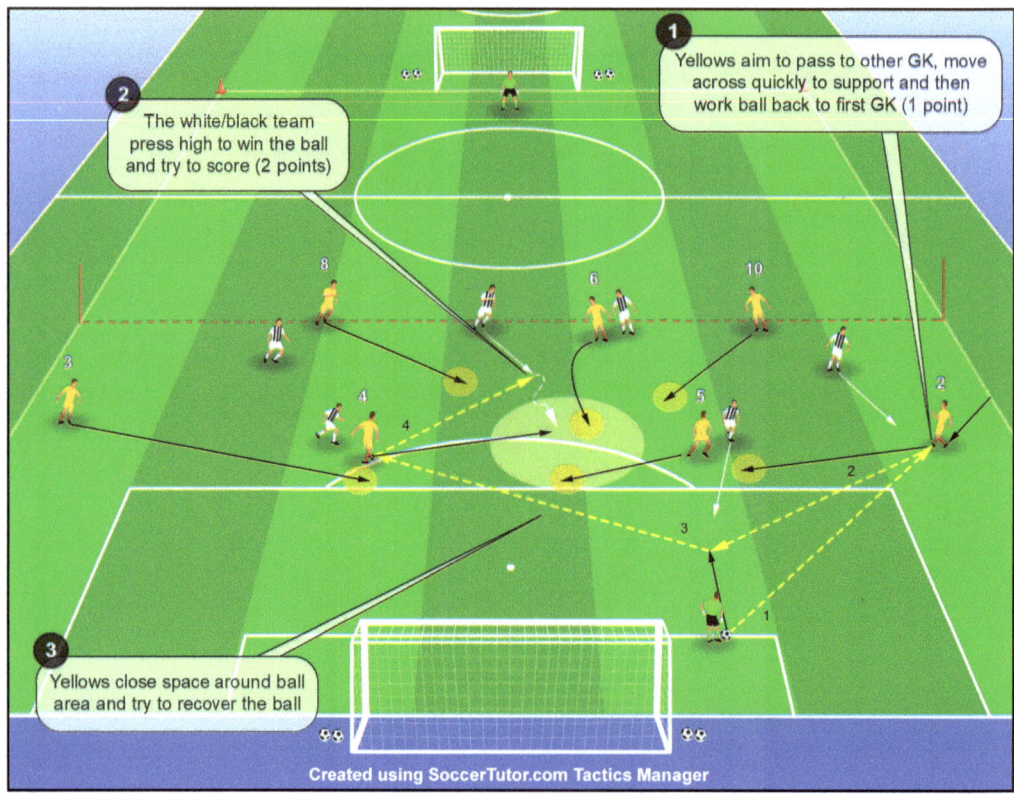

Description

We split the pitch into 2 equal halves. The yellow team have 7 outfield players in a 4-3 formation against 6 white/black players in a 4-2 formation. All the players start in one half.

1. The practice starts with the goalkeeper and the yellows aim to transfer the ball from one goalkeeper to the other and back again (1 point). To achieve this, the players must run very quickly to provide the goalkeeper with support, before then transferring the ball back again.

2. The white/black players aim to press in half the pitch, win the ball and then score a goal at that end (2 points).

3. When the yellows lose the ball, they make a fast transition to defence, closing the space around the ball carrier and protecting the goal. The aim is to recover the ball as quickly as possible.

Rules

1. All players must have moved into the other half before the yellows can transfer the ball back again to the first half.
2. Either all players have unlimited touches or just the yellows are limited to 2-3 touches.

TACTICAL SITUATION 4

JORGE SAMPAOLI TACTICS

Fast Reactions to Defend the Centre of the Pitch After Losing Possession

Content taken from Analysis of Sevilla during the 2016/2017 season

The analysis is based on recurring patterns of play observed within the Sevilla team. Once the same phase of play occurred a number of times (at least 10) the tactics would be seen as a pattern. The analysis on the next page is an example of the team's tactics being used effectively, taken from a specific game.

Each action, pass, individual movement with or without the ball, and the positioning of each player on the pitch including their body shape, are presented.

The analysis is then used to create a full progressive session to coach this specific tactical situation.

Tactical Analysis of JORGE SAMPAOLI - Transition from Attack to Defence (Low Zone)

Analysis Taken from 'Real Madrid vs Sevilla - 9th Aug 2016 (UEFA Super Cup)'

Fast Reactions to Defend the Centre of the Pitch After Losing Possession (4-3-3 vs 4-3-3)

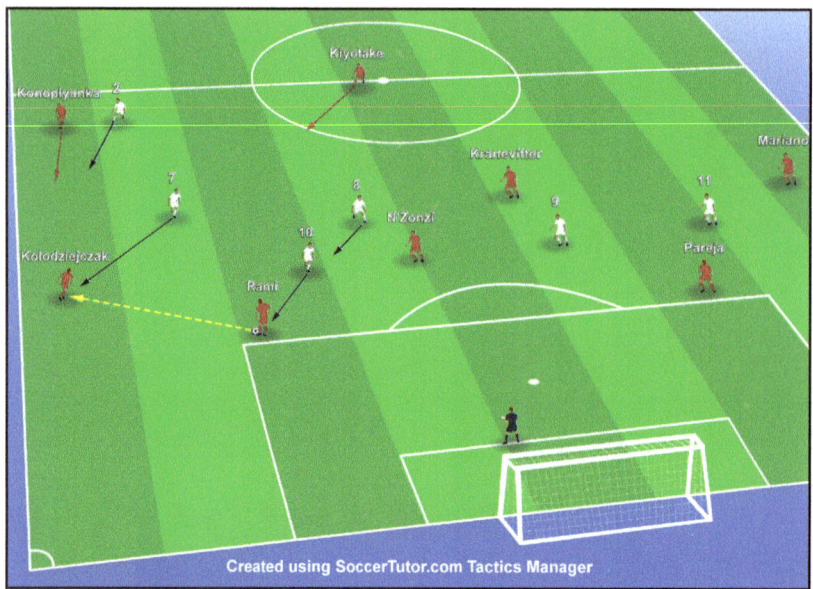

In this example, the Sevilla centre back Rami passes out wide to the left back Kolodziejczak.

The Real Madrid right winger (7) sprints across to close down Kolodziejczak.

Real Madrid's 7, 8, 10 & 2 all move towards the ball area and create a strong side with a numerical advantage.

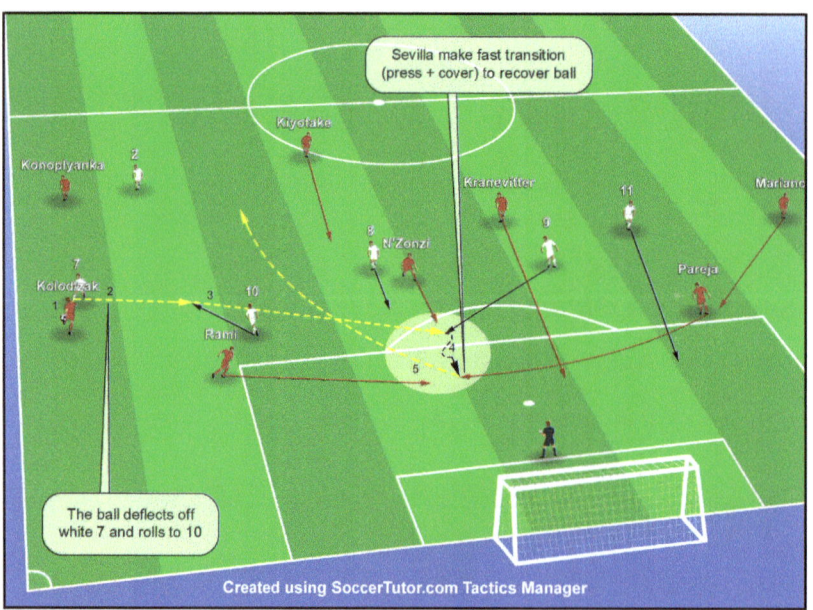

Under pressure, Kolodziejczak tries to play the ball up the line but it is blocked by 7. The ball drops for the Real No.10, who quickly passes into the space in the centre for the forward (9).

Sevilla make a fast transition with the 2 centre backs shifting inside to close the space and protect the goal. Central midfielder N'Zonzi also applies pressure on the ball carrier (9) and the centre back (Pareja) is able to clear the ball.

Session to Practice **JORGE SAMPAOLI** Tactics - Transition from Attack to Defence (Low Zone)

SESSION FOR THIS TACTICAL SITUATION (4 PRACTICES)

1. Open the Space in Possession and Close the Space in the Transition to Defence (Dynamic 8 v 8 Practice)

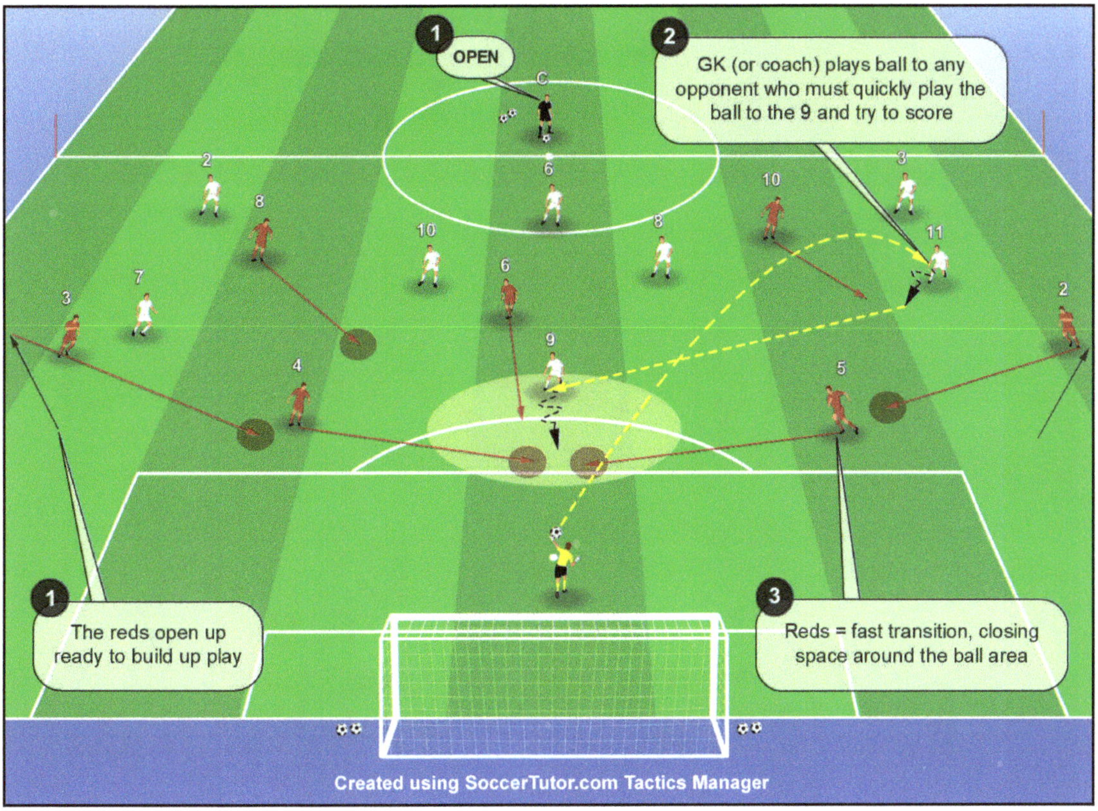

Description

The red team are in a 4-3 formation (from 4-3-3) and the whites are in a 2-3-3 formation with full backs (from 4-3-3).

1. The practice starts with the red team in a compact defensive shape, closing off the central channels to goal. When the coach calls "OPEN", the players must quickly open up and take positions ready to build up play.

2. From this point, the goalkeeper (or coach) plays a ball to any white opposing player. That white player must quickly pass to the No.9 and the white team look to attack and score.

3. The red team must make a fast transition from attack to defence, closing the space in and around the ball area in the centre as quickly as possible.

If the red team win the ball, you can either start the practice from the beginning again or they have to successfully pass the ball to the coach.

Coaching Point: In Possession = *OPEN* the Space / Out of Possession = *CLOSE* the Space.

Session to Practice **JORGE SAMPAOLI** Tactics - Transition from Attack to Defence (Low Zone)

PROGRESSION

2. Fast Reactions to Defend the Centre of the Pitch After Losing Possession in a Positional 8 v 9 Game

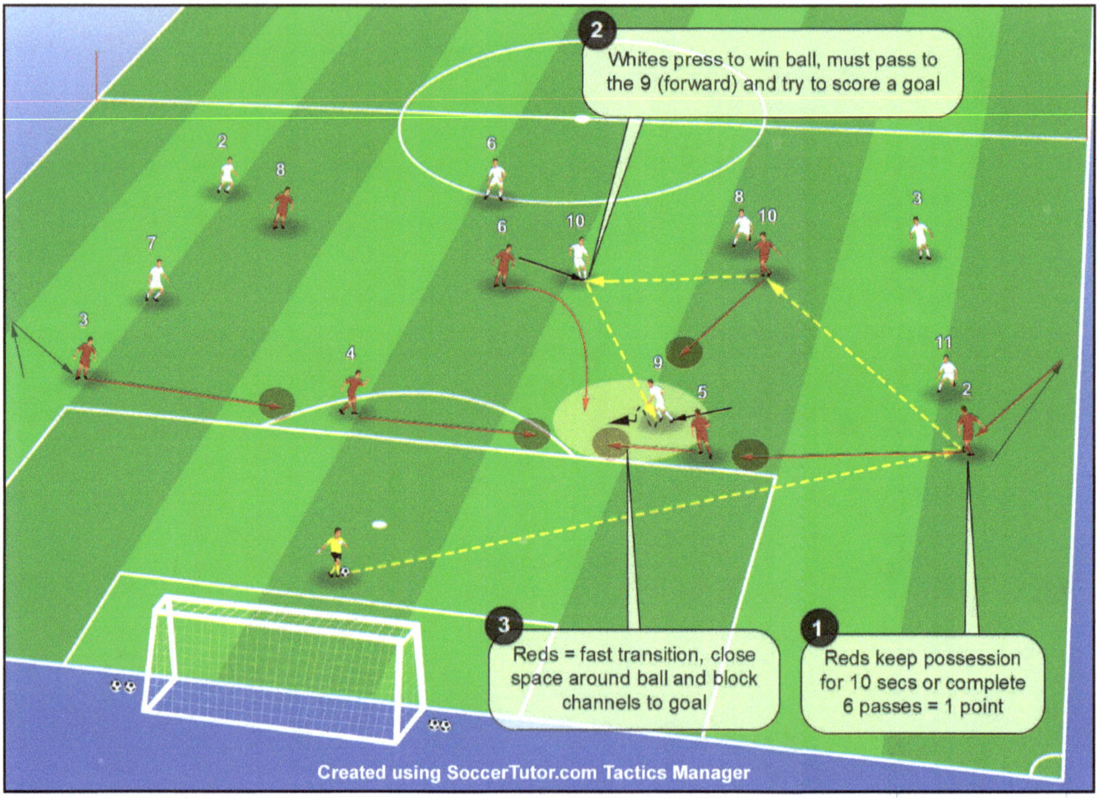

![Diagram showing the practice setup with red and white teams]

- 2: Whites press to win ball, must pass to the 9 (forward) and try to score a goal
- 3: Reds = fast transition, close space around ball and block channels to goal
- 1: Reds keep possession for 10 secs or complete 6 passes = 1 point

Description

The red team are in a 4-3 formation (from 4-3-3) and the whites are in a 2-3-3 formation (from 4-3-3).

1. The practice starts with the goalkeeper and the red team score 1 point for completing 6 passes or keeping the ball for 10 seconds.
2. The whites press to win the ball, then pass to No.9 and try to score a goal.
3. If the whites win the ball, the reds must make a fast transition to defence by closing the space around the ball in the centre and blocking the channels to goal.

After a few repetitions or a set amount of time, the practice starts again with both teams switching roles and objectives i.e. the whites start the practice building up play.

Coaching Points

1. Direct pressing from the closest player to limit the ball carrier's time, space and choices.
2. The rest of the players shift inwards as shown in the diagram, and try to create a numerical superiority in and around the ball area in the centre of the pitch.

Session to Practice **JORGE SAMPAOLI** Tactics - Transition from Attack to Defence (Low Zone)

PROGRESSION

3. Fast Reactions to Defend the Centre of the Pitch After Losing Possession in a Specific Game Scenario

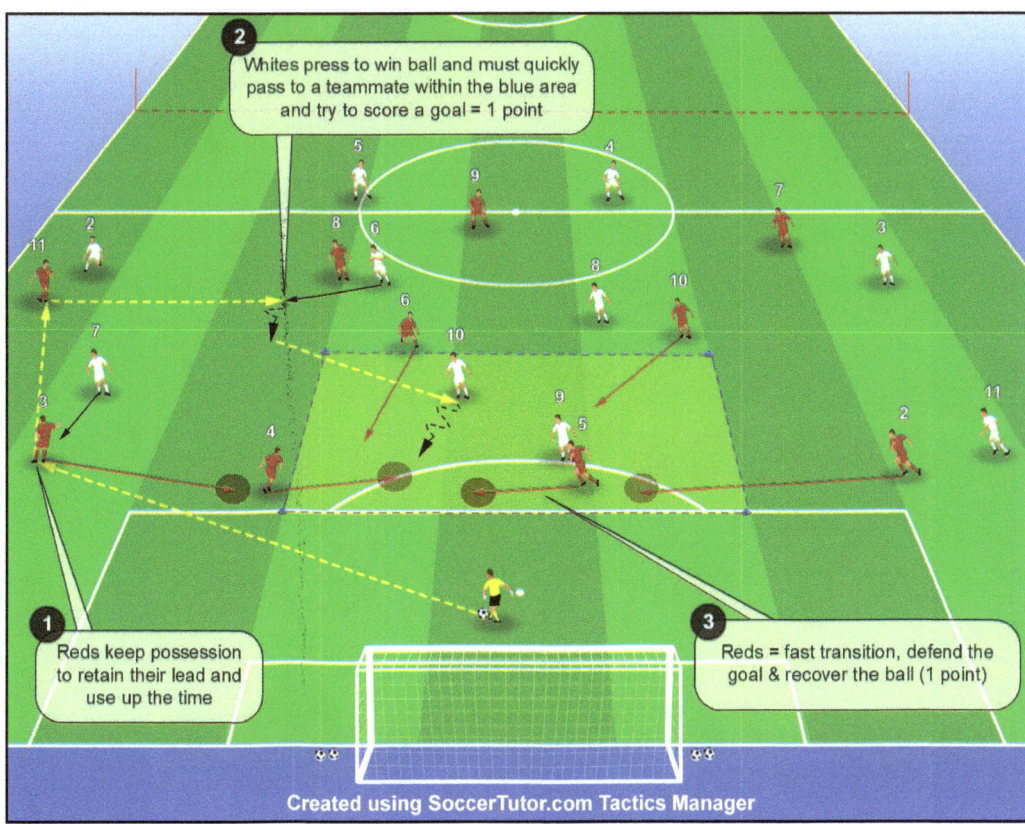

Description: In this progression of the last practice, we now play 11 v 10 in a larger area.

Game Scenario: The red team are leading 1-0 with 10 minutes left in the match.

1. The reds try to keep possession to retain their lead and use up the time.
2. The whites try to win the ball (No.6 wins it in the diagram example), pass immediately to a player in the blue box and then score a goal (1 point).
3. When the reds lose the ball, they must make a fast transition from attack to defence, defending their goal and recovering the ball (1 point) as quickly as possible.

After 10 minutes, change the team roles and objectives.

Different Rules

1. The team that starts in possession (reds) have unlimited touches and the other team (whites) are limited to 2-3 touches / Both teams have unlimited touches / Both teams are limited to 2-3 touches.
2. The white team have a limited time to finish their attack (e.g. 10-12 seconds).

Session to Practice **JORGE SAMPAOLI** Tactics - Transition from Attack to Defence (Low Zone)

PROGRESSION

4. Fast Reactions to Defend the Centre of the Pitch with Changing Game Situations in an 11 v 11 Game

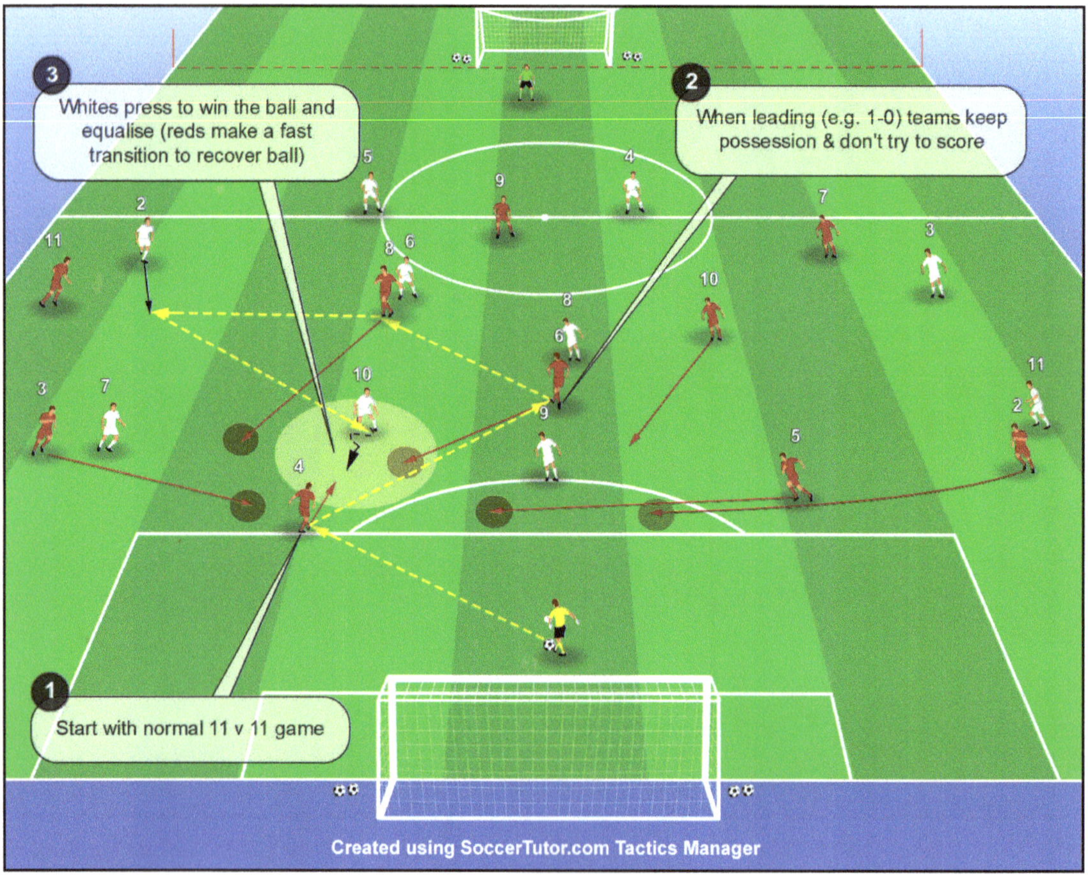

Description

In the final practice of this session, we make the area bigger again and add a large goal with a goalkeeper, as shown. We play 11 v 11 with both teams in a 4-3-3 formation.

1. We play a normal game until one team scores to make it 1-0.
2. From this point, the team that is winning (reds in diagram example) only has the aim to keep possession and protect their lead - they do not try to score another goal.
3. The team that is losing (whites) press to try and win the ball, and then score (equalise). The team that is winning (reds) make a fast defensive transition to recover the ball.
4. Once the scores are level (e.g. 1-1), we go back to a normal game until a team takes the lead again - the game continues with the rhythm and objectives of the teams constantly changing.

Rule: When a team is winning, they have unlimited touches and the other team have 3 touches.

COACHING TRANSITION PLAY - VOL. 2

CHAPTER 9

TRANSITION FROM ATTACK TO DEFENCE IN THE MIDDLE ZONE

TRANSITION FROM ATTACK TO DEFENCE IN THE MIDDLE ZONE

The red centre back (4) wins the ball from the No.10 so the white team make a transition from attack to defence

MIDDLE ZONE

For this book, we have divided the chapters by which zone the transition starts in. There are 3 zones:

1. **Low Zone**
2. **Middle Zone**
3. **High Zone**

This diagram shows an example of a team losing the ball in the middle zone. In this situation, the red team's centre back (4) wins the ball from the white No.10. There are players behind the ball and many players concentrated in the centre of the pitch (both teams).

It is again important that pressure is applied to the new ball carrier immediately, before he is able to get his head up to dribble or pass forward. The white team's defensive midfielder (6) closes down the ball carrier immediately and also blocks the pass to No.9. The left back (3), the right back (2), the central midfielder (8) and both wingers (11 & 7) all track back to mark a red player and prevent the ball being played to them.

When losing the ball in the middle zone, there is often free space in behind the defensive line. This is why the cohesive movements are so important. As shown in the diagram, all of the players move into the central area. This closes the space in which the opposition can play and prevents them from playing the ball wide or utilising the space in behind.

The players need to work together as a full team, because if just one player doesn't react quickly enough, the opposition could have an easy passing opportunity in behind with a goal scoring chance. If it is done effectively, the team will recover possession.

TRANSITION FROM ATTACK TO DEFENCE IN THE MIDDLE ZONE

What is the Tactical Situation?

- Our team have the ball approximately the same distance from our goal as they do to the opponent's goal.

- We have free space in behind our defensive line and there are many players concentrated in the centre of the pitch from both teams.

- The opposition will have many different attacking solutions if we lose the ball. They have the possibility to attack with 5-6 players and make runs in behind our defensive line.

- The opposition forwards can provide support easily and at least 2-3 players can move forward from midfield.

- We are often disorganised when we lose the ball in the middle zone. The positions that we have when losing the ball in this area sometimes make the reactions slow and ineffective.

- The negative transitions can be with an equality of numbers or we may face a numerical disadvantage.

- The opposition's counter attack takes 8 seconds on average.

What Objectives Should We Have?

- To maintain good positions when we have possession in the middle zone, so we can react quickly and efficiently when we lose the ball, thus reducing the risk.

- To quickly pass from attack to defence, trying to deny the opposition time and space - making sure to prevent passes being played in behind our defensive line.

- There should be an immediate press of the opponent's new ball carrier from our nearest player. There also needs to be fast tracking back and support from other teammates to create a strong side with a numerical advantage near the ball zone.

- The players in the centre of the pitch (centre backs, central midfielders) must be able to read the tactical situation and provide defensive balance. If there is an open ball situation, they should look to prevent the opposition from exploiting space in behind. They move back together and track the runs of the opposition players.

What Practices/Sessions Can We Create for this Tactical Situation?

- Possession situations in the middle zone versus opponents trying to defend in there and win the ball. We practice situations that lead to quick transitions from attack to defence in all possible scenarios.

- We work on fast reactions when we lose the ball in any tactical situations, anywhere in the middle zone. There should be a focus on synchronised defensive movements from our team - this depends on our formation and the strengths and weaknesses of the opposition and their formation.

TACTICAL SITUATION 1

MAURIZIO SARRI TACTICS

Tracking Back and Forcing Opponents Wide to Protect the Goal

Content taken from Analysis of Napoli during the 2017/2018 season

The analysis is based on recurring patterns of play observed within the Napoli team. Once the same phase of play occurred a number of times (at least 10) the tactics would be seen as a pattern. The analysis on the next page is an example of the team's tactics being used effectively, taken from a specific game.

Each action, pass, individual movement with or without the ball, and the positioning of each player on the pitch including their body shape, are presented.

The analysis is then used to create a full progressive session to coach this specific tactical situation.

Tactical Analysis of MAURIZIO SARRI - Transition from Attack to Defence (Middle Zone)

Analysis Taken from 'Napoli vs Feyenoord - 26th Sep 2017 (Champions League)'

Tracking Back and Forcing Opponents Wide to Protect the Goal (4-3-3 vs 4-2-3-1)

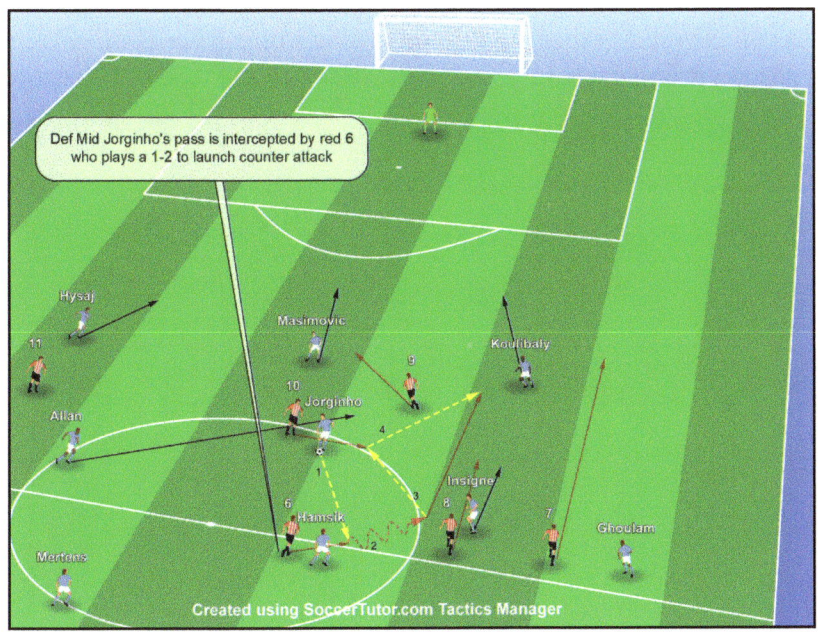

In this example, Napoli's defensive midfielder Jorginho's pass is intercepted by Feyenoord's defensive midfielder (6).

No.6 plays a 1-2 combination with No.10 and Feyenoord start their counter attack.

The Napoli players are alert and react quickly to track back into good defensive positions.

The runners are well tracked and the Napoli defenders move into the penalty area to defend the goal.

Feyenoord's No.6 has no passing options towards goal, so he passes out wide for the run of the right winger (7).

Napoli central midfielder Allan tracks No.7's run well, forces him to turn back towards the side-line and tackles him.

Session to Practice MAURIZIO SARRI Tactics - Transition from Attack to Defence (Middle Zone)

SESSION FOR THIS TACTICAL SITUATION (5 PRACTICES)
1. Tracking Back and Forcing Opponents Wide to Protect the Goal in a 5 v 4 Practice

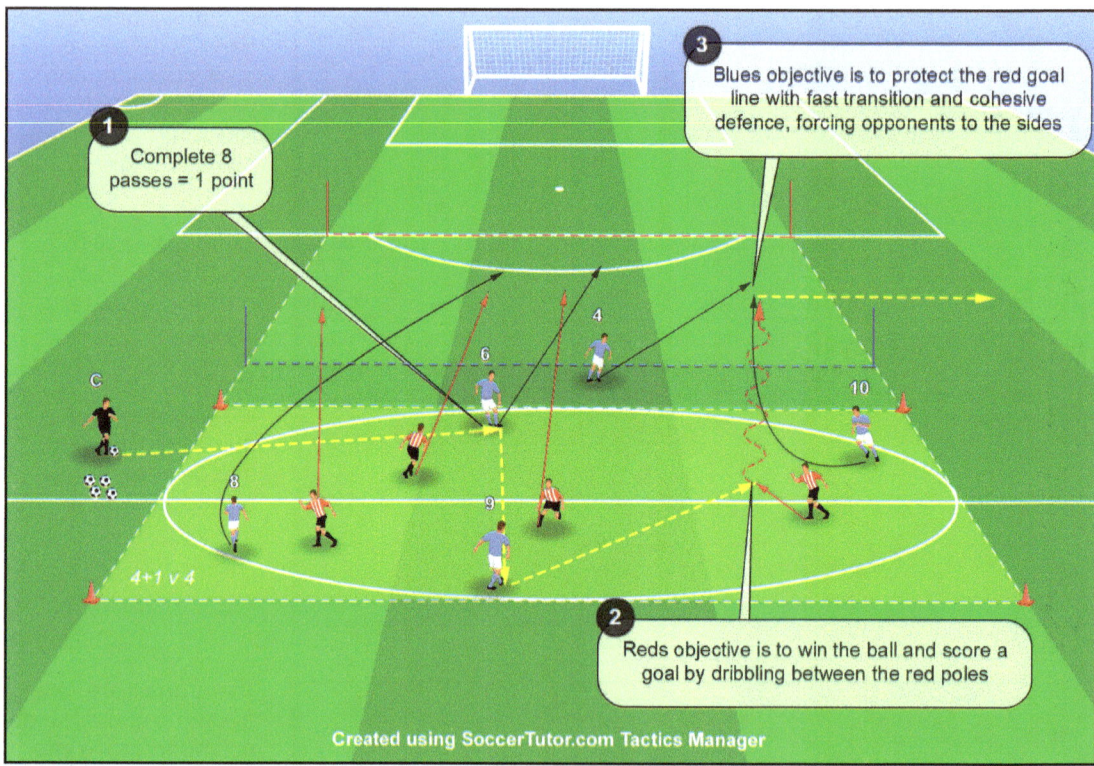

Objective: Develop fast reactions and cohesion after losing possession - track back, get behind the ball, force play wide and prevent the opposition from playing into the penalty area.

Description

We mark out a 20 x 20 yard area (white). The blues have 3 central midfielders (6, 8 & 10) and the forward (9) inside vs 4 reds. There is also a small area (blue) for the blue centre back (4), as shown.

1. The coach starts and the blues try to maintain possession with a 4 (+1) v 4 situation. They aim to complete 8 passes to score 1 point.

2. The reds try to win the ball, leave the area and launch a quick counter attack. In the diagram example, the red player who wins the ball dribbles forward. If any red player is able to dribble through the red poles, they score 2 points.

3. When the blue team lose the ball, their objective is to protect the red goal line with a fast transition. The blue players must move quickly to track back behind the ball, while maintaining defensive cohesion. They try to force their opponents out wide. If they recover the ball or kick it out of play, they score 1 point.

Session to Practice MAURIZIO SARRI Tactics - Transition from Attack to Defence (Middle Zone)

PROGRESSION

2. Tracking Back and Forcing Opponents Wide to Protect the Goal in a Functional Practice (1)

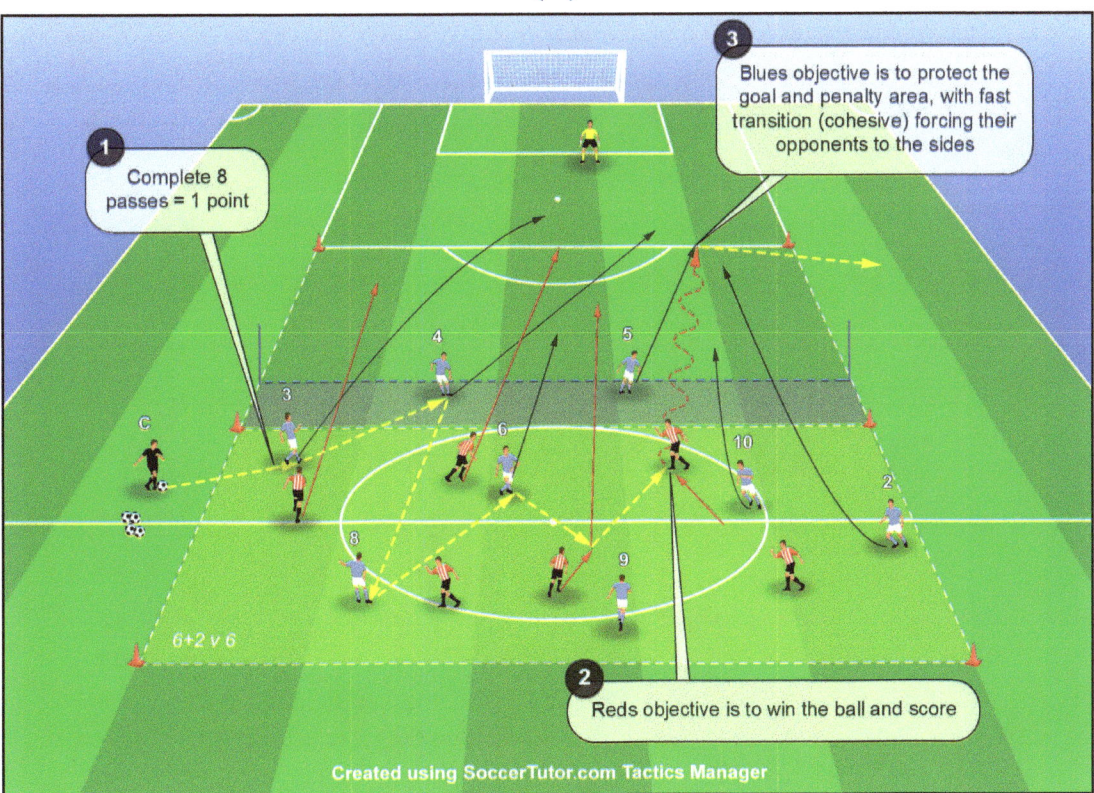

Description

In this progression of the previous practice, we make the white area slightly larger and play 6 (+2) v 6.

We add 2 red players, 2 blue full backs (2 & 3) and 1 extra blue centre back (5) who starts in the small blue zone. These are the practice objectives:

1. The coach starts and the blues try to maintain possession with a 6 (+2) v 6 situation. They aim to complete 8 passes to score 1 point.

2. The reds try to win the ball, leave the area and score a goal (2 points). We have removed the red poles from the previous practice, so the reds now try to score past the goalkeeper.

3. When the blue team lose the ball, their objective is to protect the penalty area and the goal with a fast transition to defence. The blue players must move quickly to track back behind the ball, while maintaining defensive cohesion. They try to force their opponents out wide. If they recover the ball or kick it out of play, they score 1 point.

Session to Practice MAURIZIO SARRI Tactics - Transition from Attack to Defence (Middle Zone)

PROGRESSION

3. Tracking Back and Forcing Opponents Wide to Protect the Goal in a Functional Practice (2)

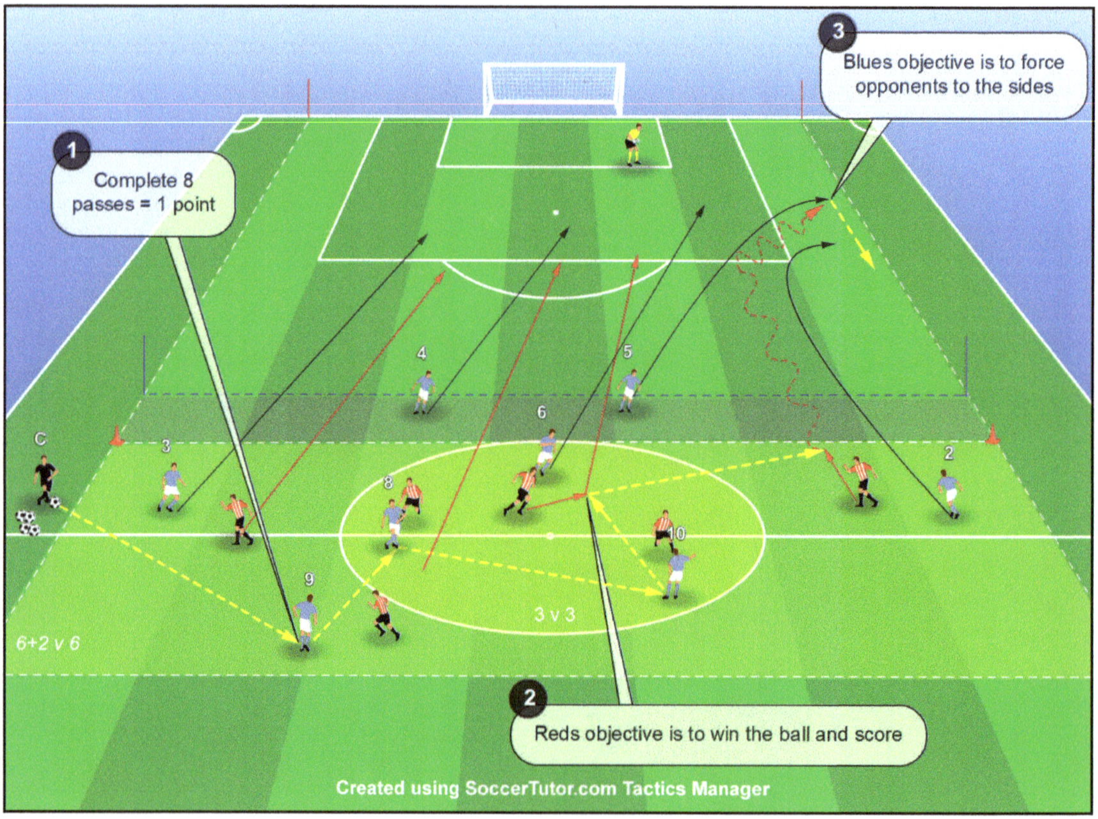

Description

In this progression of the previous practice, we make the entire area wider. The reds now have more space to exploit for their counter attacks and the blues have a larger area to defend and cover.

Within the white area, we now create a 3 v 3 situation inside the semi-circle. The 3 blue central midfielders and 3 red players must stay within the semi-circle until the reds win the ball.

The practice objectives are exactly the same as the previous practice.

Session to Practice MAURIZIO SARRI Tactics - Transition from Attack to Defence (Middle Zone)

PROGRESSION

4. Tracking Back and Forcing Opponents Wide to Protect the Goal in a Dynamic Zonal Game

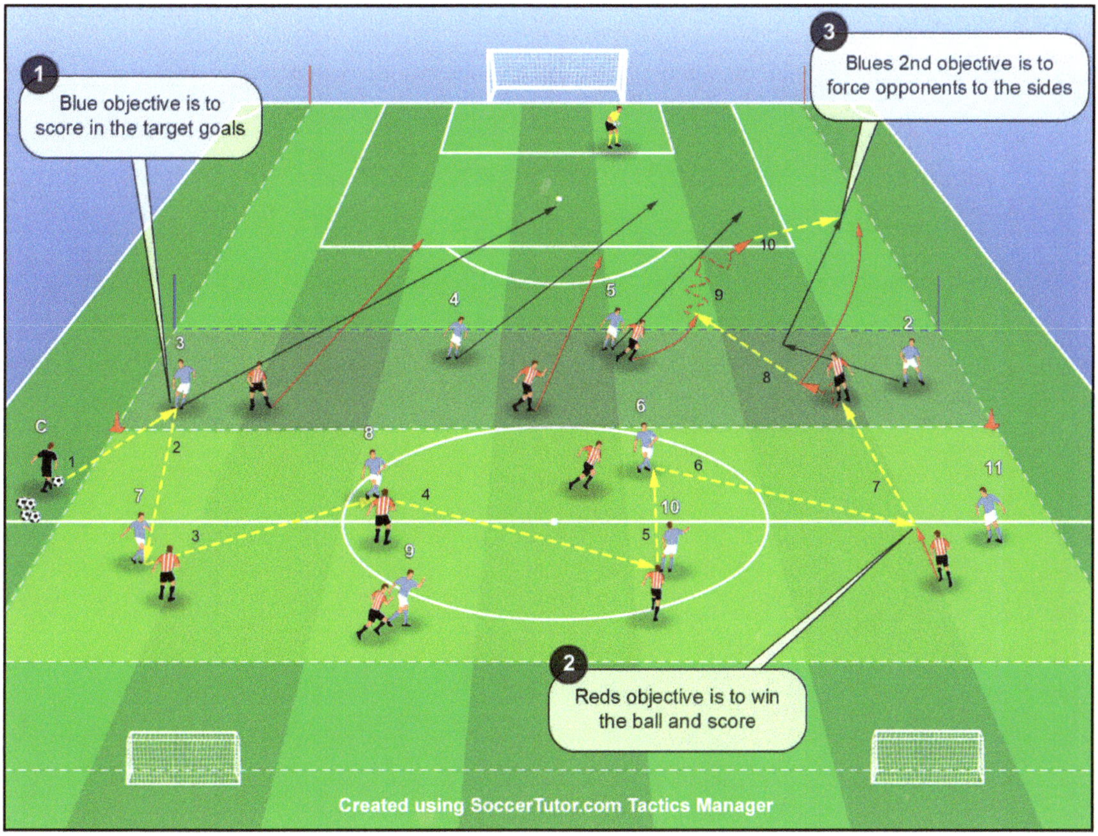

(Diagram: Blue objective is to score in the target goals. Blues 2nd objective is to force opponents to the sides. Reds objective is to win the ball and score.)

Description

In this progression of the previous practice, we now play 11 v 10 and we add 2 target goals, as shown. The blues use a 4-3-3 formation and the reds use a 4-2-3-1. In the large white area, we start with 6 v 6 and in the smaller blue area we start with 4 v 4.

These are the practice objectives:

1. The coach starts and the blues try to score in either of the target goals (1 point). In this phase, the players must stay within their respective zones.

2. The reds try to win the ball and score a goal (2 points). Once the reds win the ball, there are no restrictions concerning the zones for either team.

3. When the blue team lose the ball, their objective is to protect the penalty area and the goal with a fast transition to defence. The blue players must move quickly to track back behind the ball, while maintaining defensive cohesion. They try to force their opponents out wide. If they recover the ball or kick it out of play, they score 1 point.

Session to Practice MAURIZIO SARRI Tactics - Transition from Attack to Defence (Middle Zone)

PROGRESSION

5. Tracking Back and Forcing Opponents Wide to Protect the Goal in an 11 v 11 Game

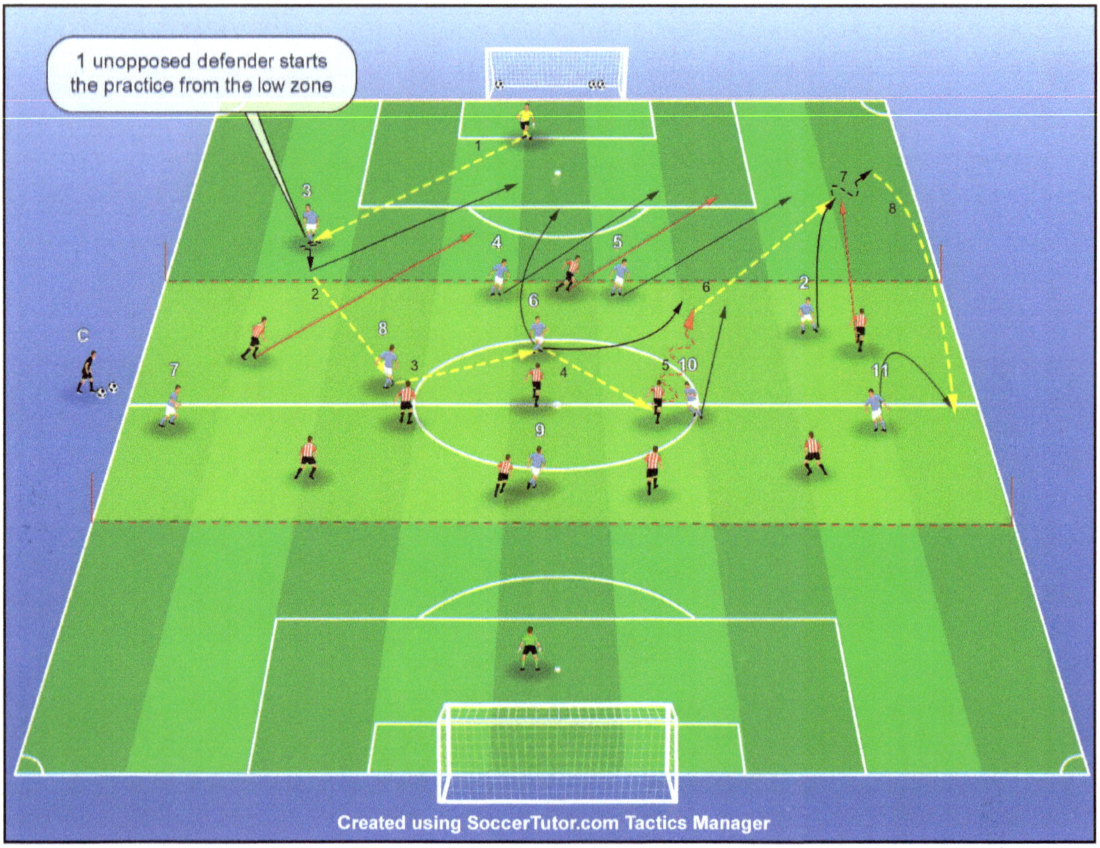

Description

In this final practice of the session, we play 11 v 11 on a full pitch and mark out the middle zone. One blue defender (unopposed) receives from the goalkeeper and the blues try to build up play and score.

The reds try to win the ball in the middle zone and then counter attack to score. The blues must make a fast transition to defence (see the coaching points for the blue team's aims).

Coaching Points

1. The defenders need to track runs and cover the space in behind to protect the penalty area and the goal. They should also be focused on forcing their opponents wide.
2. Fast collective shifting towards the ball area to create a strong side with a numerical superiority in and around the ball area.
3. Players ahead of the ball must run quickly back behind the line of the ball to provide support for the defenders and restrict time/space for their opponents (putting them under pressure).

TACTICAL SITUATION 2

JORGE SAMPAOLI TACTICS

Fast Transition with Midfielders Tracking Back to Get Behind the Ball

Content taken from Analysis of Sevilla during the 2016/2017 season

The analysis is based on recurring patterns of play observed within the Sevilla team. Once the same phase of play occurred a number of times (at least 10) the tactics would be seen as a pattern. The analysis on the next page is an example of the team's tactics being used effectively, taken from a specific game.

Each action, pass, individual movement with or without the ball, and the positioning of each player on the pitch including their body shape, are presented.

The analysis is then used to create a full progressive session to coach this specific tactical situation.

Tactical Analysis of JORGE SAMPAOLI - Transition from Attack to Defence (Middle Zone)

Analysis Taken from 'Sevilla vs Real Madrid - 15th Jan 2017 (La Liga)'

Fast Transition with Midfielders Tracking Back to Get Behind the Ball (4-2-3-1 vs 3-5-2)

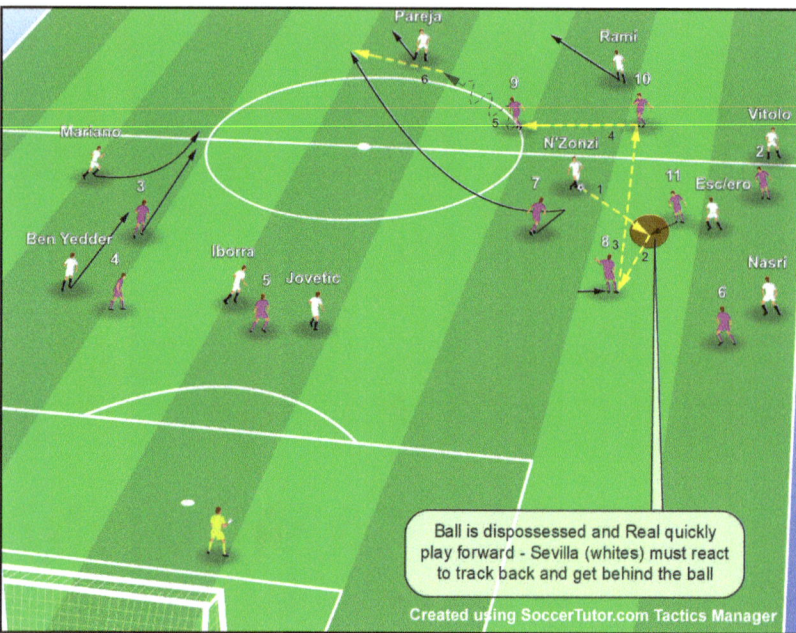

In this example, Sevilla central midfielder N'Zonzi's pass is dispossessed by Real Madrid's No.11.

Madrid work the ball forward with quick combination play, as shown.

The Sevilla players must react quickly to get behind the ball, restore defensive shape and create a numerical advantage around the ball area, to ultimately recover possession.

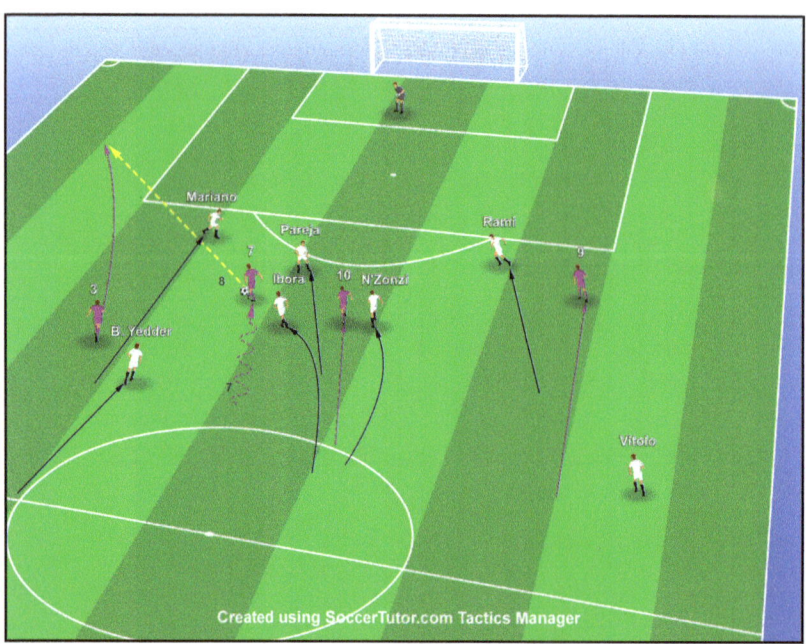

The central midfielder Iborra tracks No.7 as he dribbles forward and the other central midfielder N'Zonzi tracks the run of No.10.

The right back (Mariano) and 2 centre backs (Pareja and Rami) get behind the ball to defend the goal and force the attack out wide.

Real Madrid's No.7 passes to the left back (3) who makes an advanced run.

Tactical Analysis of JORGE SAMPAOLI - Transition from Attack to Defence (Middle Zone)

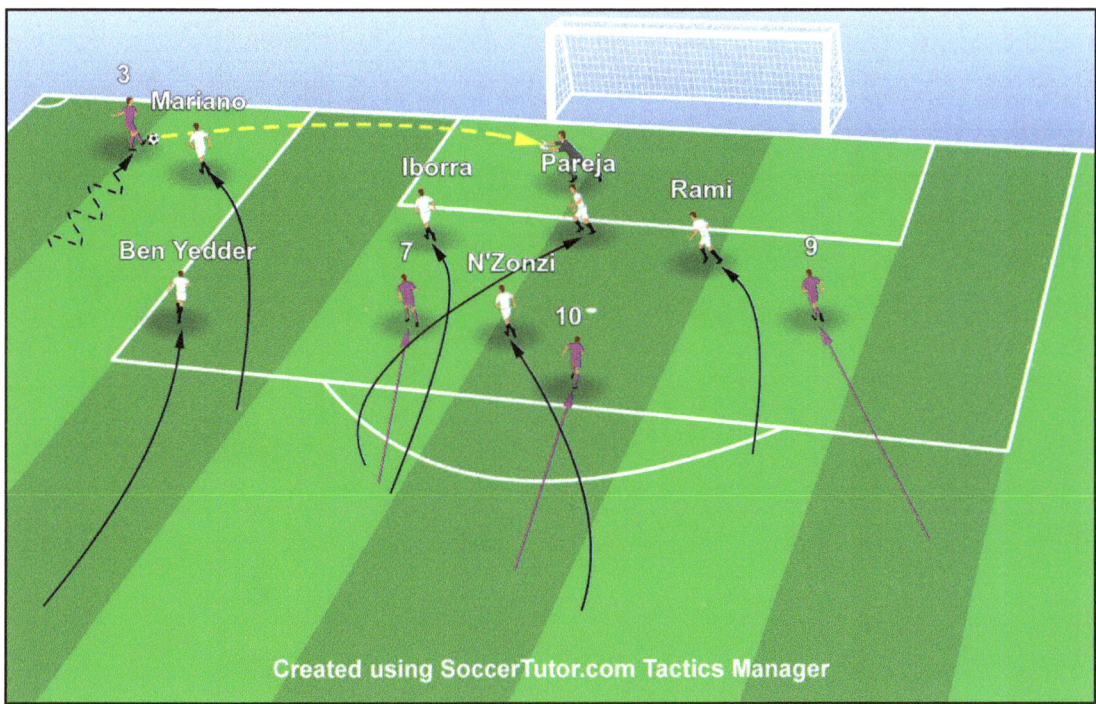

The Madrid left back (3) receives high up on the flank and the Sevilla right back Mariano runs across to apply pressure.

The other Sevilla players all track their runners or get behind the ball to take up balanced defensive positions. The result is a poor cross from No.3, which is easily caught by the goalkeeper.

Session to Practice **JORGE SAMPAOLI** Tactics - Transition from Attack to Defence (Middle Zone)

SESSION FOR THIS TACTICAL SITUATION (4 PRACTICES)
1. Fast Transition with Midfielders Tracking Back to Get Behind the Ball in a 2 Zone Possession Game

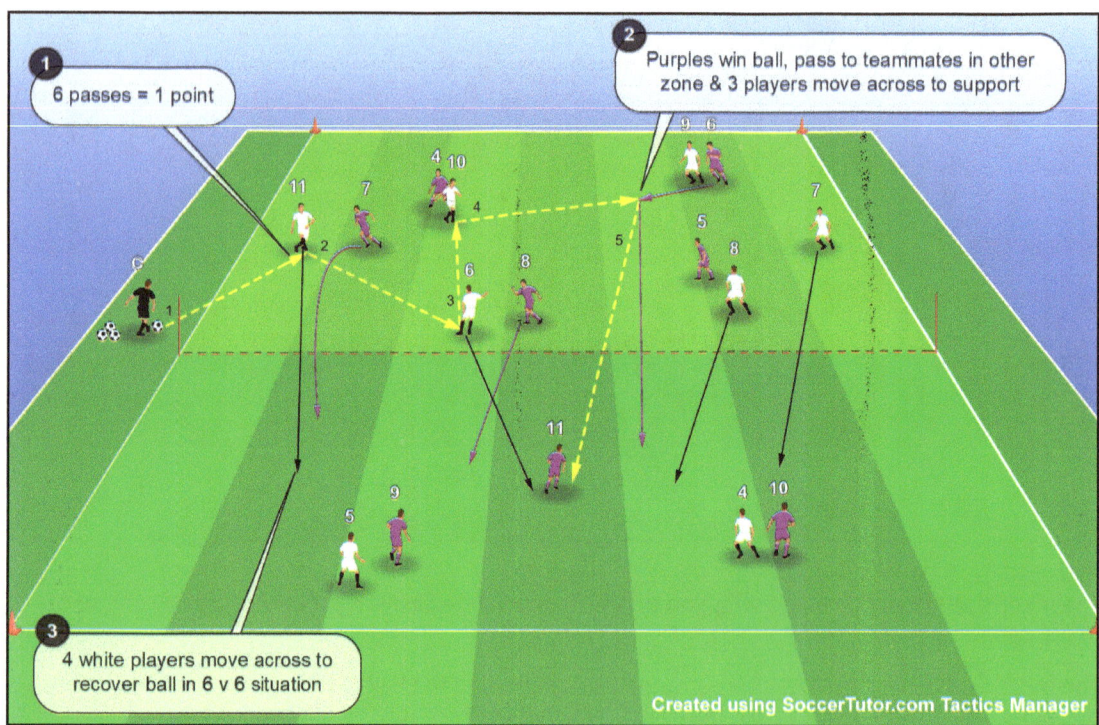

Description

In a 30 x 40 yard area, we have 2 equal 30 x 20 yard zones. Both teams have 8 players. In zone 1, we have 6 white players in a 2-3-1 formation (from 4-2-3-1) versus 5 purple players in a 3-2 formation (from 3-5-2).

1. The practice starts in zone 1 with a 6 v 5 numerical superiority for the whites as they keep possession and try to complete 6 passes to score 1 point.

2. The purple team aim to press and win the ball. If this happens, they must pass the ball to their 3 teammates in the other zone and 3 players move across to provide support to keep possession.

3. The white team make a fast transition to defence as 4 players move across to apply pressure and recover the ball as quickly as possible in a 6 v 6 situation. Once they win the ball back, they pass into zone 1 and the practice starts again with the same aims and objectives.

Coaching Points

1. In the transition from attack to defence, very quickly run back into the other zone to limit time and space for the opponents before they can organise their possession phase.

2. The closest player presses the ball carrier, others provide cover and the team create a strong side in and around of the ball area, to force the opponent to lose the ball or make a mistake.

Session to Practice JORGE SAMPAOLI Tactics - Transition from Attack to Defence (Middle Zone)

PROGRESSION

2. Fast Transition with Midfielders Tracking Back to Get Behind the Ball in a Dynamic Zonal Game (1)

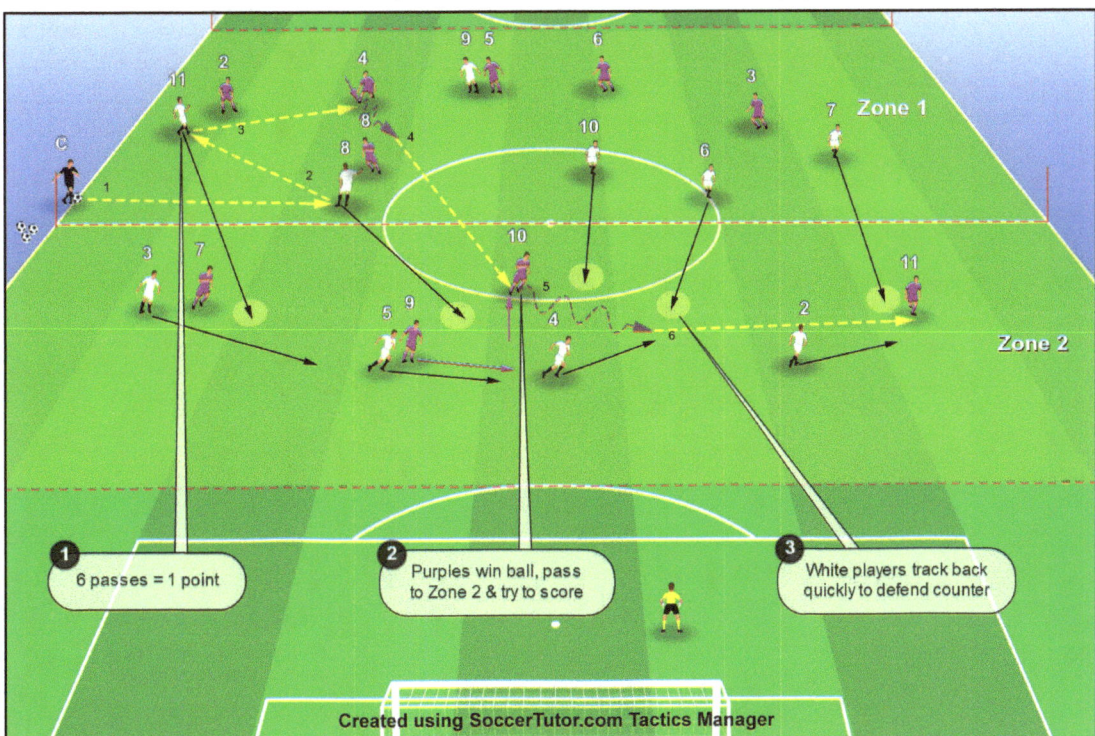

Description

We mark out 2 zones in the middle of a full pitch. The white team are in a 4-2-3-1 formation - they have the back 4 in zone 2 and all other players in zone 1. The purple team are in a 3-5-2 formation - they have the back 3, 2 wing backs and 1 central midfielder in zone 1 and all other players in zone 2.

1. The practice starts in zone 1 with the whites in possession trying to complete 6 passes (1 point).
2. The purple players in zone 1 press to win the ball and then pass to a teammate in zone 2. All players can then move freely, as they try to score a goal as quickly as possible.
3. When the purple team win the ball, the white players in zone 1 must quickly run back into zone 2 to provide defensive support and create a numerical superiority around the ball and behind the line of the ball, ultimately preventing their opponents from scoring.

Rules

1. White players are limited to 3 touches in zone 1.
2. After losing the ball, the white players must run back from zone 1 to zone 2 within 6 seconds, otherwise they are not allowed to participate to defend the opposition's counter attack.
3. The purple players have unlimited touches and time (or 10 seconds) to finish their counter attack.

Session to Practice **JORGE SAMPAOLI** Tactics - Transition from Attack to Defence (Middle Zone)

PROGRESSION

3. Fast Transition with Midfielders Tracking Back to Get Behind the Ball in a Dynamic Zonal Game (2)

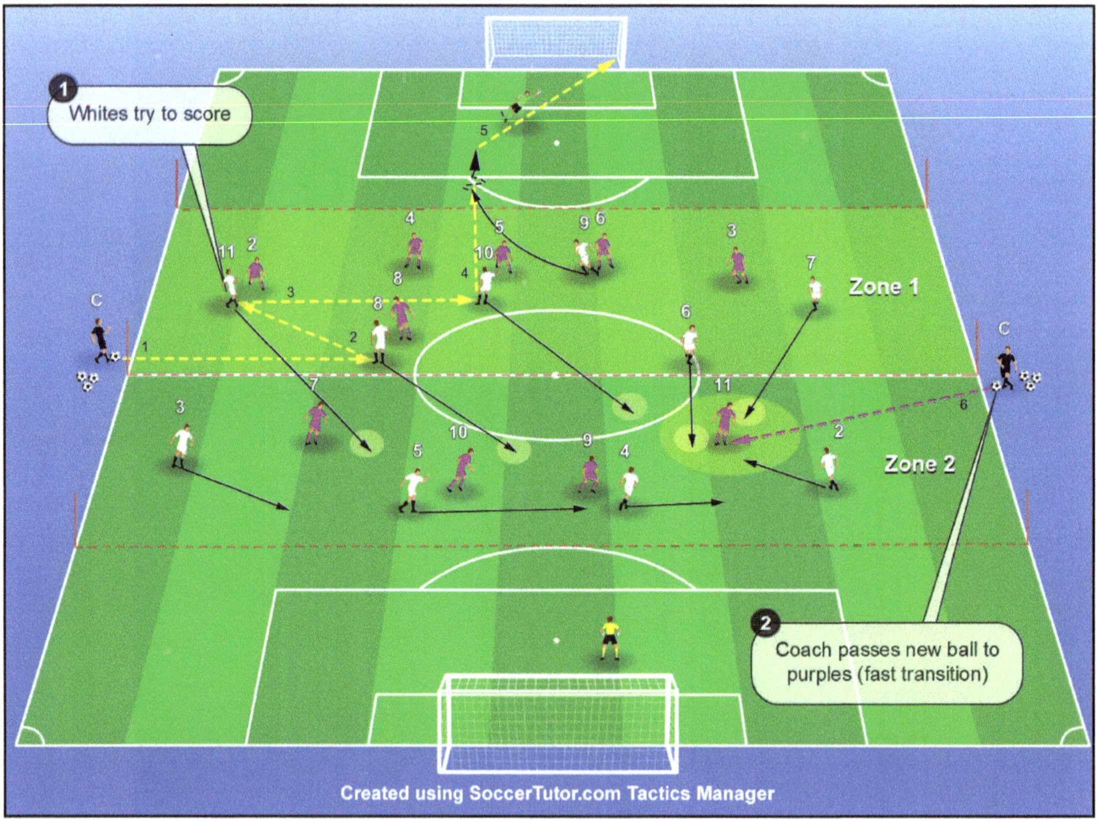

Description

In this progression of the previous practice, the white players in zone 1 now try to score a goal in the first phase. As soon as the attack finishes, the coach passes a new ball to the purple team in zone 2 for their counter attack. The other rules and objectives remain the same.

Rule: The purple defenders aren't allowed to leave zone 1 until the ball has been played outside of it.

Coaching Points

1. If the whites lose possession in zone 1, they must apply pressing immediately to avoid the purple players passing into zone 2.
2. If the coach passes into zone 2, all the white players in zone 1 must quickly run back into zone 2 to provide defensive support, limiting time and space for their opponents to force mistakes.
3. The 4 white defenders in zone 2 must show good awareness, be synchronised and communicate as a subgroup to press and cover, stop the opponents dribbling or passing into their box and protect their goal. This is until their teammates have tracked back to create a numerical superiority.

Session to Practice JORGE SAMPAOLI Tactics - Transition from Attack to Defence (Middle Zone)

PROGRESSION

4. Fast Transition with Midfielders Tracking Back to Get Behind the Ball in an 11 v 11 Tactical Game

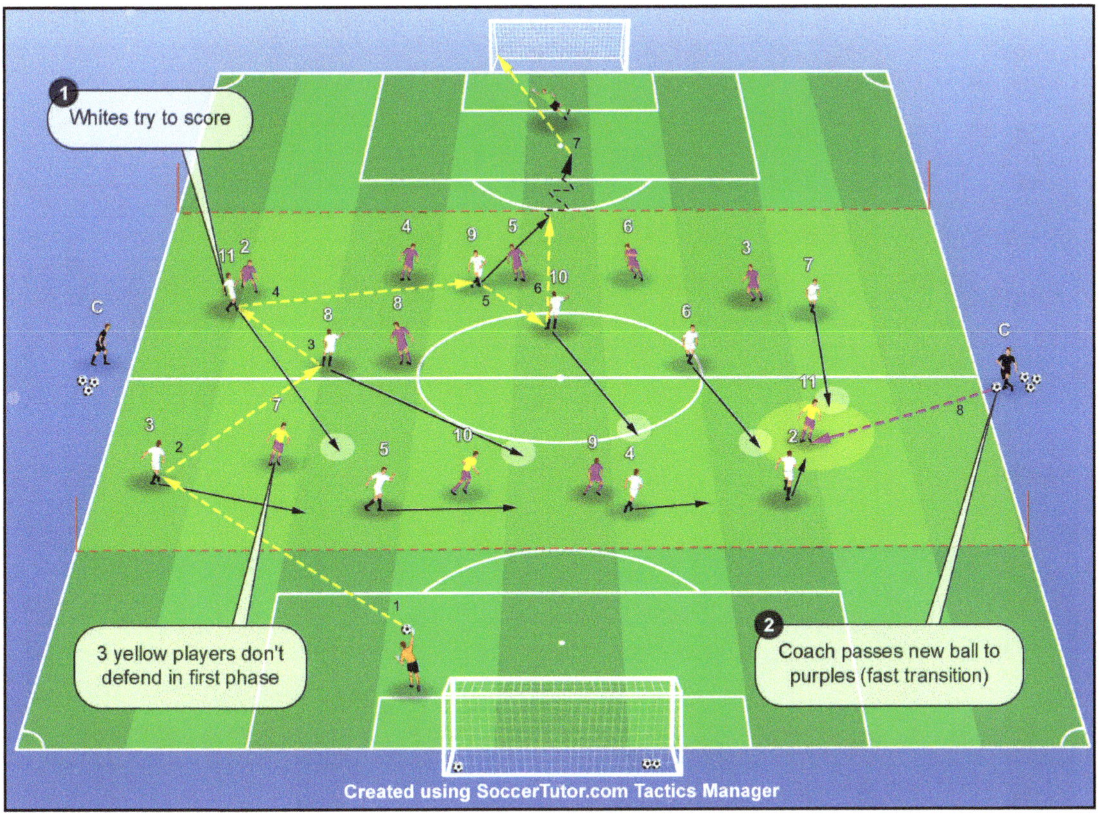

Description

In this progression, we now have just one middle zone. The purple team have 3 players with yellow bibs who are not allowed to defend in the first phase.

1. The practice starts from the goalkeeper and the whites have a 10 v 7 advantage to try and score.
2. Once the white attack is finished, the coach passes a new ball to one of the players in the yellow bibs. The purple team are free to launch a fast break attack, trying to score as quickly as possible.
3. The white players ahead of the ball must quickly track back to provide defensive support and create a numerical superiority in their defensive half, preventing their opponents from scoring. If the ball goes out of play at any time, start the practice from the beginning, but if the white team recover the ball, they launch their own counter attack to try and score a goal.

Different Rules

1. The purples (including yellow players) must complete 4 passes before being allowed to shoot.
2. The purple team can finish their attack without any limit on the amount of passes.

TACTICAL SITUATION 3

LEONARDO JARDIM TACTICS

Quickly Returning into Defensive Shape After Losing Possession

Content taken from Analysis of Monaco during the 2016/2017 season

The analysis is based on recurring patterns of play observed within the Monaco team. Once the same phase of play occurred a number of times (at least 10) the tactics would be seen as a pattern. The analysis on the next page is an example of the team's tactics being used effectively, taken from a specific game.

Each action, pass, individual movement with or without the ball, and the positioning of each player on the pitch including their body shape, are presented.

The analysis is then used to create a full progressive session to coach this specific tactical situation.

Tactical Analysis of LEONARDO JARDIM - Transition from Attack to Defence (Middle Zone)

Analysis Taken from 'AS Monaco vs Paris Saint Germain - 28th Aug 2016 (Ligue 1)'

Quickly Returning into Defensive Shape After Losing Possession

In this example, Monaco central midfielder Bakayoko's pass towards the winger Bernado Silva is intercepted. PSG are able to quickly switch play and pass forward. The ball ends up at the feet of No.11 and PSG have space to attack in behind the Monaco defence.

The Monaco players must react quickly to track back and return the team into defensive shape after losing possession.

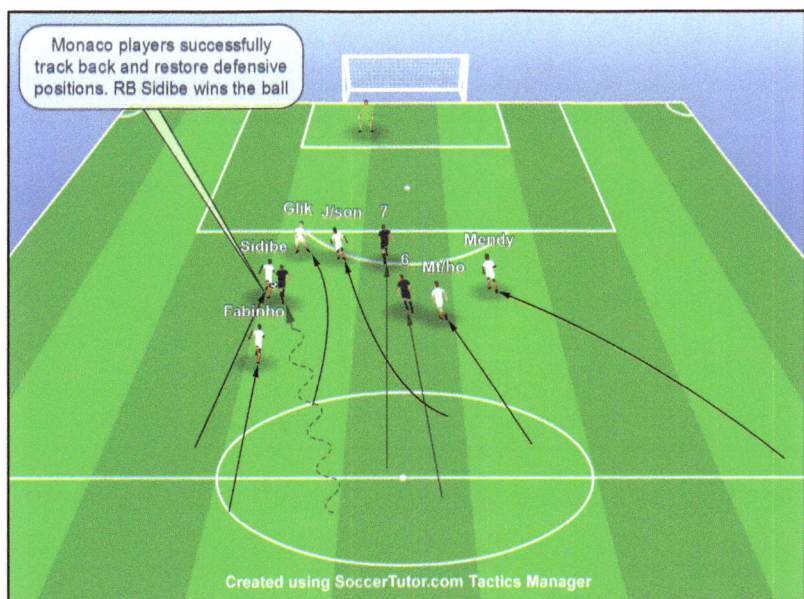

The PSG No.11 dribbles forward as the 2 Monaco centre backs (Gilk and Jemerson) make back steps to delay the attack.

The Monaco back 4 and 2 midfielders are able to quickly track back and move into positions behind the ball.

They soon have a numerical advantage around the ball area and the right back Sidibe is able to dispossess the ball carrier.

Session to Practice **LEONARDO JARDIM** Tactics - Transition from Attack to Defence (Middle Zone)

SESSION FOR THIS TACTICAL SITUATION (4 PRACTICES)
1. Unopposed Combination Play and Quickly Returning into Defensive Shape (Warm Up)

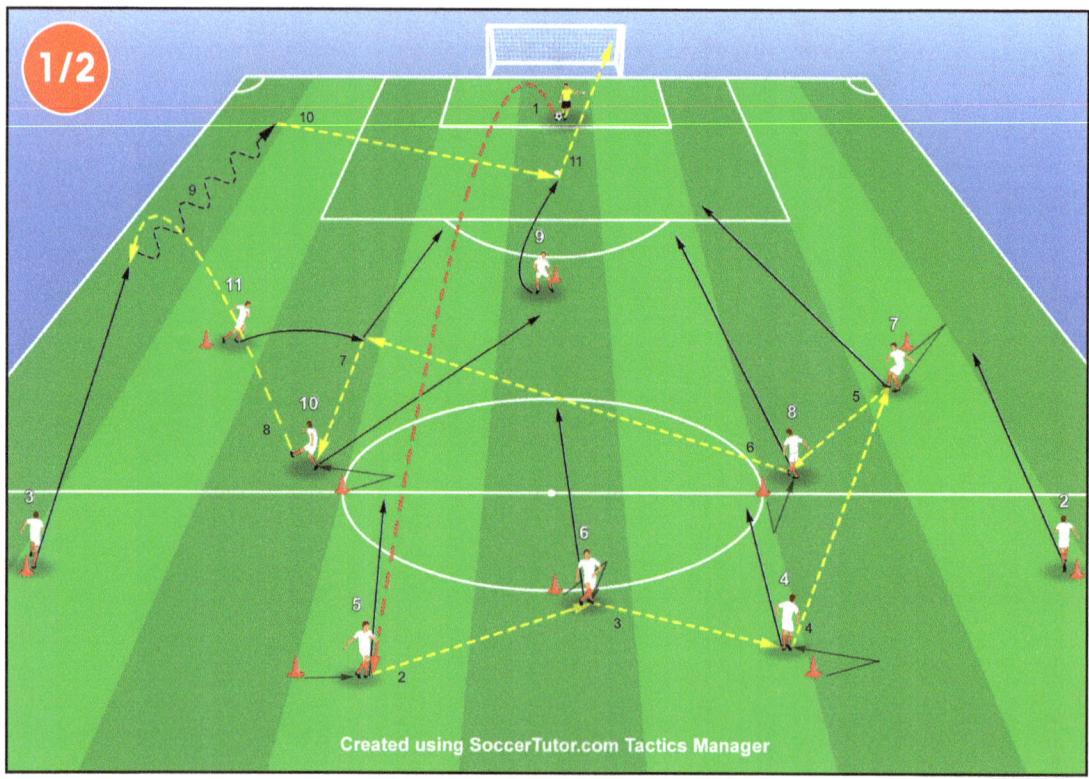

Objective: Fast tracking back to restore defensive balance and recover possession in the transition from attack defence.

Description (1/2)

We mark out the 10 positions of the 4-3-3 formation with cones as shown - please adjust to your team's formation.

Each cone represents a player's starting possession for this practice.

The practice starts with a long pass from the goalkeeper to one of the centre backs (4 or 5). The players then perform a specific passing combination (with set movements) designed by the coach.

The diagram shows our example, which includes an overlapping run by the left back (3) who crosses for the forward (9) to finish.

The practice description continues on the next page...

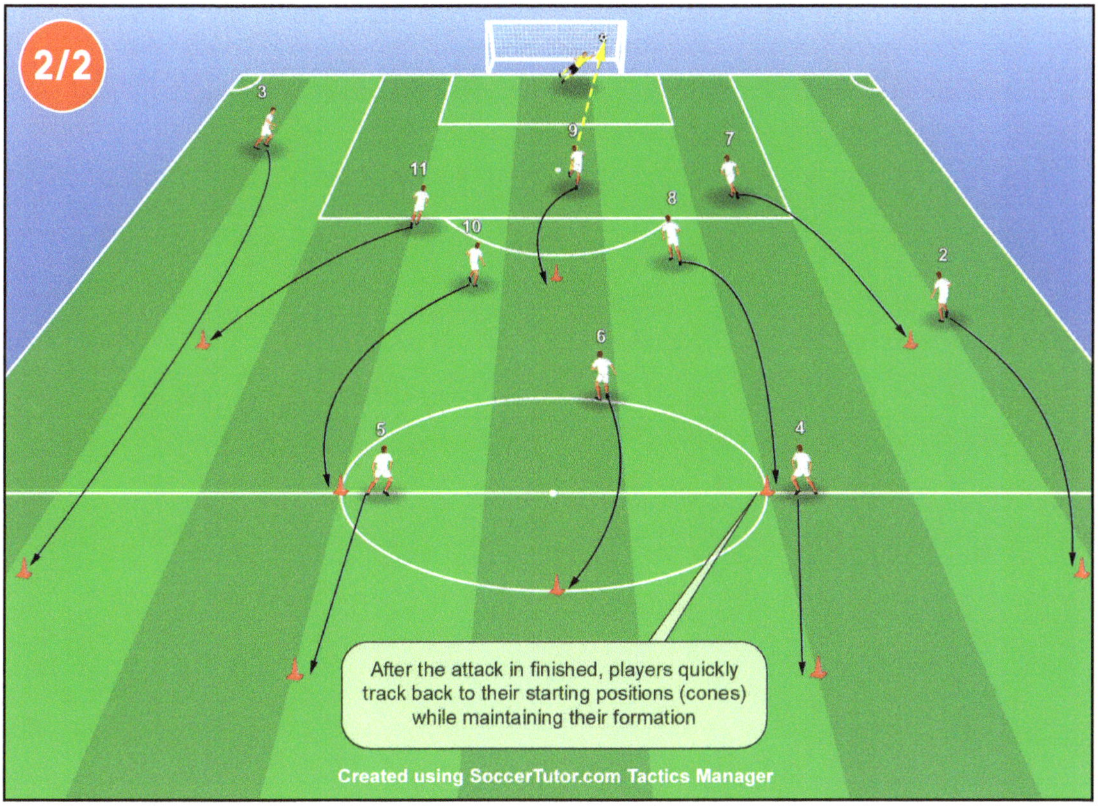

Session to Practice LEONARDO JARDIM Tactics - Transition from Attack to Defence (Middle Zone)

Description (2/2)

After the players finish their attack, we then focus on quickly tracking back.

All the players must run back to their starting positions (cones) as quickly as possible, while maintaining their formation.

Session to Practice **LEONARDO JARDIM** Tactics - Transition from Attack to Defence (Middle Zone)

VARIATION

2. Unopposed Combination Play and Quickly Reorganising in Relation to the New Ball Position

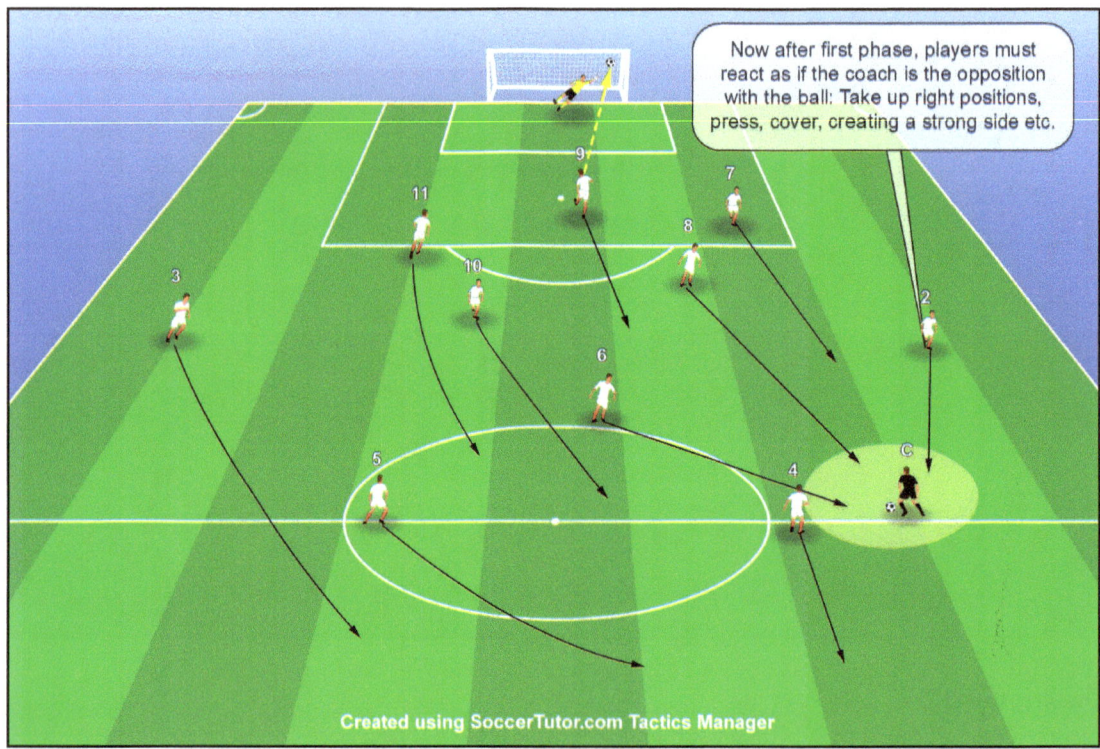

Now after first phase, players must react as if the coach is the opposition with the ball: Take up right positions, press, cover, creating a strong side etc.

Description

In this variation of the previous practice, the first phase remains the same.

1. The practice starts with a long pass from the goalkeeper to one of the centre backs (4 or 5). The players then perform a specific passing combination (with set movements) designed by the coach.
   * Please see page 174 which demonstrates this.

2. The difference in this practice is that the cones have been removed. In the second phase, when the attack is finished (when No.9 shoots in diagram example), the players must run back into the correct positions in relation to the opposition's ball carrier (represented by the coach).

Coaching Points

1. Press, cover, retrain small distances between each other.
2. Take up the correct positions in relation to the ball.
3. Create a numerical superiority around the ball area and create a strong side etc.

Session to Practice **LEONARDO JARDIM** Tactics - Transition from Attack to Defence (Middle Zone)

PROGRESSION

3. Quickly Returning into Defensive Shape After an Attack in a Dynamic 11 v 6 Practice

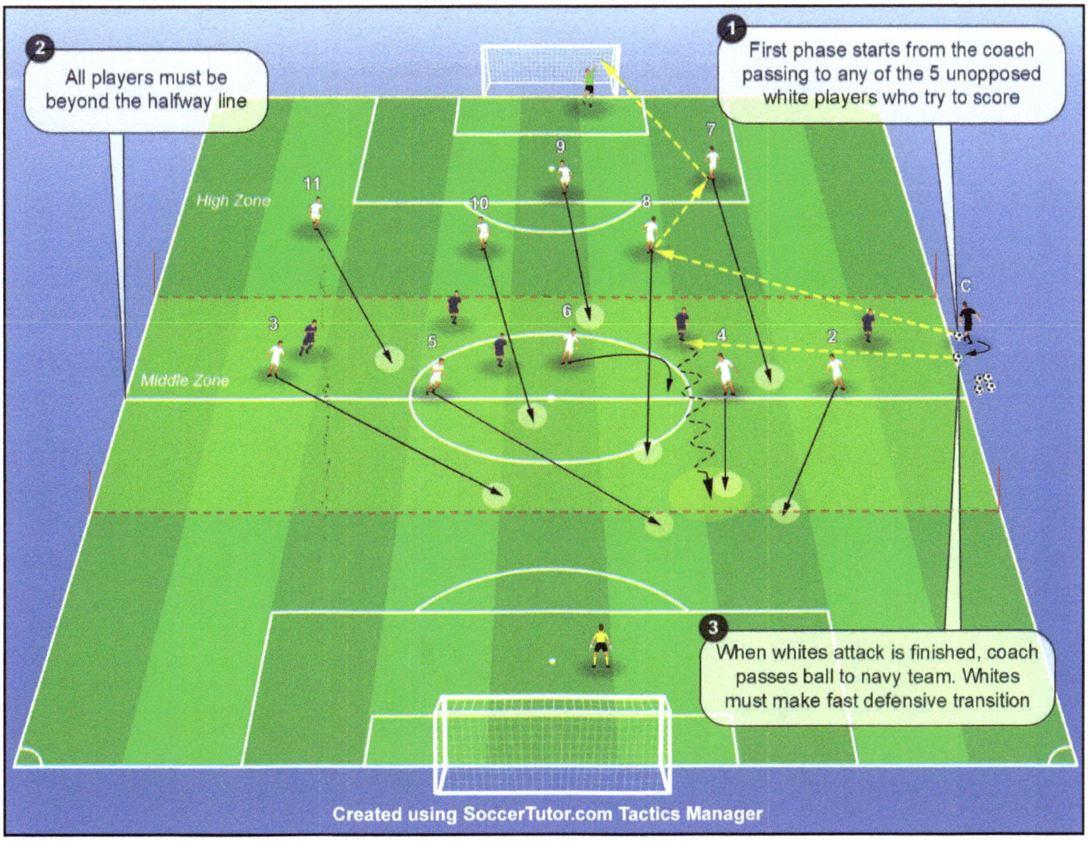

Description

In this progression, we add 5 navy opponents in the middle zone in a 2-3 formation (from 4-2-3-1).

1. The practice starts with the coach's pass into the high zone for the 5 unopposed white players who try to score. Alternatively, you can start with a long pass from the goalkeeper - the players then perform a specific passing combination (with set movements) as in the previous 2 practices.

2. In this first phase, all white players must be beyond the halfway line, as shown.

3. When the attack is finished (when No.7 shoots in diagram example), the coach passes a new ball to the navy team, who launch a fast break attack to try and score. The white defenders drop back to cover the space and delay the attack. The players ahead of the ball must quickly track back to provide support, trying to create a defensive numerical superiority and recover the ball.

Coaching Point: The 5 white players ahead of the ball must return back quickly as there is a 5 v 5 situation for the navy attack. They need to limit time and space to force mistakes/wrong decisions from their opponents.

Session to Practice **LEONARDO JARDIM** Tactics - Transition from Attack to Defence (Middle Zone)

PROGRESSION

4. Quickly Returning into Defensive Shape After an Attack in a Dynamic 11 v 11 Game

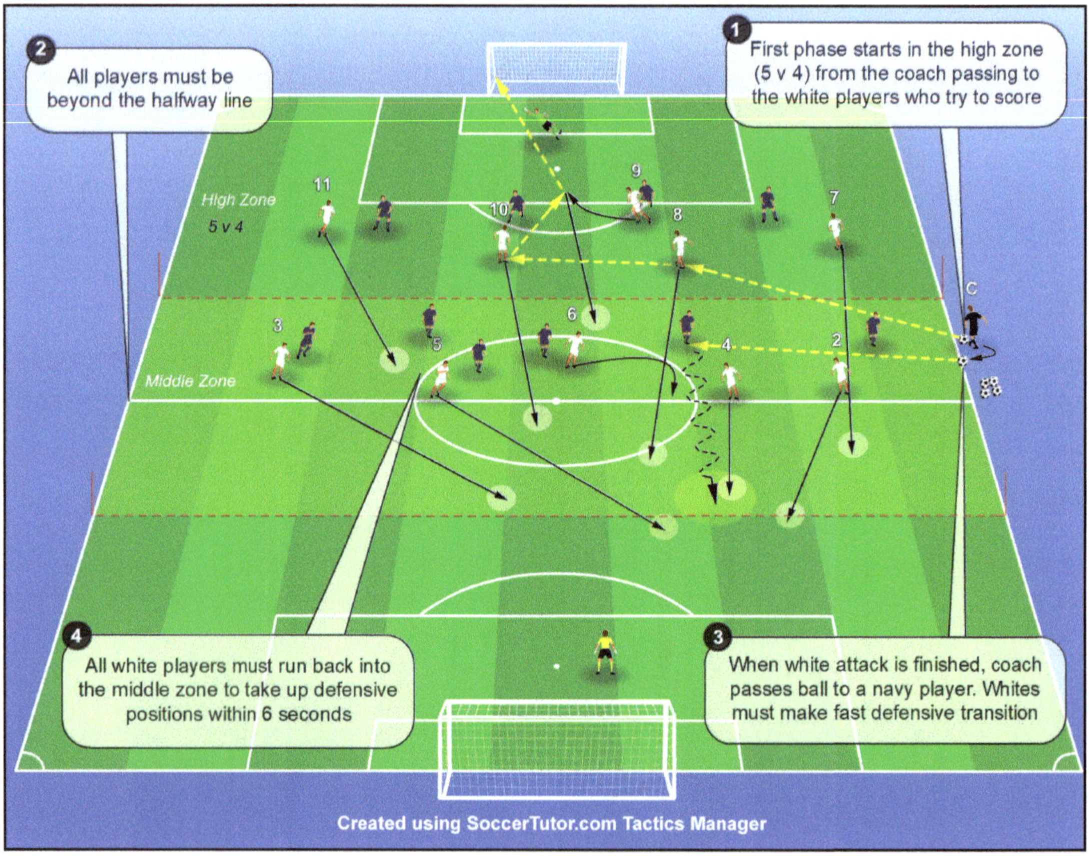

Description

In this final practice of the session, we now play 11 v 11. We add 4 navy players into the high zone and 1 extra navy player in the middle zone.

1. The practice starts with the coach's pass into the high zone with the whites trying to score a goal in a 5 v 4 situation.

2. In this first phase, all white players must be beyond the halfway line, as shown.

3. When the attack is finished (when No.9 shoots in diagram example), the coach passes a new ball to a navy player in the middle zone. The navy team launch a fast break attack to try and score. The white defenders in the middle zone drop back to cover the space and delay the attack.

4. The players ahead of the ball (high zone players) must quickly track back to provide support, trying to create a defensive numerical superiority and recover the ball. All 5 of these players must move back into the middle zone within 6 seconds of the coach playing the new ball in.

CHAPTER 10

TRANSITION FROM ATTACK TO DEFENCE IN THE HIGH ZONE

TRANSITION FROM ATTACK TO DEFENCE IN THE HIGH ZONE

TRANSITION FROM ATTACK TO DEFENCE IN THE HIGH ZONE

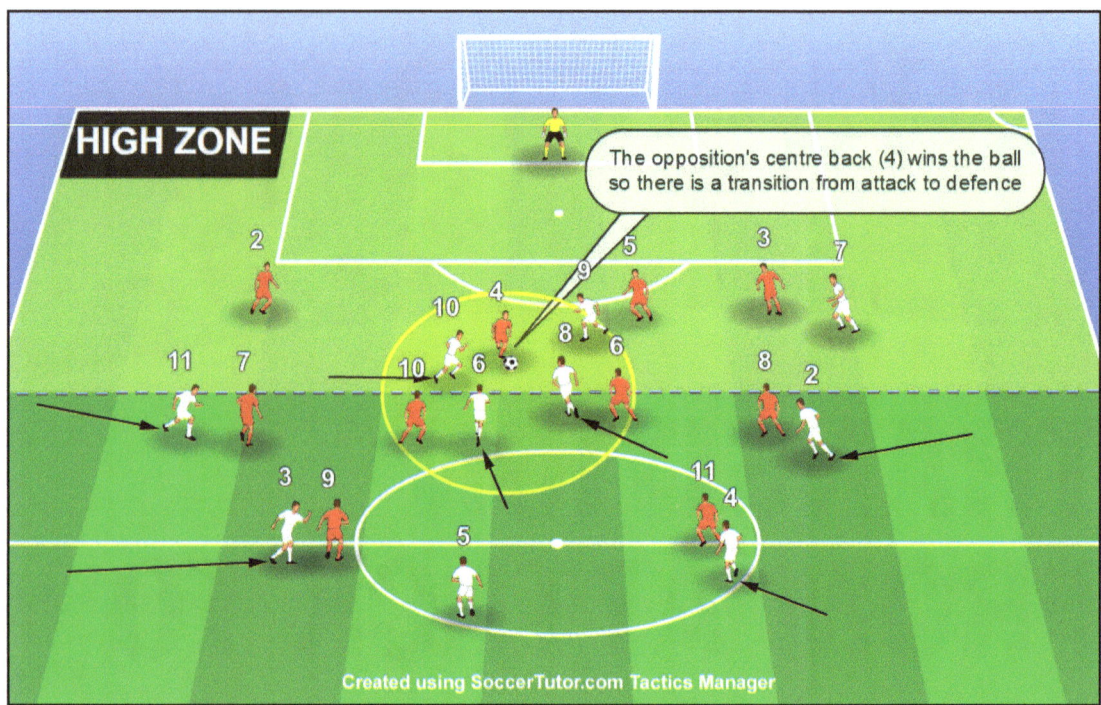

For this book, we divide the chapters by which zone the transition starts in. There are 3 zones:

1. **Low Zone**
2. **Middle Zone**
3. **High Zone**

This diagram shows an example of a team losing the ball in the high zone. In this situation, the red team's centre back (4) wins the ball. It is important that pressure is applied to the new ball carrier immediately, before he is able to get his head up to dribble or pass forward. We want to create a numerical superiority in and around the ball zone. We also have many players in the opposition half and need to prevent an early long ball in behind our defensive line, where there is lots of space to run into.

The 3 central midfielders (6, 8 &10) close down the ball carrier immediately and also block the potential passes towards the red No.6 and No.10 respectively.

All of the other players move inside to create a congested central zone and mark their opponents tightly. This closes the space in which the opposition can play and prevents them from playing the ball wide or utilising the space in behind.

The players need to work together as a full team, because if just one doesn't react quickly enough, the opposition could have an easy passing opportunity in behind with a goal scoring chance. If it is done effectively, the team will recover possession.

Players need to also be aware and have quick reactions to track back in case the first press of the ball is not effective. They need to prevent a numerical disadvantage from occurring during the opposition's potential counter attack.

TRANSITION FROM ATTACK TO DEFENCE IN THE HIGH ZONE

What is the Tactical Situation?

- We have many players in the opposition half.

- We have short distances between the lines.

- There are many opposition players in this half.

- We have a lot of space in behind our defensive line as we are high up the pitch.

- There is a short distance to the opponent's goal.

- The opposition have 1-2 players level with or near our defensive line.

- We have an equality of numbers and many potential 1 v 1 battle situations.

- The counter attacks from the opposition take 8-12 seconds on average.

What Objectives Should We Have?

- To pass very quickly from attack to defence in the area that we lose the ball, limiting the time and space for our opponents, marking players around the ball zone very tightly and blocking off potential passing lanes.

- To quickly press the player with the ball to avoid them passing or dribbling forward and forcing them to play under pressure of time and space.

- The basic aim is to win the ball or to force our opponents into making a wrong decision.

- Avoid making fouls when the opponent is under pressure of time and space and has no solutions. If a foul is committed, it stops the press and solves the problem for our opponents.

- To avoid the opposition playing long balls in behind our defensive line, which would neutralise the many players we have high up the pitch.

- To create a numerical superiority in and around the ball area and create a strong side.

- Players need to be aware and have quick reactions to track back in case the first press of the ball is not effective. They need to prevent a numerical disadvantage from occurring at the back from the opposition's counter attack.

What Practices/Sessions Can We Create for this Tactical Situation?

- High intensity possession and transition practices which force our players to react very quickly and effectively when we lose the ball in the high zone and in tight areas of the pitch.

- Practices focussed on awareness, tactical movements, decision making and high energy when possession is lost high up the pitch.

- Practices with organised attacks and tactical movements in the opposition's half against organised defences with many players behind the ball. The focus is on fast and effective transitions from attack to defence, but we need to be aware that it depends on our formation (strengths and weaknesses) against the formation of our opponents.

TACTICAL SITUATION 1

MAURIZIO SARRI TACTICS

High Press from Multiple Angles to Create a Numerical Advantage Around the Ball

Content taken from Analysis of Napoli during the 2017/2018 season

The analysis is based on recurring patterns of play observed within the Napoli team. Once the same phase of play occurred a number of times (at least 10) the tactics would be seen as a pattern. The analysis on the next page is an example of the team's tactics being used effectively, taken from a specific game.

Each action, pass, individual movement with or without the ball, and the positioning of each player on the pitch including their body shape, are presented.

The analysis is then used to create a full progressive session to coach this specific tactical situation.

Tactical Analysis of MAURIZIO SARRI - Transition from Attack to Defence (High Zone)

Analysis Taken from 'Manchester City vs Napoli - 17th Oct 2017 (Champions League)'

High Press from Multiple Angles to Create a Numerical Advantage Around the Ball (4-3-3 vs 4-3-3)

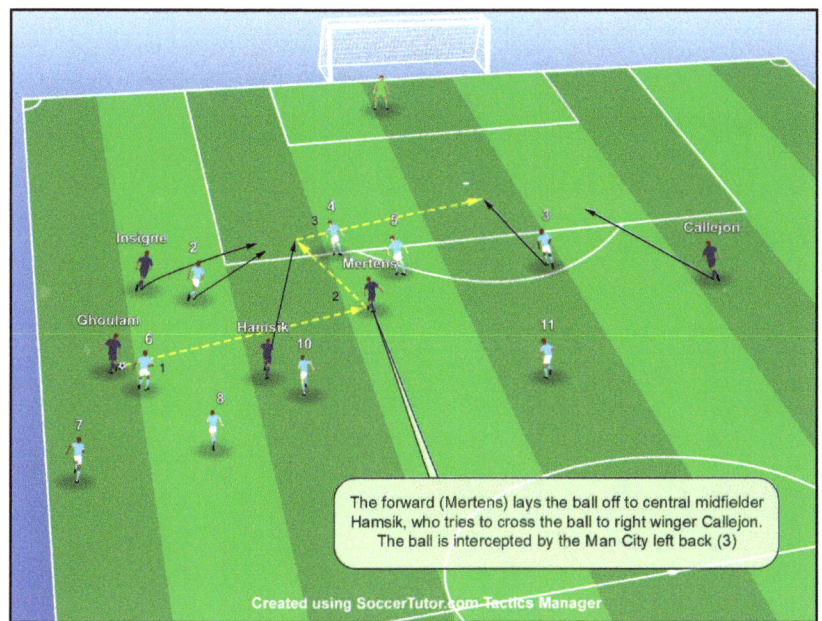

The forward (Mertens) lays the ball off to central midfielder Hamsik, who tries to cross the ball to right winger Callejon. The ball is intercepted by the Man City left back (3).

In this example, the Napoli left back Ghoulam has the ball in an advanced position and passes inside to the forward (Mertens).

The central midfielder Hamsik makes a third man run into the penalty area and receives the pass from Mertens.

Hamsik attempts to cross the ball for the right winger (Callejón) but the Manchester City left back (3) is able to intercept the ball.

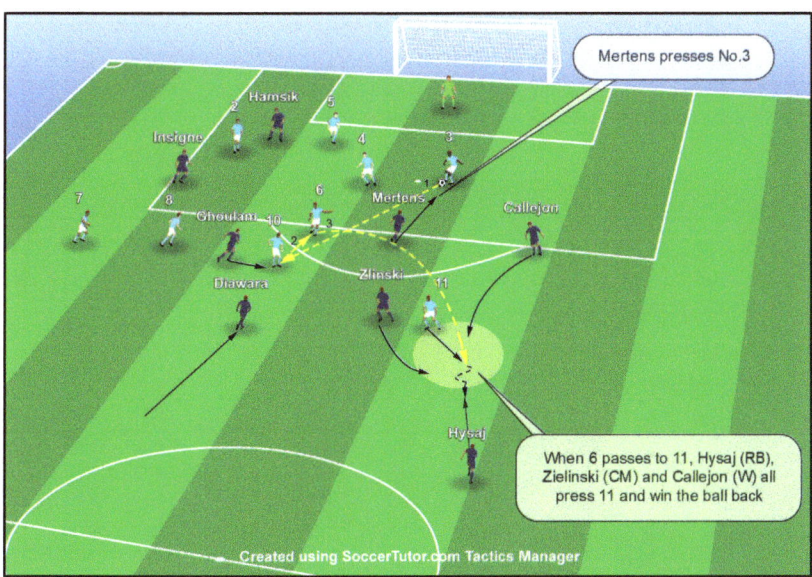

When 6 passes to 11, Hysaj (RB), Zielinski (CM) and Callejon (W) all press 11 and win the ball back

No.3 passes to the No.10 on the edge of the box, who lays it off to the defensive midfielder (6). No.6 plays an aerial pass towards the winger (11) who receives.

Napoli react quickly to the defensive transition as Hysaj (left back), Zielinski (central midfielder) and Callejón (winger) all press the ball. Hysaj wins the ball back for his team after Napoli's successful high press to create a numerical advantage around the ball.

COACHING TRANSITION PLAY - VOL. 2

Session to Practice MAURIZIO SARRI Tactics - Transition from Attack to Defence (High Zone)

SESSION FOR THIS TACTICAL SITUATION (4 PRACTICES)
1. Unopposed Combination Play + High Press from Multiple Angles to Create a Numerical Advantage Around the Ball

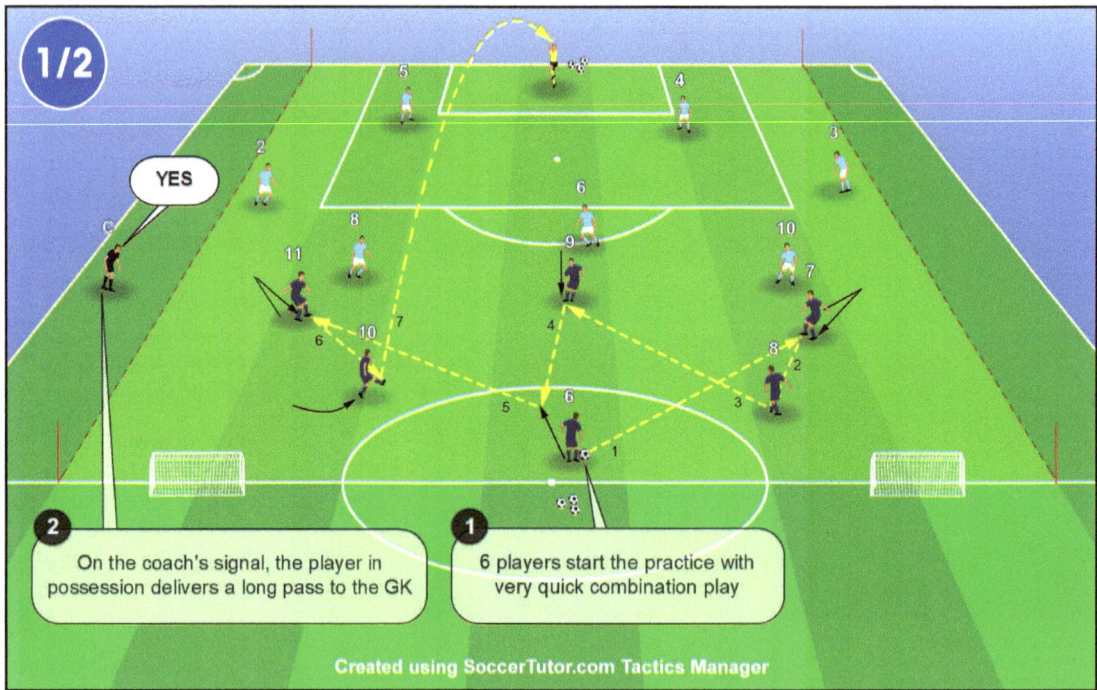

Objective: Cohesive pressing to create a strong side and close down the ball carrier from all angles to block all possible options, recovering the ball as soon as possible.

Description (1/2)

Using half a pitch (narrower), we have a navy team in a 3-3 formation and a light blue in a 4-3 formation.

1. The practice starts with the 6 navy players using very quick combination play to pass between each other, as they wait for the coach's signal.

2. On the coach's signal, the player in possession at the time (No.10 in diagram example) plays a long pass to the goalkeeper who catches it.

The other team (light blue) are not involved in this first phase and simply stay in their positions within their formation.

The practice description continues on the next page...

Session to Practice MAURIZIO SARRI Tactics - Transition from Attack to Defence (High Zone)

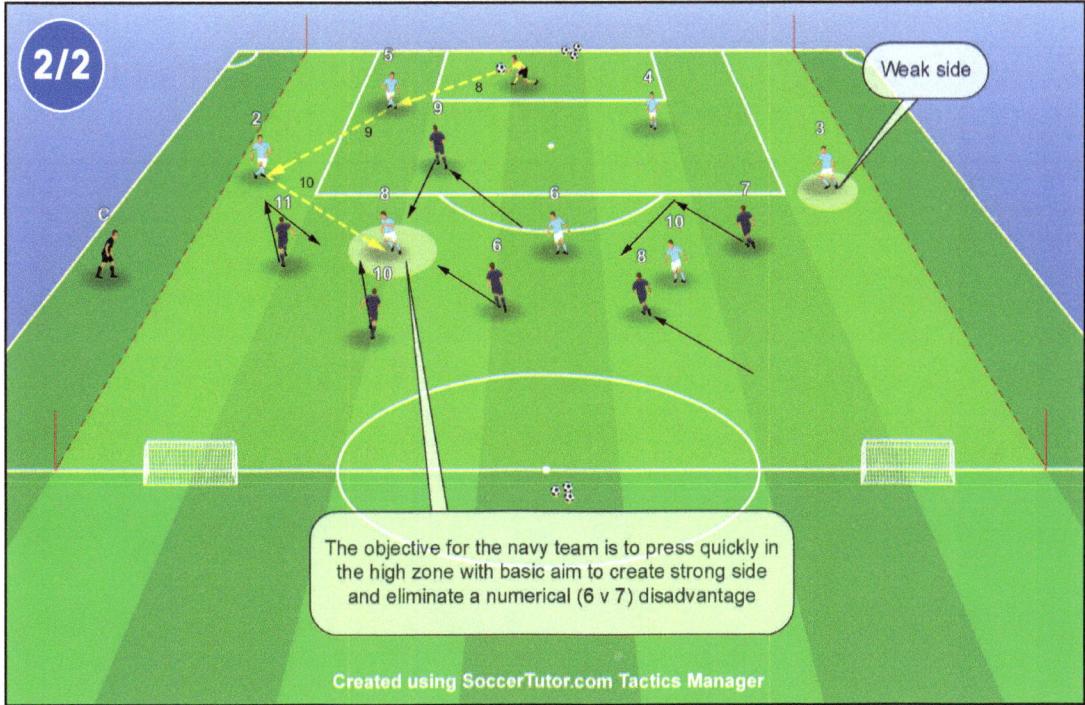

Description (2/2)

While the ball is travelling towards the goalkeeper, all 6 of the navy players move forward to apply a high press. The goalkeeper immediately passes to one of the 4 light blue defenders (centre back No.5 in diagram example) as soon as he receives the long pass.

The objective for the navy team is to apply a high press and create a strong side with a numerical advantage around the ball zone. This is used to eliminate the 6 v 7 overall numerical disadvantage that they have.

The navy team want to reduce the time and space available to the ball carrier and force their opponents into making the wrong decisions, so they can win the ball as soon as possible.

The light blue team aim to break through the pressure and then score in one of the mini goals.

Session to Practice MAURIZIO SARRI Tactics - Transition from Attack to Defence (High Zone)

PROGRESSION

2. High Press from Multiple Angles to Create a Numerical Advantage Around the Ball in a Dynamic Game

Description

Using the area shown, we mark out a high zone and a low zone. Within the high zone, we mark out 3 channels with the central channel being the largest.

The team navy are in a 2-3-3 formation (with full backs) and the light blue team are in a 4-3 formation.

1. The practice starts with the navy team in possession trying to complete 8 passes (1 point) and keep the ball for 15-20 seconds (2 points).

2. The light blue team's aim is to win the ball and launch a counter attack. If they are able to play into the end zone (navy team's low zone) they score 1 point and if they score in any of the 3 mini goals, they get 2 points.

3. When the navy team lose the ball, they must make a fast transition from attack to defence. Their focus is to apply a high press to recover the ball as quickly as possible. In the transition to defence, all of the navy players must be within the space of 2 channels next to each other. If the navy team win the ball back within 6 seconds and all players are within 2 channels, they score 1 point.

Session to Practice MAURIZIO SARRI Tactics - Transition from Attack to Defence (High Zone)

PROGRESSION

3. High Press from Multiple Angles to Create a Numerical Advantage Around the Ball in a Positional SSG

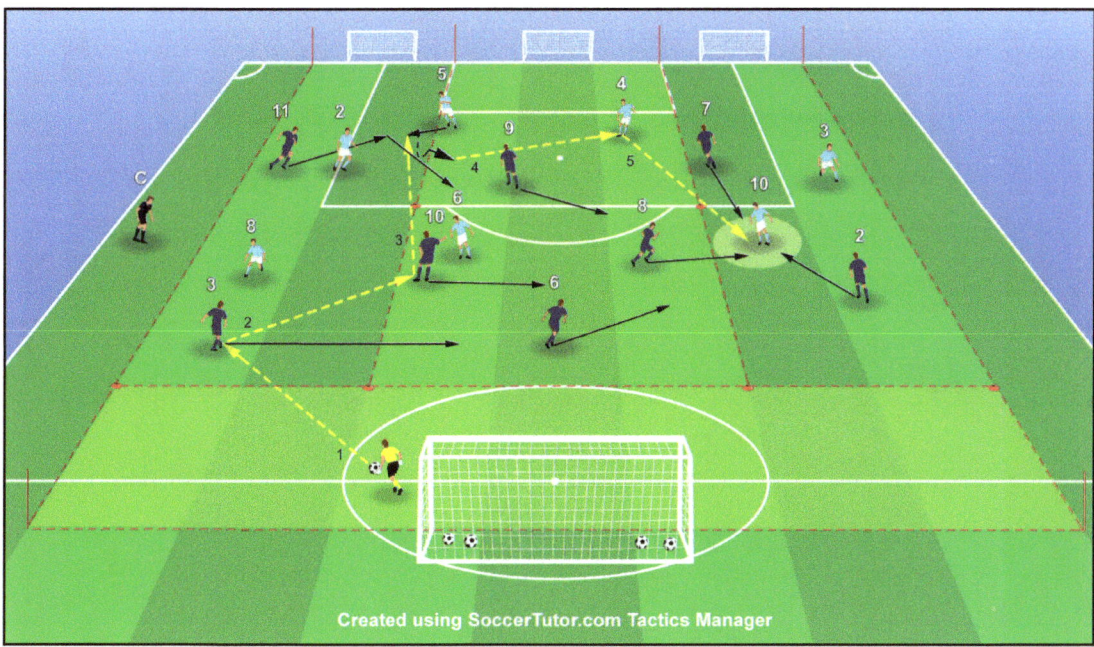

Description

In this progression of the previous practice, we add 3 mini goals for the light blue team to defend and the navy team now defend a large goal with a goalkeeper.

The practice starts with the navy team's goalkeeper and the navy team try to score in any of the 3 mini goals. The light blue team try to win the ball and launch a counter attack to score past the goalkeeper. The other aims/objectives are the same as the previous practice.

Rules

1. If the light blue team successfully work the ball into the end zone (navy team's low zone), they score 1 point.
2. If the light blues score a goal, they get 2 points.
3. If the navy team win the ball back within 6 seconds and all players are within 2 channels, they score 1 point.
4. If the navy team win the ball back within 6 seconds and then score a goal, they get 2 points.

Session to Practice MAURIZIO SARRI Tactics - Transition from Attack to Defence (High Zone)

PROGRESSION

4. High Press from Multiple Angles to Create a Numerical Advantage Around the Ball in an 11 v 11 Tactical Game

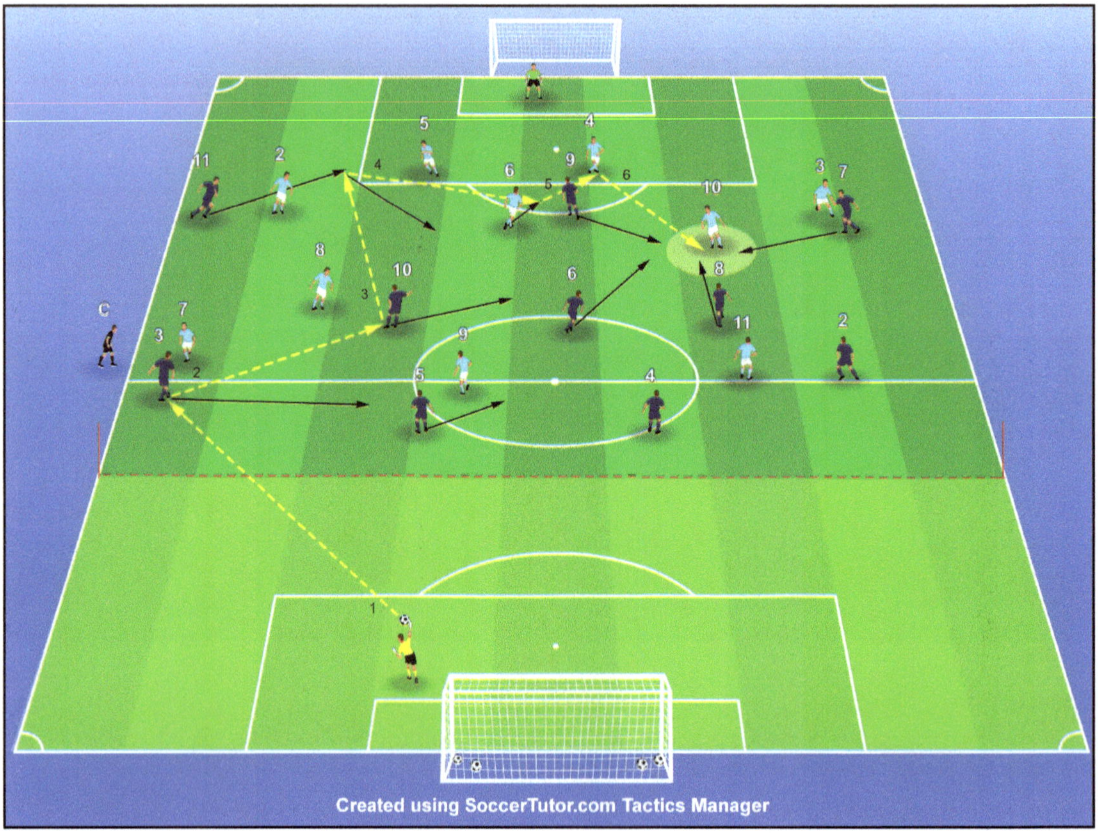

Description

In the final practice of this session, we adapt the previous practice by playing an 11 v 11 game on a full pitch. The 3 channels are removed. Both teams use the 4-3-3 formation.

The objectives and rules are the same as the previous two practices.

Coaching Points

1. The focus is on a quick transition by pressing the opponent in the same area the ball is lost and creating a numerical advantage there.

2. When making a transition from attack to defence, quickly press the ball carrier to stop them passing or dribbling forward, forcing them to play under pressure of time and space.

3. Mark players around the ball zone very tightly and block off potential passing lanes.

4. The basic aim is to win the ball or to force our opponents into making the wrong decisions.

TACTICAL SITUATION 2

JORGE SAMPAOLI TACTICS

Recovering the Ball as Quickly as Possible with a High Press

Content taken from Analysis of Sevilla during the 2016/2017 season

The analysis is based on recurring patterns of play observed within the Sevilla team. Once the same phase of play occurred a number of times (at least 10) the tactics would be seen as a pattern. The analysis on the next page is an example of the team's tactics being used effectively, taken from a specific game.

Each action, pass, individual movement with or without the ball, and the positioning of each player on the pitch including their body shape, are presented.

The analysis is then used to create a full progressive session to coach this specific tactical situation.

Tactical Analysis of JORGE SAMPAOLI - Transition from Attack to Defence (High Zone)

Analysis Taken from 'Juventus vs Sevilla - 14th Sep 2016 (Champions League)'
Recovering the Ball as Quickly as Possible with a High Press

In this situation, the right winger Vitolo dribbles forward and tries to play a through ball to the left winger Sarabia.

The pass is over-hit and the Juventus goalkeeper Buffon is able to collect the ball.

From this point, Sevilla's aim was to push their players high up the pitch and win the ball back as quickly as possible with a high press.

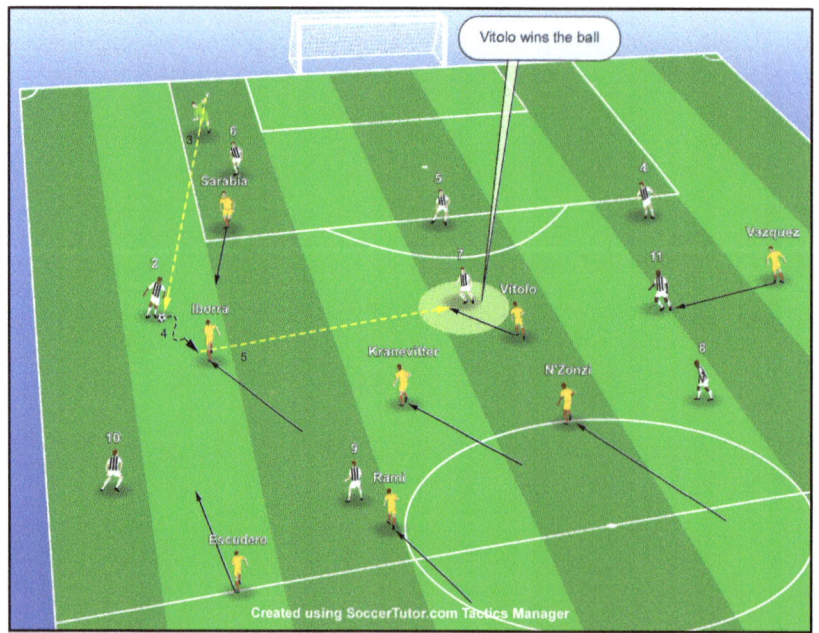

Buffon rolls the ball out to the right back (2). Sevilla central midfielder Iborra moves to press the ball carrier and the right winger Sarabia tracks back. All the other Sevilla players shift up and across to apply pressure and mark any potential receivers.

Dani Alves (2) has limited options and is forced to pass inside to the central midfielder Khedira (7) and the Sevilla right winger Vitolo is able to win the ball from him.

Session to Practice JORGE SAMPAOLI Tactics - Transition from Attack to Defence (High Zone)

SESSION FOR THIS TACTICAL SITUATION (4 PRACTICES)
1. Recovering the Ball as Quickly as Possible with Collective Pressing in a Dynamic 6 v 5 Possession Game

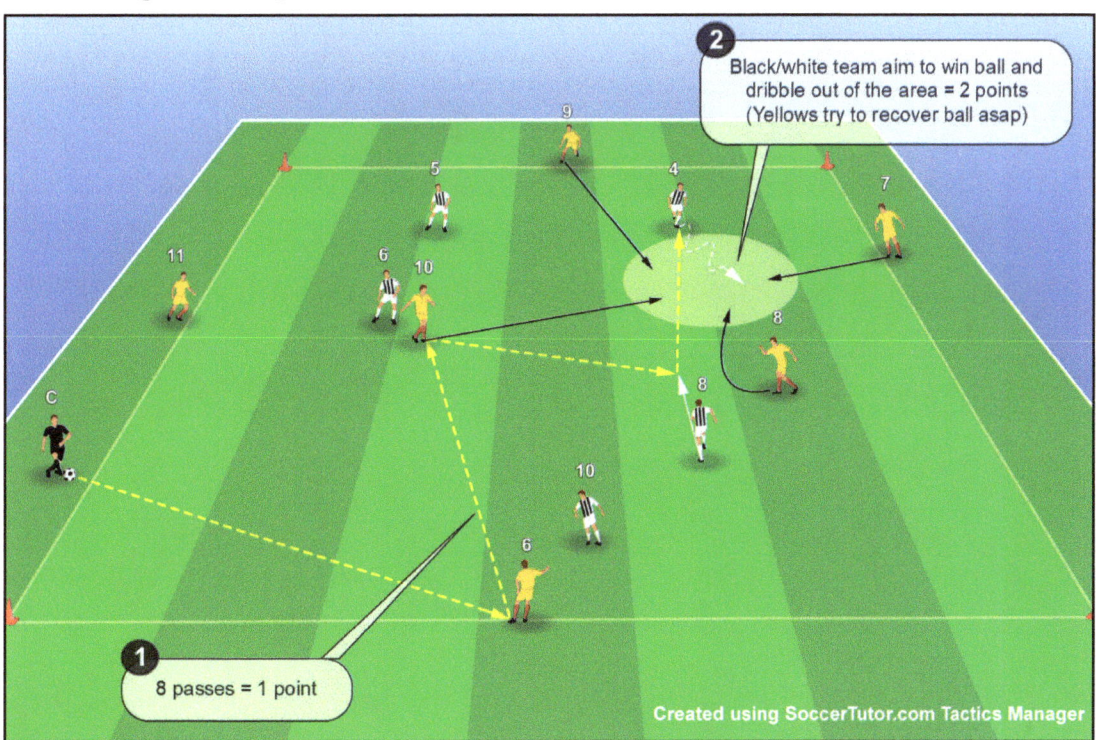

Objective: Keep possession under pressure and fast transition to recover ball with collective press.

Description

In a 25 x 25 yard area, we play 6 v 5. The yellow team are in a 3-3 formation - the defensive midfielder (6), the 2 wingers (7 & 11) and the forward (9) move along the outsides. The black/white team are in a 2-3 formation.

1. The practice starts with the yellow team trying to complete 8 passes (1 point).

2. The black/white team press to win the ball and then try to dribble it outside of the area (2 points). When the yellows lose the ball, they must make a fast transition from attack to defence, applying collective pressing on the ball carrier and the space around him. When they recover the ball, they must then open the space again to maintain possession.

Out of Possession = *CLOSE* the Space / In Possession = *OPEN* the Space.

Different Rules

1. The yellows are limited to 3 touches and the black/whites have unlimited touches.
2. The yellows are limited to 2 touches and the black/whites have 3 touches.

Session to Practice **JORGE SAMPAOLI** Tactics - Transition from Attack to Defence (High Zone)

PROGRESSION

2. Recovering the Ball as Quickly as Possible with a High Press in a Dynamic 2 Zone Game

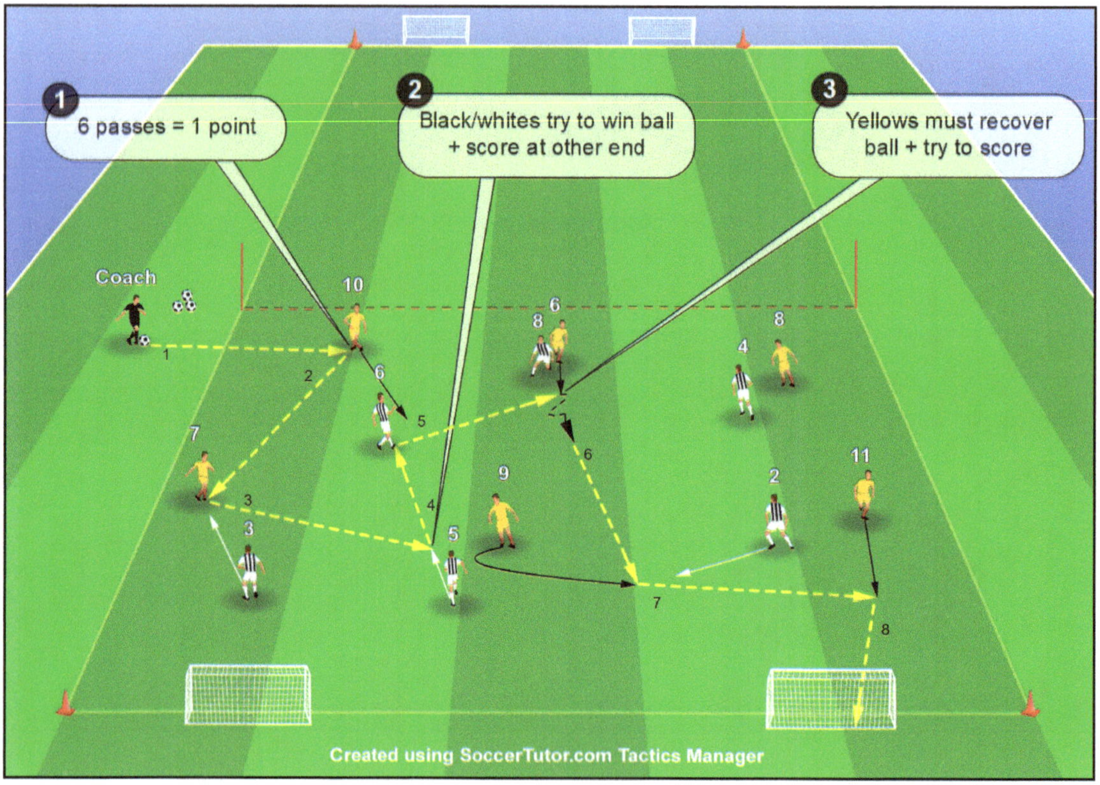

![Diagram: 1. 6 passes = 1 point; 2. Black/whites try to win ball + score at other end; 3. Yellows must recover ball + try to score]

Objective: Keep possession under pressure and fast transitions to recover the ball with high press.

Description

In a 20 x 40 yard area, we divide the pitch into 2 equal halves. We play 6 v 6 in this directional game.

The practice starts from the coach and with one team in possession (yellows in diagram) trying to complete 6 passes (1 point) and then score in the mini goals.

If the yellows lose the ball, they must make a fast transition to defence (high press) to stop the black and white team launching a fast break attack in the other half. If the yellows successfully recover the ball, they again try to score in the mini goals.

Coaching Points

1. In the transition to defence, quickly press the ball carrier to stop them passing or dribbling forward and force them to play under pressure of time and space.
2. Mark the players around the ball zone very tightly and block off potential passing lanes.
3. The basic aim is to win the ball or to force our opponents into making the wrong decisions.

Session to Practice **JORGE SAMPAOLI** Tactics - Transition from Attack to Defence (High Zone)

PROGRESSION

3. Recovering the Ball as Quickly as Possible with a High Press in an 11 v 11 Game with Passing Gates

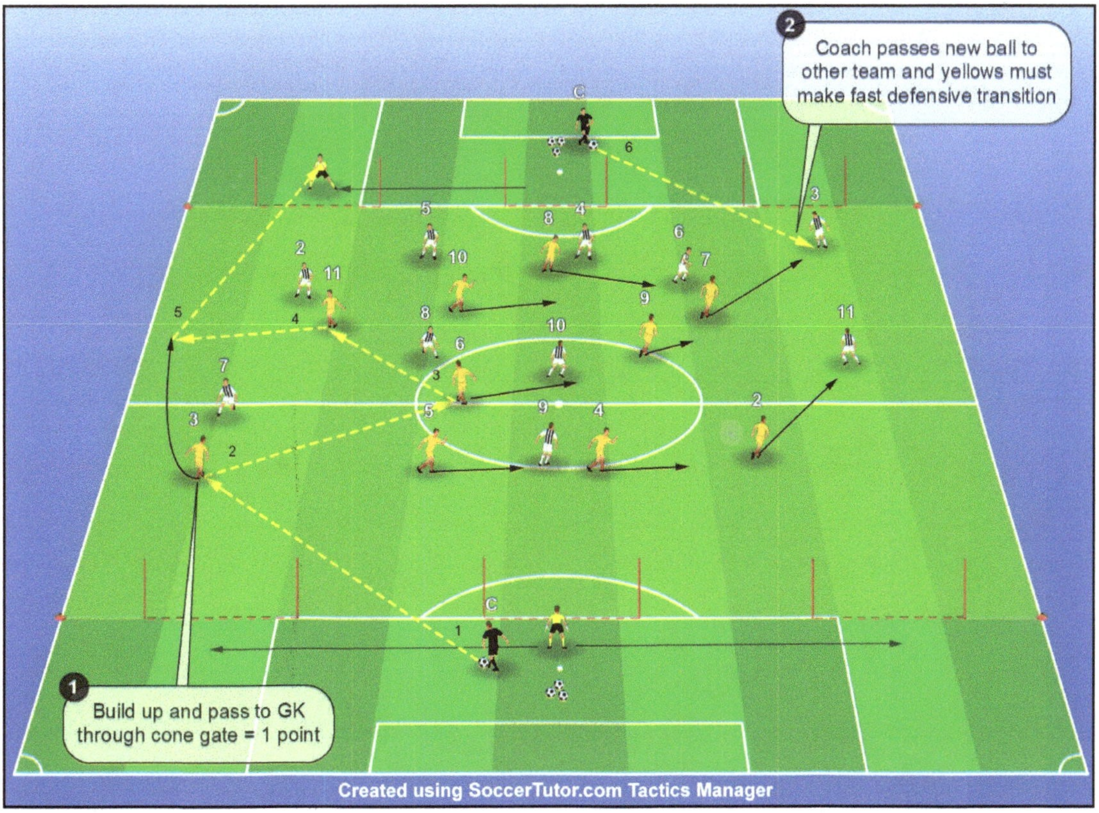

Description
We play in between the two penalty areas and create 3 large pole gates at each end. Behind each end line, we have a goalkeeper and coach with balls.

1. The practice starts with one team in possession (yellows) who build up play and try to score by passing through a pole gate for the goalkeeper to receive (1 point).

2. Immediately after this happens, the coach at that end passes a new ball to the other team (black/white), who launch a fast attack. The yellows must therefore make a fast transition from attack to defence, stopping the black/white team from scoring and recovering the ball as quickly as possible.

If the black/white team pass successfully through a cone gate to the goalkeeper at the other end, the coach at that end then passes a new ball to the yellows and the practice starts from the beginning.

Coaching Points
1. Quickly change the point of defence to stop the opponents from attacking the weak side.
2. Delay the attack initially and press collectively once some defensive balance has been restored.

Session to Practice JORGE SAMPAOLI Tactics - Transition from Attack to Defence (High Zone)

PROGRESSION

4. Recovering the Ball as Quickly as Possible with a High Press in a Dynamic Game

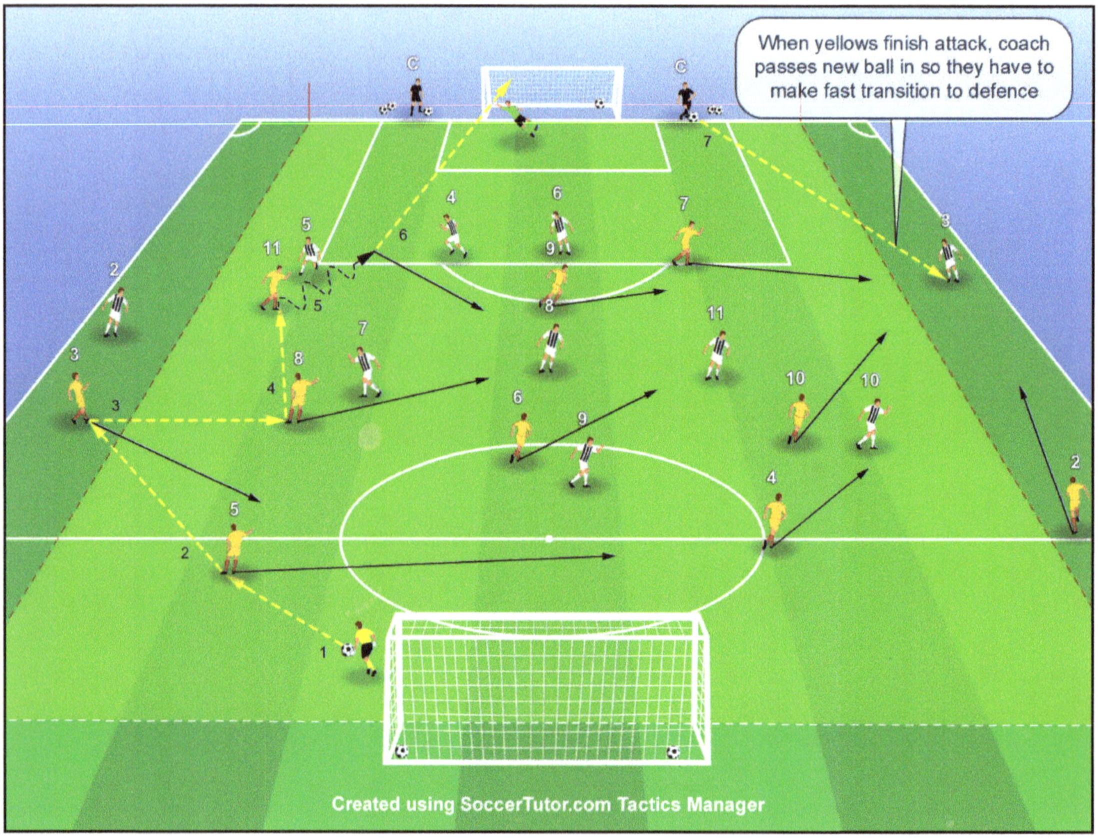

Objective: Transition to defence while switching the point (direction) of defence with a high press.

Description

In the final practice of this session, we connect all previous practices. From the previous practice, we add 2 full backs (2 & 3) for the yellow team. For the black/white team, we add 1 extra centre back (6), 2 wing backs (2 & 3) and an extra forward (10). The full backs and wing backs operate in the side zones.

The practice starts from the yellow goalkeeper and the yellow team try to score a goal (1 point). We play 11 v 9 as the black/white wing backs are not involved in this first phase.

When the attack is finished, one of the coaches passes a new ball to the black/white team. Therefore, the yellows must react very quickly to the new tactical situation, shifting across collectively to make a fast transition from attack to defence in relation to the new ball position.

All players are involved as soon as the coach passes a new ball to the black/white team and we then have an 11 v 11 game from that point.

FREE TRIAL

Football Coaching Specialists Since 2001

TACTICS MANAGER
Create your own Practices, Tactics & Plan Sessions!

 www.SoccerTutor.com/TacticsManager
info@soccertutor.com

 PC   Mac   iPad   Tablet   Web

Football Coaching Specialists Since 2001

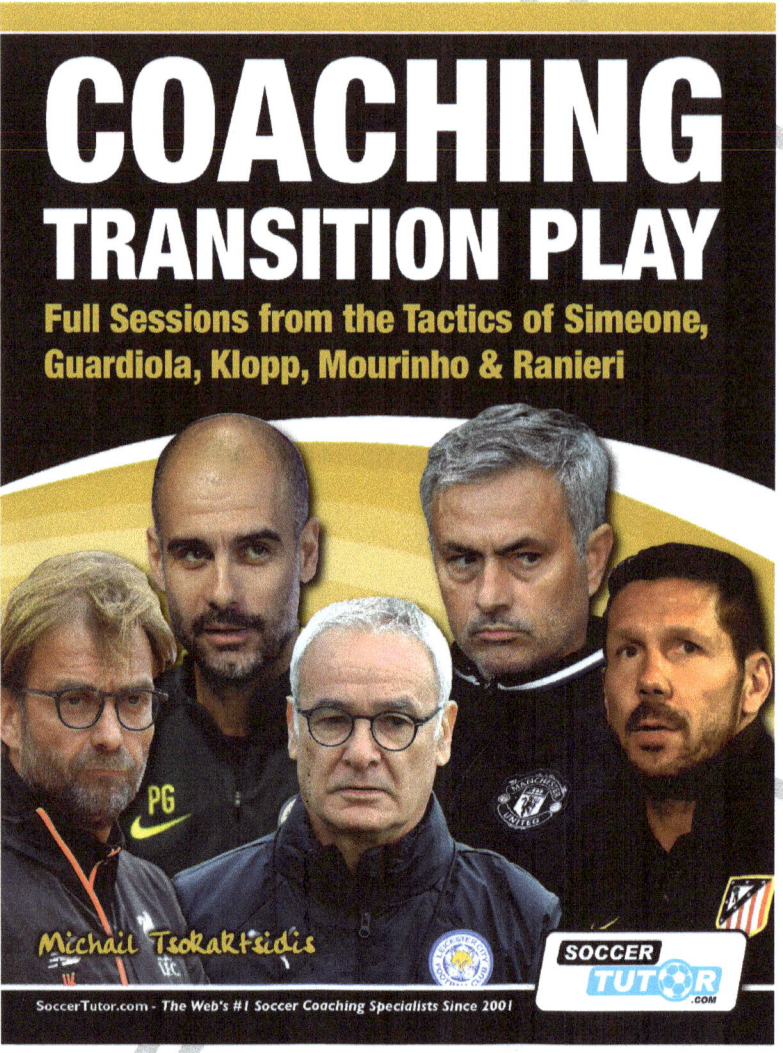

Available in Full Colour Print and eBook!
PC | Mac | iPhone | iPad | Android Phone/Tablet | Kobo | Kindle Fire

www.SoccerTutor.com
info@soccertutor.com

Football Coaching Specialists Since 2001

Available in Full Colour Print and eBook!
PC | Mac | iPhone | iPad | Android Phone/Tablet | Kobo | Kindle Fire

www.SoccerTutor.com
info@soccertutor.com

Football Coaching Specialists Since 2001

MARCELO BIELSA

Coaching Build Up Play Against High Pressing Teams

Terzis Athanasios

Available in Full Colour Print and eBook!
PC | Mac | iPhone | iPad | Android Phone/Tablet | Kobo | Kindle Fire

www.SoccerTutor.com
info@soccertutor.com

Football Coaching Specialists Since 2001

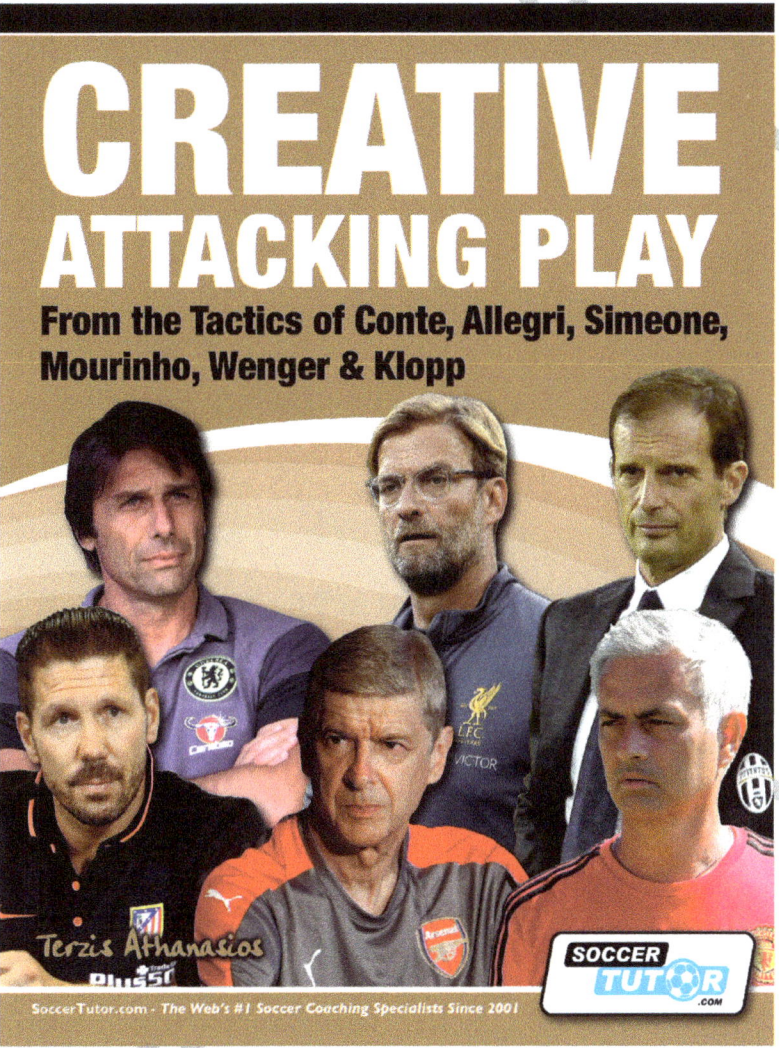

Available in Full Colour Print and eBook!
PC | Mac | iPhone | iPad | Android Phone/Tablet | Kobo | Kindle Fire

www.SoccerTutor.com
info@soccertutor.com

www.ingramcontent.com/pod-product-compliance
Lightning Source LLC
Chambersburg PA
CBHW061129010526
44117CB00023B/2995